2018 AICA
International Congress
Taiwan
Art Criticism in the Age
of Virtuality
and Democracy

虛擬性與民主時代的
藝術評論

2018 國際藝評人協會 台北世界年會

16-18 November 2018,
in Taipei.

Contents

Preface

Congress theme for 2018 AICA International Congress Taiwan:

Art Criticism in the Age of Virtuality and Democracy

Chi-Ming Lin, and the scientific committee of AICA Taiwan

Based on observations of important tendencies in the actual world, we would like to address some key issues concerning the role of art criticism related to these new developments.

Firstly, the virtual is not the opposite of reality but rather an increasing part of our reality. Presently, communities, social relations, everyday life, the body, and even biological life are in the processes of mass virtualization. Life itself has been supposed as an algorithm, AI as a brain without body, while space-time's relationship is virtualized in VR technology. A virtual enterprise need no longer convene its employees onsite, but rather can delegate work to be done remotely, thus re-articulating the time-space relationship of its workers.

Secondly, if we make an observation of a longer duration, there seems to be an unquestionable expansion of democracy which can be confirmed by the democratic transitions beginning in the mid-1970s, which span from Latin America to Taiwan and South Korea, through the end of the cold war, and to following transitions in Eastern Europe, the Color Revolution and the Umbrella Movement in Hong-Kong in the fall of 2014. Nevertheless in more recent years, the phenomenon of the retreat of democracy can also be observed in the uprising of the populism worldwide.

Moreover, these two tendencies may be related. The Congress Theme "Art Criticism in the age of Virtuality and Democracy" has two sub-themes:

1. Art criticism in the age of virtuality
2. Art discourse facing challenged democracy

1. "Art criticism in the age of virtuality" will address the situation in which the rapid pace of development in computer and media technologies is creating new working environments and new possibilities for art, each with their own particular problematics. How does this process affect the description, interpretation and evaluation of contemporary art? More precisely, does art criticism develop new methodology and new languages concerning its analysis and new problematics in its debates? What does it mean for art and art criticism that new media reaches crowds of new readers around the world, often "for free"?

2. "Art discourse facing challenged democracy" will discuss the following questions: how is art discourse constitutive of the collective representations and imaginary of democracy? In the situation of democracy under challenge, how are these social-political phenomena reflected in new developments of censorship and self-censorship, or post-truth? For new problems brought out by transitional justice, what kind of function can art discourse play?

Acknowledgment

AICA Taiwan would like to express our special thanks of gratitude to all 35 of the contributors for submitting their impressive works, and the President of AICA International-Lisbeth Rebollo Gonçalves, Honorary President- Jacques Leenhardt, Secretary General-Allthorpe-Guyton Marjorie, Treasurer-Mathilde Roman, and Office Assistant- Nathalie Rousselle for their great help. This book would not have been possible without the financial or the organizational support of the Ministry of Culture, Ministry of Science and Technology, Ministry of Foreign Affairs, and the Ministry of Education of Taiwan(R.O.C). Also, we appreciate the kind support from Taipei City Government, Taipei Fine Art Museum, National Taipei University of Education: Department of Arts and Design, Critical and Curatorial Studies of Contemporary Art at NTUE, Museum of NTUE, Department of Music. Special thanks to the sponsorships from the private association-Xue Xue Foundation, Taishin Holdings and Foundation for Arts and Culture, Cathay Century Insurance, Egret Foundation, and Bonyu Ltd.

We are grateful to both jury panels for "AICA Prize for Distinguished Contribution for Art Criticism" and "AICA Incentive Award for Young Art Critics": Hsiang-Lin Lai, Kuang-Yi Chen, Po-Shin Chiang, Ya-Chun Chin, Tzu-Chieh Chien, Ching-Wen Chang, Yang YEUNG, Nhung WALSH, Chien-Mei LIU, Jeannine TANG, Damian Smith, and

Mariko Takeuchi. Also special thanks to AICA Taiwan Preparatory Committee and the Scientific Committee-Hai-Ming Huang, Hsien-Hung Yang, Shui-Peng Cheng, Chau-Hsin Chen, Ching-Wen Chang, LI-Fu Chen, Lin-Yen Tsai, Mu-Ching Wu, Pei-Ni Hsieh, Chi-Hsiang Chen, Yi-Hua Wu, Hung-Yi Chen, Man-Ray Hsu, Hong-John Lin, Sheng-Hua Zheng, Chih-Yung Chiu, Wen-Hao Huang. Furthermore, We thank the President of AICA Taiwan and the editor in chief of this book, Chi-Min Lin along with the editing working team-Tien-Han Chang, Shih-Ting Wang, Cheng-Hao Liou, E-Fahn Wang, Shih-Hsuan Chou, and Sean Gaffney- for their efforts.

Contributors

Bundy, Jean is an Alaskan art critic who writes on social and environmental issues. She's also a painter showing work at Pleiades gallery, New York City, which allows her to empathize with artists she critique. She hold degrees: BFA, University of Alaska; MFA, University of Chicago; MFAW, The School of the Art Institute of Chicago; PhD, Institute for Doctoral Studies in the Visual Arts. The Arctic varies in Pacific Rim ethnicities, and isn't free from discrimination, political or cultural insensitivities, which allows a plethora of writing perspectives. Plus-side economics of tourism and the oil industry possess negativities that become microcosms of global issues found elsewhere. Art is the great communication tool for aesthetically providing greater awareness of bureaucratic debacles facing humanity. Cultural and environmental damage are evidenced by global warming, along with the paradox that cleaning up Nature generally involves political appeasement. Suppressing art's voice not only angers, it delays solutions. Violations to the earth can be as destructive as violations to mankind. Art written, painted, or performed is a means to address social and civic issues and should be allowed a voice, regardless of a country's agendas. She recently became an AICA-International board member, also serving on their Censorship committee.

Bonde, Lisbeth is a full time, freelance art critic based in Copenhagen. Lisbeth hold a master's degree in Literature and Art history from the University of Copenhagen. She've written 9 books on art – mainly on Danish contemporary art and practised art criticism since 1992 after having finished her master's degree. In 1994, Lisbeth was appointed editor of the art section at the Danish daily broadsheet newspaper Information and she continued to work and write there until 2002. The next eleven years she continued to practice as an art critic on a regular basis for Weekendavisen – also a broadsheet newspaper which is being published on a weekly basis. Today she's contributing on a regular basis to a wide variety of media – including a broad sheet daily newspaper – Kristeligt Dagblad – and to the most widespread design magazine in Scandinavia Bo Bedre with her monthly art guide and to the most widespread Scandinavian online art magazine: kunsten.nu.

Cramerotti, Alfredo is a writer, curator and broadcaster. He is Director of MOSTYN, Wales, and Head Curator of APT, Artist Pension Trust. He organized *Sean Scully: Standing on the Edge of the World* at the Hong Kong Arts Centre (2018), *Leviathan* by Shezad Dawood, in conjunction with the 57th Venice Biennale (2017), *EXPO VIDEO* Chicago (2015), three national pavilions at the Venice Biennale (Mauritius in 2015, Wales and Maldives in 2013), and the biennials *Sequences* VII in Iceland (2015) and *Manifesta 8* in Spain (2010).

Cramerotti is Visiting Lecturer at universities throughout Europe and the Americas, as well as regularly publishing, broadcasting and speaking at public events. His scholarship involves the theory and practice of "The Hyperimage", investigating digital culture's impact on artistic and curatorial practices, and "Aesthetic Journalism", addressing the relationship between contemporary art and interview, fiction and reportage. He is Editor of the *Critical Photography* book series and his own publications include the books *Forewords: Hyperimages and Hyperimaging* (forth. 2018), *Unmapping the City: Perspectives of Flatness* (2010) and *Aesthetic Journalism: How to inform without informing* (2009).

Chen, Chieh-Jen was born in Taoyuan, Taiwan, Chen Chieh-jen currently lives and works in Taipei, Taiwan. Chen employed extra-institutional underground exhibitions and guerrilla-style art actions to challenge Taiwan's dominant political mechanisms during a period marked by the Cold War, anti-communist propaganda and martial law (1950 – 1987). After martial law ended, Chen ceased art activity for eight years. Returning to art in 1996, Chen started collaborating with local residents, unemployed laborers, temporary workers, migrant workers, foreign spouses, unemployed youths and social activists. In order to visualize contemporary reality and a people's history that has been obscured by neo-liberalism, Chen embarked on a series of video projects in which he used strategies he calls "re-imagining", "re-narrating", "re-writing" and "re-connecting."

Chan, Felix Ho Yuen from Hong Kong (b.1994), graduated from New York University's Gallatin School of Individualized Studies in 2017, with a focus on avant-garde art in China and Japan, and the social history of photography. He is currently curatorial assistant at The Walther Collection, an art foundation dedicated to the critical understanding of historical and contemporary photography and related media. Past curatorial and editorial contributions include "Post-Pop: East Meets West" (2014, Saatchi Gallery), "Life and Dreams: Chinese Contemporary Photography and Media Art" (The Walther Collection and Steidl, 2017). He is currently assisting Brian Wallis in organizing a series of exhibitions investigating aspects of vernacular photography at The Walther Collection Project Space in New York. He lives and works in New York.

Crawford, Holly is an artist and art historian (www.art-poetry.info). She is the Director of AC Institute (www.artcurrents.org) in NYC. Institutional critique and power structures, are the area of her major focus in art and art history.
Projects: If I'm,Who are You? Critical Conversations in a Limo, Outsourced Critics, Open Adoption for Art, Orphans Offered Up, May I have your autograph? Hospitality Suite, Tracking, 13 Ways of Looking at a Blackbird, Offerings, Punctuation Performance, The Dinner Party, The Road: The Century Freeway, Offerings, Water!, Water$ Water? and Voice Over. Exhibited: Research Pavilion at Venice Biennale, Ars Electronica, Tate Modern, Beyond Baroque, The Armory Art Fair, PhotoNY, Photo San Francisco, Polish National Sculpture Garden, Melbourne International Arts Festival, Riverside Art Museum, Downey Art Museum and other galleries and non-profits. Publications: 7 Days, My Art Life (ed), Attached to the Mouse, Disney & Contemporary Art, 2006; Artistic Bedfellows, Histories, Theories and Conversations in Collaborative Art Practices editor 2008, and catalogue essay, "Disney and Pop" in Once Upon a Time Walt Disney Studio, 2006 and essay Who Can Play?, in Popular Culture Values and the Arts, ed. Ray B. Browne and Lawrence A. Kreiser, Jr.

Chan, Kang-Jung was born in 1971, Chan Kang-Jung is a Taiwan lawyer and a managing partner of a law firm as well as a PhD student in the Department of Arts and Design in National Taipei University of Education. He also works as a chairman/ supervisor of some companies and non-profit organizations, including finance, cultural and creative industry, media, tourism industry and agriculture. He is deeply interested in political and social issues and involved in interdisciplinary collaborations as well.

Cepeda, Rui Gonçalves is a PhD candidate at the University of Manchester on the management of contemporary art and spaces for participation. Prior to working in his PhD, he led several art and cultural festival in Portugal. From 2013 onwards he has been working as an art curator and producer for small-scale art organisations in England and has been exploring the media reaches of the online world. Since 2007, he has been focusing his practice both as art producer and critic on exploring processes in which artistic collaboration and confrontation operate, in delivering moments that are community-building mechanisms, and in implementing communicative actions that inform powerful stories while giving individual communities their own voice. In 2012, he became an AICA International member, and, in 2015, integrated AICA International as a Board Member. Presently is a member of the Archives and Living Memory Commission. He has organised and presented displays and performances by Tatsumi Orimoto, Per Barclay, Jane and Louise Wilson, Adam Chodzko, Cristina Lucas, Rosângela Rennó, Wang Nindge, Zhao Liang, and about the Kharkiv School of Photography. He is a frequent contributor to international art magazines and newspapers.

Gacina, Mira was born in 1978 in Skopje, Macedonia, is an art historian, art critic and senior curator at Museum of Contemporary Art in Skopje. From 2013 she serves as a President of AICA Macedonia. From 2017 Gakina is an Director of the Museum of Contemporary Art in Skopje. She graduated from the Institute of History of Art and Archaeology at the Faculty of Philosophy in Skopje (2006) and completed her postgraduate studies at the University of Zagreb, Faculty of Philosophy (2010). She received her PhD in Art Management on the subject "Management of the cultural institutions – case study MoCA Skopje" (2017). From 2006 till 2009 she was teaching assistant at the Faculty of Fine Arts in Skopje on the subject„History and Theory of Art". She has curated a number of exhibitions in the country and abroad and presented her work in New York, Krakow, Texas, Prishtina, Berlin, Ljubljana, and Zagreb. She is the chief curator of the Biennale of Young Artists organized by MoCA Skopje in addition to publishing her writing in publications, catalogues and art and culture books and magazines as "Large Glass", "Art Republic", "Brooklyn Rail", "From Consideration to Commitment: Art in Critical Confrontation to Society" among others. She was curator in residence as part of the Prohelvetia Cultural program in Zurich, Bern and Geneva; "Close connection", curatorial program in Amsterdam; International Partnership among Museums program organized by the American Association of Museums at Weil Gallery - Texas; She was UNESCO scholarship holder for the program "The best in the cultural heritage", Dubrovnik. She is also a member of the Board of Directors of the Association for Contemporary Art and Curatorial Practices "Project Space Press Exit Skopje".

Grosser, Sabine is Professor of Aesthetic Learning at Kiel University of Applied Sciences (since 2013); after her postdoctoral thesis at the University of Paderborn, she represented a professorship at the University of Hildesheim (2009-2011); from 1997 - 2002 she worked as DAAD Senior Lecturer at the University of Kelaniya (Sri Lanka).
She studied Art / Visual Communication, German Studies and History at the Universities of Marburg, Kassel and Tucson (USA) and did her PhD on Blinky Palermo (Peter Lang Verlag 1996). She is involved as a writer, curator and artist in numerous exhibitions and

projects (eg. from 1992 - 1997 in the Produzentengalerie Kassel) and teaches at universities in Germany and abroad. She received numerous prizes and awards for her work (including Lise-Meitner scholarship, DAAD scholarships, Landesstipendium Hessen, Dierich Prize).

Since 1989 she writes about contemporary art. Main topics include contemporary art and culture and their communication (including media developments, aesthetic and cultural education, image-, culture- and reception theories as well as cultures of remembrance). With her publication on „Kunst und Erinnerungskultur Sri Lankas im Kontext kultureller Globalisierung. Eine multiperspektivische Betrachtung als Beitrag zum transkulturellen Diskurs" (Athena Verlag 2010) she strengthens her transnational perspective.

Huang, Chien-Hung is Associate Professor in Institute of Trans-disciplinary Art, Taipei National University of Arts. He has published numerous books, including COQ(2009), An Independent Discourse (2001), Trans-Plex Agenda (2011), EMU (2012), and Smile of Montage (2013). Huang has curated shows such as Chim↑Pom's Beautiful World and Crush on EMU (2012), Schizophrenia Taiwan 2.0 (2013), Post-Movement (2014), and Discordant Harmony (2015).

Huang, Hsin-Chien is a new media creator with backgrounds in art, design, engineer and digital entertainment. His career endeavor explores cutting edge technologies in art, literature, design and stage performing. Hsin-Chien was awarded the grand prize of "New Voices, New Vision" new media competition in 1994, the Muse Award of America Association of Museum in 2009, and the Light of Taiwan's Honor from Taiwan's President Ma in 2011, the Fifth Public Art Award from the Ministry of Culture Taiwan in 2016, Best VR Experience in 74 Venice Film Festival.

Hughes, Henry Meyric is the Honorary President of AICA in Paris, Chair of the International Awards for Art Criticism in London and Shanghai, and a member of the Scientific Advisory Board of Les Archives de la critique d'art and of the International Scientific Committee of The International Review of Contemporary Art Criticism in Rennes. He worked for 24 years with the British Council in Germany, Peru, France, and Italy, ending up as the Director of Visual Arts in London before leaving to become Director of the Hayward Gallery in London in 1992. Since 1996, he has worked as an independent curator and arts writer. He was a co-founder and the founding president of Manifesta: The European Biennial of Contemporary Art (1993-2007). He has been a frequent curator and commissioner at the Venice Biennale and Bienal de São Paulo and has (co-)curated numerous national and international exhibitions of modern and contemporary art, including the 30th Council of Europe exhibition Critique and Crisis/The Desire for Freedom: Art in Europe since 1945 (Berlin and international tour, 2012-14). He has been special adviser on exhibitions for the Council of Europe and has been decorated by the Czechoslovak, French, and German governments.

Keesling, Jamie is a a an independent writer, Art History faculty member at the School of Visual Arts, and membership manager for AICA-USA. She lives and works in Brooklyn, New York.

Kelly, Liam is the Emeritus Professor of Irish Visual Culture at Ulster University, Belfast. He holds a BA (Hons) degree in the History of European Art from the Courtauld Institute of Art, University of London, and a Ph.D from Trinity College, Dublin.

His publications (selected) include 'The City as Art: Interrogating the Polis', 1994; 'Thinking Long, Contemporary Art in the North of Ireland', 1996; 'Miquel Navarro 1973-96' (co-ed.) 1996; 'Liam Gillick - Big Conference Centre' (co-ed), 1997; 'Art and the Disembodied Eye', 2007; 'The School of Art and Design, Belfast 1960-2009', 2009 and 'Brian O'Doherty Collected Essays',(ed.),University of California Press, California, 2018.

He was Director of The Orpheus Gallery, Belfast, 1986-92 and The Orchard Gallery, Derry 1996-99. From 1981-86 he was a member of the Visual Arts Committee of the Arts Council of N.Ireland; member of the Executive Committee, Association of Art Historians (U.K.) 1990-93 and co-convene r of their conference 'Contestations' in Belfast, 2007; member of the BBC N.I. Audience Council 2007-2010; board member Ormeau Baths Gallery, Belfast (2008-12). He is a former Vice-President of The International Association of Art Critics (AICA), organising their annual congress "Art and Centres of Conflict: Outer and Inner Realities' in 1997 and was the inaugural Chair of the AICA Commission on Censorship and Freedom of Expression.

Kaźmierczak, Małgorzata was born in Kraków, Poland (1979). PhD. in History (2010). Since 2004 an independent curator of art events in Poland and USA, especially performance art festivals (e.g. Scores – National Museum in Szczecin, Poland 2016, Anarchy and New Art. 100 years of Dadaism, Center for Polish Sculpture in Oronsko, Poland, 2016, Imagine as part of the International Drawing Triennale, National Museum in Wroclaw, Poland, 2015). Art critic (e.g. Gazeta Wyborcza, Obieg, Exit, Opcje, Fragile, Art and Documentation). Since 2011 an editor and translator of http://livinggallery.info,

2012-2014 Managing Editor of the Art and Documentation journal. Co-editor of: Friends
from the Seaside and Visual text as a Form of Meta-art. Between 2006-2012 chairwoman
of the Foundation for the Promotion of Performance Art "Kesher" in Krakow, a member
of the Art and Documentation Association and AICA. Between 2014-2016 director of the
City Art Gallery of Kalisz, 2016-2017 director of the Library and a lecturer at the Art
Academy in Szczecin, since 2017 an Assistant Professor and Chief Editor of the
Publishing House at the Art Academy of Szczecin. Currently an Assistant Professor at the
Faculty of Art of the Pedagogical University of Krakow.

King, Natalie is an Australian art critic and curator with more than two decades
experience in international contemporary art, realising landmark projects in Taiwan, Italy,
India, Indonesia, Japan, Korea, Singapore and Vietnam. Current roles include Enterprise
Professorial Fellow, Victorian College of the Arts, University of Melbourne; Curator &
Editor of *Tracey Moffatt: My Horizon*, Australian Pavilion at Venice Biennale 2017 with
Thames & Hudson. Recent projects include Chief Curator, *Melbourne Biennial Lab:
What happens now?* City of Melbourne at Melbourne Festival 2016; *Conversations:
Entang Wiharso & Sally Smart*, National Gallery of Indonesia, Jakarta; *Whisper in My
Mask: TarraWarra Biennial 2014* and *Episodes: 13th Dong Gang International Photo
Festival*, Korea. King has curated exhibitions for the Kaohsiung Museum of Fine Arts,
Taiwan; Bangkok Arts and Cultural Centre, Thailand; Singapore Art Museum; the
National Museum of Art, Osaka; Tokyo Metropolitan Museum of Photography; and the
Museum of Contemporary Art, Sydney. She has conducted in-depth interviews with Ai
Wei Wei, Pussy Riot, Candice Breitz, Joseph Kosuth, Pipilotti Rist, Hiroshi Sugimoto,
Bill Henson, Jitish Kallat, Hou Hanru and Cai Guo-Qiang amongst others. She is widely
published in arts media including *Flash Art*. She is a Member of AICA and CIMAM,
International Committee for Museums and Collections of Modern Art.

Khazam, Rahma is an art critic, art historian and researcher. She studied philosophy and
art history before receiving her Ph.D. from the Sorbonne in aesthetics and art theory.
Rahma regularly participates in international conferences relating to her main research
areas, namely contemporary art and architecture, modernism, image theory, speculative
realism and sound art. Her writing has been published in exhibition catalogues, edited
volumes and contemporary art magazines such as Frieze and Springerin and she is
currently preparing a book on the work of the French artist Franck Leibovici. She is a
member of AICA (International Association of Art Critics), NECS (European Network
for Cinema and Media Studies) and EAM (European Network for Avant-Garde and

Modernism Studies) and received the AICA France Award for Art Criticism in 2017. Recent publications include: "From the Object to the Hyperobject: Art After the New Art History" (2017), in Newest Art History/Wohin geht die jüngste Kunstgeschichte?, Proceedings of the 18th Conference of Austrian Art Historians, http://www.voekk.at/de/node/143 and "Art, Knowledge, and the In-Between" in Paulo de Assis and Paolo Giudici (eds.), The Dark Precursor: Deleuze and Artistic Research, Vol. II, Leuven University Press, 2017.

Lin, Chi-Ming is the professor at the Department of Arts and Design of National Taipei University of Education, Doctor of Ecole des Hautes Etudes en Sciences Sociales, Paris. He is specialized in the field of Theory of image, contemporary French thoughts, the Cross-boundary study of arts and Contemporary Aesthetics. His publications are published in Chinese, French, English, and Italian. One of his recent book titles is Multiple and Tension: On History of Photography and Photographic Portrait. Art critic and curator, he is now President of AICA Taiwan, board member of Taiwan Art and Technology Association. Director of National Taiwan Museum of Fine Arts since October 2018.

Muñoz, Ernesto holds degree in theory and Art Criticism, Critic and Art Theorist from University of Chile, Faulty of Art, Literature of Theory and Art Critic. His labor background includes Emotional Traits Exhibition, Lima Link Gallery; curator El Pais Geometrico, Cultural Institute of Las Condes; Biennial of Santa Cruz, Curator; Peruvian Art Today, Isabel Aninat Gallery; First Biennial of Montevideo; Fourth Ibiza Biennial; Chilean Art In Switzerland; Puente Aereo, Modern Art Museum In Buenos Aires; Chile Image, Nine Photographers At Borges Cultural Center, In Buenos Aires; Chilean Art, in the Museum of contemporary Art of Sao Paulo; Tenth Festival De Cali, Colombia; Biennial of Mexico Engraving; Recovered Images, in IDB of Washington D.C.; Overseas, Mitland Art Center, Birmingham, England; Arco Fair, Madrid; Biennial of Art, Johannesburg Chilean Photographers Resident In Paris; New Delhi Triennial; Istanbul Biennial, (Curator In Two Opportunities); Curatoris 13x13, University of Talca, Santiago Headquarters.

His curated exhibitions with foreign artists to Chile includes Puente Aereo, Argentine Artists in Chile; Uruguayan artists about Tango; Viva Brasil, Eight Brazilian Artists; Peru Obra Abierta, Twelve Peruvian Artists; Ecuadorian Art in the House of Culture of Ecuador; Roberto Obregon, Pedro Tangliafrico and other Venezuelan artists; Panamanian Art of Today; Latin American art at the Summit of the Americas; Contemporary Mexican Art; The End of the Margins, Bolivian Art; Marite Zaldivar, Paraguayan Artist; Cobra

Group, Collection of 140 Pieces; Contemporary English Art; German Art, Scenographies in Art; South African art; Croatian Art Today.

His curated exhibitions with Chilean artists to Chile includes Competition Coordinator, Securities Placement; The Hidden Look, Museum of Contemporary Art; The Emerging Reality, Inaugural Exhibition of La Galera Gavriela Mistral; Enrique Lihn, Drawings of The Poet; New Generations, Museum of Contemporary Art; Recreating Goya.

Nolan, Joe is a student at the University of Notre Dame. Joe Nolan is currently researching the intersections of art criticism and philosophy for a thesis on contemporary art that will be completed by May 2019. His area of undergraduate study is the intellectual tradition of Western culture, from Plato to Virginia Woolf. He finds this perspective indispensable for any discussion of contemporary art, especially in trying to understand the art of highly educated MFAs, which, increasingly, references the roots of Western culture, even while opening avenues to other cultural idioms.

Popova, Jovanka was born in 1980 in Skopje, Macedonia, a curator and program coordinator at press to exit project space since 2012 and curator collaborator at the Museum of Contemporary Art Skopje since 2017. She is a member of the Board of the Macedonian Section of the AICA International Association of Art Critics and she is executive director of JADRO Association of the independent cultural scene, Macedonia. She completed her B.A. and M.A. at the Faculty of Philosophy – Institute for History of Art in Skopje, where she was an Assistant for the subject "Macedonian Contemporary Art". She has curated exhibitions in the contemporary art field in Macedonia and worked on international curatorial projects. She has also presented her work at the Humboldt University, Central European University Budapest, Goethe University Frankfurt, Hankuk University of Foreign Studies, Seoul, Kunst Historisches Institut, Florence, Bahcesehir University, Istanbul, Trondheim Academy of Fine Arts and other institutions. She serves on the board of the West Balkan Residency Program coordinated by <rotor> Association for Contemporary Art, Graz and apexart, New York. Lives and works in Skopje.

Papastergiadis, Nikos is Professor at the School of Culture and Communication at the University of Melbourne. He studied at the University of Melbourne and University of Cambridge. Prior to returning to the University of Melbourne, he was a lecturer at the University of Manchester. Throughout his career, Nikos has focussed on issues relating to cultural identity and worked on collaborative projects with artists and theorists of international repute, such as John Berger, Jimmie Durham and Sonya Boyce. His current research focuses on the investigation of the historical transformation of contemporary art and cultural institutions by digital technology. His sole authored publications include Modernity as Exile (1993), Dialogues in the Diaspora (1998), The Turbulence of Migration (2000), Metaphor and Tension (2004) Spatial Aesthetics: Art Place and the Everyday (2006), Cosmopolitanism and Culture (2012), Ambient Perspectives (2013) as well as being the editor of over 10 collections, author of numerous essays which have been translated into over a dozen languages and appeared in major catalogues such as the Biennales of Sydney, Liverpool, Istanbul, Gwanju, Taipei, Lyon, Thessaloniki and Documenta 13. He is a Fellow of the Australian Academy of the Humanities and co-chair of the Greek Centre for Contemporary Culture, Chair of the International Advisory Board for the Centre for Contemporary Art, Singapore, and Visiting Professor at Nanyang Technological University, Singapore.

robotlab founded in 2000 by Matthias Gommel, Martina Haitz and Jan Zappe at the ZKM Center for Art and Media in Karlsruhe, Germany. robotlab develops artistic installations and performances with industrial robots which are normally used for industrial production. Integrated as ready-mades into the group's art projects the robots invade consistently new thematic or cultural contexts. Thus, their works discuss the human-machine relationships on many different levels. In robotlab's installations the role of the machine is always defined as that of an autonomous, creative agent. www.robotlab.de.

Rodríguez, Bélgica is considered an expert in the field of Latin American art. She received her MA in Art from the Courtauld Institute of Art in London, England, (tutor: John Golding) and her Ph.D. in Art History, with honors, from the Sorbonne University in Paris, France (tutor: Marc Lebot). In 1987, Dr. Rodríguez was elected President of the AICA (International Association of Art Critics), and after her tenure, she was named Honorary President. Between 1984 and 1995 she was Director of the National Gallery of Art in Caracas, Venezuela, and Director of the Art Museum of the Americas, OAS in Washington D.C. She began teaching art history and Latin American art at the School of Art at the Central University of Venezuela in 1978. For four years, Dr. Rodríguez was in charge of the section on 19th and 20th-century Latin American art and architecture for the Handbook of Latin American Studies. An accomplished art critic, writer, art historian, and curator, she has published widely on the subject of art and has participated in conferences, seminars, juries, and roundtable discussions worldwide. She is currently preparing an extensive study on Latin American art of the 20th century, the second volume on Central American art, and one hundred years of sculpture in Venezuela.

Rusca, Elisa is an art historian working as curator and writer. PhD candidate in Visual Cultures at Goldsmiths, University of London, she is specialised in photography and new media. Chair of the AICA Web committee since 2015, she was assistant curator at the Collections of the Musée de l'Elysée, Lausanne, Switzerland for five years and since 2010 she curates contemporary art exhibitions in Switzerland, Italy, Germany, Brazil, Slovakia and Poland. With Broken Dimanche Press Berlin she edited the book Oblio (2014). She collaborated with Nathalie Herschdorfer to the editing and writing of the New Dictionary of Photography (Thames & Hudson, 2015). She presented her research on contemporary visual cultures (depiction of power and violence), hacktivism, technology and poetry at CNRS Paris, the National Museum for Contemporary Art, Seoul, the National Museum for Contemporary Art, Prague, MASC Florianopolis, Brazil, Kunst Werke Berlin and ETOPIA, Centro de Arte y Tecnología, Zaragoza, Ischia International Festival of Philosophy, and the Academy of Fine Arts Prague among others.

Read, Richard is Emeritus Professor of Art History and Senior Honorary Research Fellow at the University of Western Australia. He has published in major journals on the relationship between literature and the visual arts, nineteenth and twentieth-century European, American and Australian art history, contemporary film, theories of perception and complex images in global contexts. He published the first book on the English art critic Adrian Stokes, which won a national prize in 2004. His book project on The Reversed Canvas in Western Art was funded by an Australian Reseach Council Discovery Grant. In 2016-17 he helped bring the Continental Shift exhibition of nineteenth-century American and Australian Landscape Paintings to the Art Gallery of Western Australia and the Ian Potter Gallery, University of Melbourne with teaching units and international symposia. Co-edited with Kenneth Haltman, papers from these projects are to be published by University of Chicago Press as *Wilderness and Colonization in Nineteenth-Century Australian and American Landscape Paintings* in 2019. He lectures internationally and writes art criticism locally.

Sural, Agnieszka is a writer, curator and producer in the fields of visual and performing arts, and architecture. From 2016 she's a contributing editor for the Flash Art International. Between 2012–2017 she was an editor on the culture.pl. She was a curator (together with Julia Staniszewska) of the Witryna gallery project in a window shopping in Warsaw (2007–2014) and the interdisciplinary platform Temps d'Images Festival at the Centre for Contemporary Art Ujazdowski Castle (2005–2011). She's a co-author and editor of books: "Polish Phrase Book with Art in the Background" (with Maryna Tomaszewska) and "Witryna 2007–2009" (with Julia Staniszewska). She runs the

Witryna Foundation and works independently with artists and public and private institutions in Poland and abroad. She lives and works in Warsaw.

Serexhe, Bernhard is an art historian, author, independent international curator, and certified expert for electronic and digital art. Dr. Serexhe studied sociology, psychology, educational science, and art history, and holds a doctorate in art history from the University of Freiburg (DE). He has published extensively on architecture and heritage history, art and media theory. Since 1995 he has been a consultant on media policy to the Council of Europe. From 1994–2016 he was the co-founder and chief curator of ZKM | Media Museum Karlsruhe. He has held teaching positions at the Russian Academy of Fine Arts in Saint Petersburg (1999), the University of Bern (2000–2001, 2008), the University of Basel (2001), the University of Arts and Design Karlsruhe (2001), the University of Karlsruhe (2002–2006), and the Stuttgart State Academy of Art and Design (2011). From 2008–2012 he was Professor for Aesthetics and Media Theory at the Istanbul BILGI University. From 2010–2012 he was initiator and leader of the EU-funded research project Digital Art Conservation. Since 2016, he has been curating ongoing international exhibitions, consulting for international art institutions, and providing expertise on the preservation of digital media art.

Smith, Damian was born in Melbourne, Australia, Damian Smith is a curator and art critic with more than twenty years experience in the field of contemporary art. He is the Director of Words For Art, an international consultancy specializing in contemporary culture and discourse. He is a Curator for China Art Projects, Beijing promoting contemporary Chinese art internationally. He is Editorial Consultant for the Global Mind Project, an arts and neuroscience venture that has garnered critical acclaim through its representation in major international surveys of art-science hybridity. As an art critic and writer he has published more than one-hundred articles on contemporary art, including peer reviewed papers for leading international journals and art museums. He is a Member of the International Association of Art Critics and his advice is regularly sought for projects in the global arena. He has held numerous positions in both the public and commercial sectors and has curated more than thirty exhibitions. His interests include contemporary Australian, Chinese and Tibetan art, the history of Modernism in the antipodes and hybrid and new-media practice.

Stein, Judith E. is the co-president of AICA-USA, writer, and curator who studied at Barnard College and the University of Pennsylvania. She is the author of *Eye of the Sixties, Richard Bellamy and the Transformation of Modern Art* (Farrar, Straus & Giroux,

2016), which earned the Athenaeum Literary Award. As curator at the Pennsylvania Academy of the Fine Arts, she organized *Red Grooms, A Retrospective*; *The Figurative Fifties, New York School Figurative Expressionism,* (with Paul Schimmel;) and *I Tell My Heart: The Art of Horace Pippin*, which traveled to the Metropolitan Museum of Art. Dr. Stein's articles, interviews and reviews have appeared in *Art in America*, *Art News*, and *The New York Times Book Review*. Among her honors is a Creative Capital/Andy Warhol Foundation Arts Writers Grant; a Pew Fellowship for literary non-fiction; and a Lannan Foundation writing residency in Marfa, Texas.

Streitfeld, Lisa Paul has been professional critic for two decades, ranging from mainstream to avant-garde to global critic for Huffington Post Arts (2010-2017). She received her doctorate in media philosophy in 2016 from European Graduate School. Currently based in New York and Berlin, Dr. Streitfeld gave presentations on the critic and the Heisenberg Uncertainty Principle at AICA Dublin, as well as Berlin and Los Angeles. Her background as an experimental novelist and screenwriter catalyzed her journey as critic, curator and New Media artist to uncover the central principle of a new modernism based on an authentic gender equality. In 2007-08, her five-chapter public Lab experiment in hermeneutics, www.thealchemyoflove.com, sped her on a multimedia trajectory culminating in a multimedia virtual/gallery project (2013-2017) taking her from Berlin to Tel Aviv – culminating in an Oxford presentation. In pursuit of a Web 3.0 virtual collaboration with the ubiquitous celebrity, she pushed the boundaries of criticism in public space and virtual exchanges. During the death of her trade of newspaper criticism, she pioneered a new model of critical sponsorship through virtual channels – HUFFINGTON POST, WORDPRESS, GOFUNDME and MEDIUM – in a quest to restore through virtuality the timeless pursuit of the avant-garde: to be timeless.

Sanc, Marilena Preda is a visual artist. Professor at the National University of Arts, Bucharest. Marilena Preda Sanc is an interdisciplinary artist who creates drawing, painting object, photography, artist book, media installation, video, performing arts and mural art. She is the author of art writings focused on Feminism, Electronic Art and Public Art.
From 1980 her work has been presented internationally at museums, conferences, symposium, broadcast venues and galleries.
Integrating the traditional forms of art and the new media arts, her art works visualizes and investigates the body/mind/soul/behavior in relation to nature and social/political and representational space. Her art work explores the feminism problematic as gender/ageism and woman as leader in an eco-feminism key.

Tang, Audrey is a civic hacker and Taiwan's Digital Minister in charge of Social Innovation, Audrey is known for revitalizing the computer languages Perl and Haskell, as well as building the online spreadsheet system EtherCalc in collaboration with Dan Bricklin. In the public sector, Audrey served on Taiwan national development council's open data committee and K-12 curriculum committee; and led the country's first e-Rulemaking project. In the private sector, Audrey worked as a consultant with Apple on computational linguistics, with Oxford University Press on crowd lexicography, and with Socialtext on social interaction design. In the voluntary sector, Audrey contributed to Taiwan's g0v ("gov-zero"), a vibrant community focusing on creating tools for the civil society, with the call to "fork the government".

Tsai, Raylin is Inspector of the Supervisory Board of Public Service Pension Fund, Examination Yuan, Senior researcher of the National Academy of Civil Service. Professor of I-Shou University, Taiwan (1997-2016). Adjunct professor of Graduated Institute for Theater Arts, National Sun Yat-sen University, National Taiwan University of Arts, and Taiwan Police College. Board member of International Association of Art Critics (2013-15), and executive committee member of Aica Taiwan (since 2000). His interests research fields are Aesthetics, Art Theory, Philosophy, Religion Study, and Culture Administration.
His works includes *On Egological and Non-egological Phenomenology* (1987); *Noema and Meaning* (1992); *Poetic and Rational, Two Attitudes towards Aesthetics* (2000); other books and various papers on Philosophy, Aesthetics, and Art Criticism.

Wójtowicz, Ewa is media arts researcher and art critic, teaching at the University of Arts in Poznań, Poland. Author of monographs: Art in Post-media Culture (2016) and Net Art (2008).

Wang, Yu-Juin is an international consultant for social innovation, independent culture critics and adjunct assistant Professor of Liberal Education at the Taipei Medical University (TMU), Taiwan. She holds a PhD in Physics (Stony Brook, USA), master in Philosophy and is a PhD candidate in Political Science (both at the University of Trier, Germany). She has conducted post-doctoral research in Chalmers University of Technology in Goeteborg, Sweden. She is currently committed to the <Taiwan/German dialogue in social innovation & social enterprise (SISE)> project, which encourages exchange of NGOs, citizen groups and corporates to disseminate the core values of Sustainable Development Goals (SDG). She is awarded the 2018 <German/Taiwan Friendship Medal> by the German Institute Taipei.

Forking Democracy

Audrey Tang

Unlike many people today, I'm an optimist. This strange condition began when I was 15 years old. That was 1996; I discovered that the future of human knowledge is on the Web, and my textbooks were all out of date. So I told my teachers: I want to quit school and start my education on the World Wide Web. Surprisingly, the teachers all agreed with it.

A year later, I founded a startup working on Web technologies, and I got to join this fabulous Internet community that runs with this crazy idea — an open, multi-stakeholder political system that powers the Internet to this day.

Today, as Taiwan's first Digital Minister, I'm putting into practice the ideas that I learned when I was 15 years old: Rough consensus, civic participation, and radical transparency. Surprisingly, it's working. And it's transforming our society.

Two years ago, our President Tsai Ing-wen said an inspiring statement in her inauguration speech. She said: "Before, democracy was a clash between two opposing values, but now democracy must become a conversation between many different values." Indeed, in conventional thinking, social benefits and business profits, for example, are opposite forces and often contradict each other, forcing the government to make tradeoffs. However, the idea of social innovation brings forth a brand new way of thinking.

For people working on social innovation, the core objective may be achieved by developing business models to address social issues or environmental issues, and the government's role has changed. Instead of being the arbiter torn between different sides, we are now asking a different set of questions. We ask: "What are our common values despite different positions?"; and we ask: "Given the common values, can we find solutions for everyone?" This is the spirit of co-creation, a spirit for the subversion of paradoxes. Civic technology — the branch of technology that enables millions of people to listen to each other, instead of one person speaking to million people — is a core ingredient to co-creation.

Indeed, in the past couple of years, Taiwan has been consistently ranked as the top country internationally on open data, internet participation, women's digital access, digital inclusivity, et cetera. All this was because we adopted open data and crowdsourcing as national direction since 2014 — it was catalyzed and epitomized by an Occupy movement in March 2014. There was a live demo of mass participation — We occupied the Parliament for 22 days.

At the time, the MPs in Taiwan were refusing to deliberate a Trade Service Agreement with Beijing, so the occupiers got into the Parliament at night and stayed there. For 22 days, we demonstrated how to deliberate a Trade Service Agreement with the whole society. There were over 20 NGOs participating. The Greens, the Labors, the Independents, everybody. We supported this whole deliberation with radically transparent broadcasting, live streaming, logistics system, which we exported to Hong Kong for the Umbrella Movement in the same year, and was powered by this community called g0v.

g0v is a civic tech community with a call to "fork the government." We take the government websites, which all end in gov.tw, and make better open alternatives that end in g0v.tw. For example, the annual national budget is hundreds of pages long, in a PDF file, and very hard to read.

The g0v community's very first project was budget.g0v.tw, which shows the national budget in a way that everybody understands, and you can drill down to each and every budget details. Today, this system is adopted by seven city governments and powers the participatory budget platform for the Taipei City at budget.taipei. Anyone can just look at this map, find the part of city budget they care about, type in any question they want to ask, and a career public servant actually comes forward and answers that part of the question. It becomes a direct dialogue platform, not through the city council, but for the career public servants to communicate with citizens.

So why are there so many civic hackers in Taiwan, like me, who spoke to my clients during the Occupy movement — Apple, Oxford University Press, Socialtext — saying, "OK, I have to take a three-week leave because democracy needs me?" I think it's because of our generation — I'm 37 today — we are the first generation that has enjoyed the freedom of speech after three decades of martial law and dictatorship.

That freedom arrived in 1989, the year of personal computers. For us, the personal computer revolution and freedom of speech is the same thing. Our first presidential election by popular vote in 1996 is also the year that the World Wide Web got popular.

Internet and Democracy, not two things, one and the same thing in Taiwan. So for the past 30 years, when we see "free software," we always think of freedom of assembly and freedom of speech, never "free of cost."

We know that freedom is never free of costs. Our parents' generation, our grandparents' generation paid dearly for it -- and we need to use the software freedoms to keep it free, as we did during the Occupy movement in 2014. The movement caused a revolution, although a peaceful revolution. There was a radical transformation of social expectations at the end of 2014, and many Occupiers just found themselves elected mayors when they did not expect it.

Because of this, the Prime Minister resigned, and the new Prime Minister, an engineer, said, "OK. From now on, crowdsourcing, open data are just going to be the national direction." Occupiers and the civic tech people who supported them were then invited as mentors, advisors, to the public service to solve issues like Uber.

Uber is very interesting because it is a meme — a virus of the mind. The meme was called "Sharing Economy," and it says that algorithms dispatch cars better than laws, so we don't have to obey laws. The meme spreads through apps, from drivers to passengers to drivers, and you can't really argue with a meme, just like you can't argue with the flu. It's not in the same category. There are protests, the taxi drivers surrounded the ministry of transport, demanding negotiation. But how do we negotiate with a virus of the mind?

For us, the solution is through a deliberation that involves thousands of stakeholders. It's a scaling down of the deliberation we just did with half a million people, so we think we can do it.

Deliberation, thinking deeply about something together, is an effective vaccine against a virus of the mind. When everyone — passengers and drivers, academics and public servants — listened to each other and formed a consensus, we become immune to divisive PR campaigns in the future. A proper deliberation, with the "Focused Conversation Method," involves four stages.

The first stage is "Facts", where we collect evidence, first-hand experiences, objective data. Then, after that is confirmed, we move to collect everybody's "Feelings" about those same facts. You may feel angry. I may feel happy. It's all OK. After people converge on their feelings that resonates with everybody, we then talk about "Ideas" — The best ideas are the ones that address the most people's feelings. Then we translate them into legalese and sign them into "Decisions."

However, if the decision-making process is not transparent, people on the street would speak a different language than people in the government — so they're not even agreeing on basic facts, let alone each others' feelings. In that situation, ideas become "Ideologies" — viruses of the mind so potent, that they can blind people to new facts and to each other's feelings.

So our first step is open data, that is, making all the facts available, and ask the private sector and civil society to share what they have. Next, we created an interactive survey on Pol.is, to ask about how they feel. Four groups of people soon emerged: Taxi drivers, Uber drivers, Uber passengers, and other passengers. The Pol.is system shows each group how their shared sentiments are received by other groups.

The interesting thing is, it lowers people's antagonism. Because you see all these people on different sides are your Facebook and Twitter friends, you just didn't talk about this over dinner. At the beginning, the people were all on the corners, but because we say we only give binding power of anything that people can propose that convince a supermajority — that's 80 percent of people — the participants converged on feelings that resonate not only with like-minded people but across the aisle.

Instead of distracting, we attract consensus. After we get a set of feelings that resonate with practically everybody, it's now much easier for the government to meet with all the stakeholders, and check with them, one by one. Here is the consensus of the people. Do you agree? If you do agree, how do we translate that into law? They are bound to the words they said during the live-streamed consultation, and the stakeholders agreed. When we ratified their agreements in August 2016, everybody knew that it's coming. Everybody anticipated it. Uber now operates legally under the new framework, but so did the taxi companies, who are now adopting the same model that Uber is using for dispatching its cars.

So this method works. The next question is: Can we scale this process of listening?

So right after the ratification, I joined the cabinet as the Digital Minister, to explore this possibility through PDIS, the public digital innovation space. It's like Policy Labs in the UK. It's a digital service at the national level. We have designers. We have programmers. We are automating away a lot of those chores that the public servants are doing, in order to make participation possible. Even more interesting than the technological contributions, is the culture that we are bringing to the government.

For example, I'm a radically transparent digital minister. By that, I mean that all the journalists, all the lobbyists, everybody gets to ask me questions, but only publicly. If I get questions from a private email, I will reply and say if it's OK to give my answers publicly. If not, I just give them links to what my previous statements are.

It's not just to the lobbyists and journalists but also for internal meetings. For all the hundreds of internal meetings that I have had since I became the digital minister, everything was transcribed. There was the written record for everything everybody said during meetings, and we sent them to participants afterward to check for 10 days, and publish.

The effect of this is very surprising. The bureaucrats actually become very innovative and risk-taking. They propose some very good ideas under this condition. That's because previously, before I introduced this kind of radical transparency, they would get the blame if things go wrong, and the minister would get the credit if things go right.

Now, with this completely accountable record, if things go right, they get the credit, because their name is on the transcript. Because it's an experimental method, if things go wrong, it's all the digital minister's fault. Under this condition, they become very innovative and open to a lot of interesting ideas.

One of the ideas is adopting this thoroughly free software platform called Sandstorm, as our public service internal platform. We use the same tools, like Etherpad, like Trello, like Slack, how the free software community is organizing ourselves these days, we also use it in the public service.

Previously, the roadblock was the cyber security issue, but we were able to find this community platform called Sandstorm, that solves the cyber security problem. It gets audited by our cyber security department so that all the free software that runs on top of it doesn't suffer from cyber security attacks and issues. We were able to adopt a lot of free software working methods, just by adopting this Sandstorm free software platform.

We have a lot of interesting systems proposed by young public servants, like an app for ordering lunch together, or to plan travels together, or whatever. It's really good to have this choice. Also, we had an e-petition platform as a way for people to participate. It was like the "We the People" platform in the US. It did not receive much attention because, for cross-ministry issues, people would get those very blank, very bureaucratic answers that don't really solve their problems, but just explains why they can't do much about it.

After I became the digital minister, we asked each ministry to send a team, at least one person, to serve as participation officer. We assembled this virtual team of 50 people online, using Rocket.Chat and all those tools for online engagement. Now, in Taiwan, when people start a petition, they know instead of just a dutiful response, they will actually get to meet with all the relevant ministries in Taipei, or we will travel to those rural areas and islands if they are petitioning for local development.

We solved a lot of very interesting problems like this, without exposing any public servant to risk. So we relieved their fear, uncertainty, and doubt around civic participation. For example, we have a petitioner last May who petitioned that for Mac and Linux users, the national income tax filing software is "explosively unfriendly" to use and so instead of just explaining the problem, we invite everyone who complained the loudest to co-create the new tax filing system for this year.

Through this kind of co-creation, people learned that they can contribute their expertise, not just as complaints, but as co-creation efforts. By collaborating with the civic sector, we are building a robust environment suitable for social enterprises to grow, where the power of civil society could be brought into full play.

The venue we hold these collaboration meetings, the SIL because we organized five co-creation workshops, to which 100+ social enterprises were invited to communicate their conceptions and expectations for the Lab. As such, we achieved a blended consensus and created a space fulfilling all purposes. For example, the Lab stayed open till 11:00 p.m., and so did the café and kitchen — a resident chef was also arranged.

Moreover, I personally provide my office hour at the Lab every Wednesday, from 10am to 10pm. Provided my visitor agree to have our conversation posted online, anyone interested in social enterprises is welcomed to have a discussion with me. The different regional cities' social enterprises, the innovators, gather around me. It's just me that travels. Everybody else remains in Taipei, but we still have good video conference and transcription that makes it very easy to see the local problems being surfaced and being resolved in a very quick fashion because all the related eight or nine ministries are there.

Once the people solve it, the other unrelated ministries also understand, "OK, so this problem is to be resolved in this kind of way." "g0v Air Pollution Observation Network" is such an example.

By combining the diversified talents in network communities, this project utilizes the simple air quality sensor "airbox," which is becoming very popular, and applies IoT technologies, so that all interested people can participate by providing real-time air quality information, whether on their own balconies, at school, or in the office. Little by little and bit by bit, thousands of contributors accumulated a massive database, which is closer to that of the air quality in the actual places where people are active.

An exceptional advantage of Taiwan is the full support, instead of rejection, of the government. As part of the forward-looking infrastructure plan, we launched an "IoT for Public Good" program with a 4-year budget of TWD 4.9 billion (USD ~150 million). In the program, an enormous amount of environmental data on air products, meteorology, water resources, earthquakes, disaster relief, etc. are integrated into a high-speed computing environment, so that we can collaboratively discover the correlations between social activities and environmental phenomena more quickly. We are also working with our Industrial Technology Research Institute to assist with the manufacture of domestic, affordable, high-quality PM 2.5 detectors, so communities can yield data of a higher accuracy.

Why does the Taiwan government encourage such social innovations? Currently, there arc many misunderstandings between governments and their people due to a lack of transparency and insufficient information.

Using the air quality in Taiwan as an example, establishing effective dialogs about public policies is difficult until the sources of daily air pollution are disclosed to the whole society — including what pollution comes from outside Taiwan, from fixed sources in Taiwan, and from mobile sources, etc. We are proud that "airbox" related products and application experiences have been introduced all over the world.

So to speak, by uniting the strengths of both the government and the public, Taiwan proved to be capable of not only solving its own problems but also providing such solutions to other countries in similar situations as a reference.

Moreover, we have a "Sandbox Act" in Taiwan, so if you experiment in FinTech, or in self- driving vehicles, you can apply for an experimentation for 12 months up to 3 years. You get to break some laws during that period, but you need to explain why these laws need to be broken to achieve the common good.

During the experiment, we assemble a multi-stakeholder panel that collectively decides, using civic tech and consensus-gathering methods, whether the society thinks this is a good idea moving forward, or if it's a bad idea. If it's a good idea, regulations and laws get changed because of this social innovation. If it's not a good idea — at least the risk is limited and everybody learns something from it, so we can try a different model next time.

Through this way, Taiwan contributes our experience to the planetary civic society, focusing not just one or two sustainable development goals, but especially on SDG17, cross-sectoral, international, and cross-discipline collaboration.

In conclusion, I'd like to share a prayer with you about the subversion of paradoxes:

When we see "internet of things", let's make it an internet of beings. When we see "virtual reality", let's make it a shared reality. When we see "machine learning", let's make it collaborative learning. When we see "user experience", let's make it about human experience. When we hear "the singularity is near", let us remember: the Plurality is here.

The Matrix of Visibility and Legitimacy: Art and Democracy in the Age of Digital Participation

Nikos Papastergiadis

The condition of spectatorship and the modes of social interaction are inextricably interconnected. A transformation of one produces a reconfiguration of the other, and vice versa. Consequentially, aesthetics and politics are forever intertwined. This lecture is structured in three parts. First, I will contrast the contemporary nexus between spectatorship and participation against the traditional and modern forms of aesthetic contemplation. This general reflection will then be situated in a brief outline of the artistic experiments with the boundaries of perception and action that have been conducted since the early parts of the twentieth century. In the second part, I will explore a collaborative artwork that addresses the condition of visuality in a media-saturated urban environment. Finally, I will reflect on how Groys's account of flow in modern and contemporary art blurs the schematic distinctions between traditional, modern and contemporary spectatorship, and provides a useful standpoint for commenting on the contradictions between democratizing potential of new media and the wider politics of visibility.

I: Conditions of Spectatorship and Modes of Sociality

If the traditional position of the spectator stood before a work of art, the modern subject moved around the work, and the contemporary participant engages with the work, then we can see a spectrum that covers a range of positionalities - from passive to active observation, as well as a distinction between physical and virtual mobility. Of course, this schema is an idealization, in reality the three perceptual modalities are neither diametrically opposed, nor organized in a developmental sequence. All encounters with art are interactive. At a minimum, art stimulates a leap from perception to meaning making. Whether it is a visceral response, a deep cogitation, or a fanciful flight of the imagination, art requires a bridge between sensory experience and understanding. Even if the configuration is weighted differently in their respective epochs, there is a now discernible difference between contemplative spectatorship and engaged participation. This difference can be captured by the contrast in the traditional ways of seeing art, as if our vision of the artwork operated like a singular ray of light that zoomed in to a specific area of focus, to the contemporary modes of ambient attention, which gathers information from near and far in the way a satellite dish picks up signals. However, after the explosion in digital communication, the possibilities for interaction are extended beyond the individual's mental activity and physical touch. Participation in art is increasingly experienced in a media saturated outdoor context and driven by algorithmic codes that extend the levels of interface. In a digital age, participation not only occurs in complex public spaces but relies on embodied communication devices that literally enable signs to pass through a multitude of bodies. Is it still accurate to speak of spectator in these events? Is the person reflecting on and contributing to the production of a specific object that can be grasped as an artwork, or does this level of participation blur the process by which the work of art is entangled in a web of real and virtual events?

First let us unpack the process of traditional spectatorship. The gaze of the spectator was directed towards a fixed object such as a framed painting. This may appear as a straightforward relationship, however, from Ernst Gombrich to Boris Groys the problem of spectatorship - in terms of the uncertainty over the physiological, psychological and sociological dimensions of perception - has haunted art historians. Standing before a painting, the traditional spectator received the sensation of an image and registered it as information. This double activity requires the mind to perform a combination of extractive and projective tasks such as ascertaining, identifying, decoding, deducing, and comparing. From a suitable distance the spectator's gaze apprehends the overall composition, and also zooms in to grasp the inherent message. Also, as there is no perception without selection, elements in the artwork are both isolated and related to each other. In this traditional model of spectatorship the locus of meaning originates in the artwork. It is presumed that the artist has intentionally arranged the signs and the work of the spectator is to penetrate, extract and re-construct the meaning. By performing this role, which is part witness and part interpreter, the spectator produces a kind of focus that suspends the flow of time and holds back any interference from the surrounding space. The result of spectatorship ranges from pure aesthetic pleasure and spiritual revelation, to a reflection on political issues, as well as an exercise in frivolous entertainment and commercial opportunism (Belting, Huizinga). In a perfect system of communication the artist's intention and the spectator's attention are mutually aligned. In this configuration there is a one to one experience between the spectator and the artwork. Whether it occurs in the flash of revelation, or through a slow contemplative process, the appreciation of art is personal. It is experienced as if the artist intended it to be unique for the spectator. Thus, the structure of a traditional painting was organized with an ideal spectator in the artist's mind. The painting is not complete until the ideal spectator feels as if it was made for him or her.

In the context of modernity the spectator's position and perspective undergoes a series of radical challenges. As modern artists experimented with the innovations in optics and aligned themselves with revolutionary movements, spectators found themselves as either victims of 'shock' tactics, or students in a journey or perceptual transformation. During the early part of the 20th century the Dadaists in Zurich, and much later, with the Happenings in New York, artists staged performances that aimed to shock their audiences out of the seats of pure spectatorship and liberate themselves from the 'hang ups' of bourgeois patriarchal conduct. The image was meant to offer a starting point for wider imagination, clarification that opened up possibilities, insight that deepened understanding, or even in the aggressive acts of confrontation, the rage that they inspired was justified as a means to dispense with the distortions, unzip hypocrisy and reveal the manipulation of the truth. The introduction of another relatively simple idea – collage, the assembly of disjointed fragments – which had an immense influence on cinema, literature, music and design, was not only expressive of the dynamic ruptures of this epoch, but also one of the most powerful methods in toolkit for transforming the cultural condition of spectatorship. (Willett 2018:83) In the modern period the spectator is alerted to the fragmentary and partial nature of viewing. Spectators were expected to unshackle themselves from what Gombrich called the conventional "equation between life and the image", and discover how the habituation of our senses, the perpetuation of conceptual bearings and inherited social hierarchies, constrained both the understanding and production of new sensory realities. (1982) If the traditional spectator enjoyed was both detached from the work of art and equipped with a sovereign, objective and omniscient gaze, the modern spectator was decentered and flung into whirling forcefields.

Although more cerebral the developments in minimalism and conceptual art also disrupted the traditional condition of spectatorship. While viewer once again stood in front of a minimalist painting, he or she was faced with an image that was entirely constituted by a limited use of color and bereft of any narrative. There were no figures in a landscape, or symbols that needed to be interpreted and decoded. The ascetic visual experience of a minimalist painting was not guided by a story. On the contrary, the viewer was invited to participate in the mood of the painting, and immerse him or herself in an abstract world. There was no singular point that determined the perspective, and, as Sol LeWitt admitted, meaning making was uncoupled from authorial intention: "The artist may not necessarily understand his own art. His perception is neither better nor worse than that of others." (No 25 of the Sentences on Conceptual Art, LeWitt 2003, 850) The challenge of revelation through the negation of narrative content was taken to further extremes in conceptual art. The communicative function of art was distilled into the most direct expression of an idea. By eliminating symbolic content art became a "poetic instrument of communication rather than as an object of contemplation" (Groys 2016: 130). However, Groys also pessmistically claimed that, in the absence of a pedagogy that can rein in sensory experience, the realm of the aesthetic simply hovers and then dissipates: "to be able to experience an aesthetic enjoyment of any kind, the spectator has to be aesthetically educated. This education necessarily reflects the social and cultural milieus into which the spectator was born and in which he or she lives. In other words, an aesthetic attitude presupposes the subordination of art production to art consumption – and likewise, the subordination of artistic theory and practice to a sociological perspective." (2016: 124) In more general terms the avant-garde sought to make a break with not just the mimetic function of the image, as a realist depiction of nature, but also with any inherited visual tradition. The spectator did not look at a modern painting to read an image, but rather was confronted with new optical, intellectual and social challenges. As the function of the image becomes less certain, so does the status of spectatorial knowledge. (S. Wright) Kant argued that as the image was bound in a nexus between information and pleasure, but the avant-garde, by disrupting the link between the visible and the comprehensible, exposed the black hole in the era of mobility.

In the context of contemporary art the spectator's gaze becomes even more mobile and the role of active participation in the event of art becomes all the more central. The focus of effort shifts even further from detached optical reception towards social engagement - tracking multiple signals and tracing social relations. Although, as in the condition of the modern spectator, the process of meaning-making is not confined to decoding messages, it is extended to engaging with interactive devices, absorbing an abstract ambience and participating in social events that are experienced in real-time. The explosion of mobile communication devices has also produced a proliferation in the inventory of aesthetic environments. From mediated body prosthetics, the incorporation of domestic interiors as incubators for trans-national artistic experiments, the seepage from the museum's thresholds to the surrounding streets, the tele-matic linking of large screens in urban spaces, the routinization of art fairs, festivals and biennales, art is now worn, carried, encountered, and transmitted on a scale and in ways that were previously unimaginable.   Sensory experience is distributed more widely through the body, and the border between the artwork and its environment becomes tremulous. As time-space is not just a source of references, and the body of the viewer is not confined to the role of receiver, then a new nexus between spectator and participant is forged, and new frameworks for making meaning are mobilized. From this context the locus and limits of meaning are not embedded in the formal boundaries of the artwork, or structured by the artist's intentions, but are projected into a wider field of participant association and engagement. Liam Gillick recognized that the elevation of the principle of participation inverts the traditional distinction between the objective existence of the artwork and the subjective experience by which art starts to work. In his own prosaic terms, he compared the activation of art to the light in the fridge, "it only comes on, if you open the door". Being positioned amidst and accepting responsibility for activation the participant-spectator also occupies a novel time-space relationship to art. The suspension of temporal rhythms and insulation from spatial flows, that marked the traditional experience of an artwork, are now blurred. The artwork is not a special moment in time, but is flung into the flux of time-space. The object is not just drawn from everyday life, but its location is on a continuum with the ephemeral and contingent forces of ordinary space. The boundaries of the work are dissolved into a vague sense of an event, whose beginning and end is not always discernible, and which compels the participant-spectator to presume that they have entered from an interminable middle and that they occupy a mediating role. These characteristics are heightened in social engaged and interactive project where the work of art is not just thrust into an open field, but is caught up in a concatenation of communicative practices and entangled in a cultural formations that fold together background influence with the foreground of presence, that not only extend the subject matter of art, and multiply the locations for art, but also disturb the evaluative measures that distinguish art from life.

When the production and experience artwork is no longer confined to a discrete object in a church, palace or the neutral white cube of a gallery, that, in one way or another can be the focus of attention, but is now dispersed across multiple media platforms, immersed in an environment that is saturated with information, and dependent on the ongoing and unpredictable interactions with other people and things, then, what is the direction of the focus, where does the experience begin and end, what is the sum of the whole? This extension of the points of perception, multiplication of the sites of experience, and dispersal of the media for communication displaces the nexus between artistic production, critical interpretation and social validation. It presents us with a scenario where the work is permeable, fluid, incomplete and open.

Through this nexus of spectator-participant the transformative effect of art is not organized as a shock to jolt forth the new, but rather in ideal terms, instantiates an experience of being in common, or what Raunig (2018) calls a process of concatenation where event, experience and collective action come together to produce a multitude of possibilities. As the hands and minds engage, the process of manufacturing – making with hands – connects with other aspects of everyday life, and blurs traditional distinctions between the original and the copy, the raw and the refined, as well as the "untouchability of the art object" (Huhtamo: 2007, 71). The linear relationship that defined the traditional role of spectatorship is now entangled a complex feedback system. Where does the critic stand in relation to an interactive installation by Rafael Lozano-Hemmer? Does every critic need to stay for the duration of Douglas Gordon's 24 hour Psycho? Is there an ideal vantage point from which the ambience of James Turrell's mist is perceived, analyzed, compared and evaluated, or is this question as misguided as the attempt to plot fluids as if they were just a multiplication of mobile solids? If the image is not confined to the external surface of an entity, as if it were a deceptive layer that was superimposed on the real thing, then how does critique proceed when it is no longer a matter of peeling away deceptive surfaces, or correcting distorted associations? How do we make sense of images that drift without explicit reference points, intermingle with diverse elements, and are so deeply interwoven into the identity of an element, that it is no longer meaningful to refer to an image of something, but to recognize the image as the thing and process by which meaning is made?

II: Making the Matrix Visible

These questions came into sharp relief when Gerard Byrne and Sven Anderson invited me onto a project that they call The Visibility Matrix. The aim of the project was to develop a "multiscreen synchronized video exhibition" that was constructed as an "elaborate video playback network". The project was not seeking to produce a "re-thinking of video as a discrete image", because, I assume that Anderson and Byrne think that this would simply truncate and subsume video to the hegemonic frames of the still image. Rather, they aim to explore the use of video in its own terms as an "active signal". Video is thereby registered as an emitting source of signs. Given that the material capacity of video is ideally suited towards reproduction and networking, it is a medium that has the unique capacity for plasticity.

Anderson and Byrne noted that from the 1960s to the 1980s there was a wide range of art and technology projects that deployed multiscreen video projections, communication networks and algorithmic compositional principles. Many of these projects were indebted to cybernetic philosophies and telematics tools for elevating the role of feedback, and the artists were forerunners in the claim that art can be conjoined with democratizing politics and vernacular practices. (Roy Ascot, Steina and Woody Vasulka, Edward Shanken: Cybernetics and Art) The exhibition included a selection of videos by Juan Downey. These pioneering experiments provided the groundswell from which the contemporary communicative platforms have emerged. Multi-screen assemblages are now a ubiquitous feature of urban design and public culture is primarily conducted via mediated networks.

However, Anderson and Byrne stress a key distinction between the contemporary condition and the context of experimentation in the final decades of the 20th Century. They claim that the earlier projects were still defined by an epistemology of the singular. Whether the earlier works were either developed as a contrast to the still image, or as a reconfiguration of film, the frame of the artwork was conceived in terms of singularity. The excess of flows and interactions had not yet engulfed the objective conditions of production, perception and communication. The point from which a work was seen, the ways in which it was grasped and interpreted still presupposed the singular perspective. This condition is now blurred. The modes of human subjectivity have undergone a radical transformation as the communicative devices have become a kind of virtual prosthesis to the mind/body. Anderson and Byrne go so far as to claim that it is impossible to return to these singularities, and that the point of their project is not reclamation of previous modalities, but a proposition of an "alternative to the composite formed by the subject + smartphone + online-video-sharing platform that has come to represent the current standard of visibility." (Notes for Editorial Board, January 2018)

While Anderson and Byrne claim that there is no going back, there is an implied critique of the fantasy of mobile communication without cost in our culture, and they are convinced that the status quo is not without an alternative. In the broadest terms, the project promised to offer a "lens through which to experience a proliferation of ideas around visibility, video, networks and distribution in the gallery context". To what extent can video serve as a "counterpoint" to the role of networking technologies and the gallery function as an agent that transforms the conditions of visibility in contemporary visual culture?

This is a paradoxical aim – for it while it acknowledges that images have already saturated the environment, and that information is ambient, it is everywhere and in everything, and yet the primal space for framing and contemplating the still image, the gallery, is now to be repurposed as the apparatus for reconfiguring a relationship to blurred experience of text and images in everyday life.

The presentation format mirrors the trope of proliferating screen-spaces that have come to dominate arenas as diverse as airport lounges, shopping malls, and the family dinner table. Our approach is to use the gallery to reconfigure, fragment, expand and intensify these idioms of public address.

If the camera once served as a box with an aperture for looking and framing the view of the world, and thereby organizing the direction and scope of perception, then I imagine that Anderson and Byrne are proposing to scale up the gallery as the apparatus for holding and giving form to the phenomenon ambience. In short, the gallery is not a neutral surface upon which an object is placed in order to provide a context for reflection and appreciation, but it is the environment in which images and texts flow in and out of our consciousness. Inside the gallery space-time is blurred, rather than the gallery serving as a space in which time is suspended, and in this bracketing of time and space, the object of art is contemplated. In the context of ambience, space and time are blurred because perception and engagement are entangled in a co-constitutive process. This is in contrast to the interpretative stance of modern gallery and classical museum where judgment is developed through a linear sequence of perception and deliberation. It is this complex nexus of visual perception, production, circulation and experience that Anderson and

Byrne call the visibility matrix.

Towards this end I was invited to be part of an editorial board that would funnel, filter and comment on material by other artists. The need for such an editorial board is, I assume part pragmatics, and part critical. Anderson and Byrne wanted a range of inputs that exceeded their direct scope of knowledge, but they were also faced with the challenge that all programmers confront when they seek to introduce artistic context into a public environment such as the large urban screens. When the program is not organized around specific viewing schedules and positions, then there is not only problem of anticipating a fragmented and oblique experience, but also challenge of having to commission work that will fill the extended screen time. Large screen operators all want to be more than a relay for television stations, but they also complain of the expense of commission works that can fill the hunger of their own beast. Some screens have developed strategies where they have commissioned artistic content profiled during targeted events, serve as a curated platform for artists and citizens to profile their own work, and draw on digital archives.

Gerard explained (email 22/01/18) that the book I edited Ambient Screens revealed a shared interest in the function and impact of "screen-space" on our cultural conceptions of visibility, and that he hoped that I was happy to join this editorial board. Of course, the overlap was significant, and the project provided an opportunity for a new collective endeavor to explore common objectives with like-minded peers. However, from the outset the vocabulary we used presented us with risks and traps. As an editor, I recognized the absurd disjunction between the ambition of the project, and it actual budget, and deduced that I would be forced to call on my nearest and dearest circle of friends. Indeed with such an iterative subject and modest budget any capacity to survey the scene was already impossible and flawed. At best, any response would be contingent and suggestive, rather representative let alone exhaustive.

Retracing my own recent encounters in Australia, Indonesia, Singapore, Greece, United Kingdom and Sweden I selected an eclectic but related group of artists. Carlos Capelan, once pointed out that with video, artists could use the camera as a spraying device for expanding the horizons of visibility. Ross Gibson was a collaborator on the Ambient Screens project, and an artist with an ongoing fascination with both indigenous cosmologies and eerie documentation of crime scenes. Eugenia Raskopoulos uses video and multiple screens to explore the experiences of cultural displacement and the mis/takes in translation. Tin Tin Wulia came to mind because of her obsession with alternative mappings of global belonging and the function of telematics technologies to stage co-presence in multiple sites. Danae Stratou, with her partner Yani Varoufaki, made an epic video on the pernicious impact of walls in conflict zones, and the perverse reality of their multiplication in a globalizing world. Mary Zygouri has worked with archives that contain the fragments of pioneering feminist performances in Greece. Charles Lim has used video to document the unstable boundaries between sea and land. Dennis Del Favero a pioneer in construction of video works and immersive environments has zoomed into prosaic details of social history and zoomed out in the realm of the nebula. Finally, Diego Ferrari has a practice in which he has interfered with the camera's shutter speed to both split the construction and blur the projection of images.

From these artists Anderson and Byrne were not seeking completed artworks to assemble as in a survey show or a mini-biennial. They were conscious of the integrity of artistic contributions and the potential that their material could be re-presented through a method that also extended the capacities of video to reconfigure spacetime. The resulting work presented a challenge towards the conventional mean for attributing and distributing authorship as it experimented with the associative pattern making in an algorithm and the interspersibility of video content on multiple screens.

Upon entry into the foyer of the Douglas Hyde Gallery in Dublin I noted a stack of old television monitors. The grainy and abstracted images that flickered on the boxes reminded of the early video works that Anderson and Byrne were referencing as the pioneering experiments. I did not recognize the content but walked towards the cluster of flat screens in the lower gallery. This seemed more familiar territory. Over a dozen screens where arranged throughout the space, usually in triangulated formations so that the three screens were at right angle to each other. This complex surface provided the screen for the material submitted by the artists. At first the gallery was an austere environment. On the second visit I had the benefit of choosing a fold up chair and positioning myself in a more strategic position. The screens were busy with content but there was no obvious viewing position. The material came to you from multiple directions. It was possible to stand in the middle and feel surrounding but multiple facets, a jagged and jarring experience. Or else, you could walk around the perimeter and catch glimpses from the radius. I chose at first to sit in a corner and gain a diagonal view. The viewpoint of images ranged from drone's eye views to underwater vision of the submarine cables. There was a strange fascination with industrial life and urban ruins. A thrilling display of rally driving at a hairpin corner reminded of the skills of taxi drivers in Naples.

In the second gallery I noted the return the old television monitors. There were a number of stacks of various configurations. In the middle of this gallery there was another seat with headphones. This was an obvious cue. I sat down and in the middle of the stack one monitor showed in full version what all the others were revealing in fragmented and abstracted form. It was a screening of Juan Downing video Moving (1974). Downing is one of the pioneers of video art. He was trained as an architect in Chile, but after travelling in Europe he became an artist that experimented in photography, drawing, electronic sculptures, performances and video. In the early 1970s, with a Sony Portapak, Downey embarked on numerous trips to Mexico, Guatemala, Chile, Peru that resulted in a project called Video Trans Americas (VTA) Series. The videos were screened in the exhibition Landscape Studies in Video at Long Beach Museum of Art (1975), and then as an installation at Whitney Museum of American Art (1976).

Moving is one of the early videos in Downey's VTA series. The central story documents a road trip in the United States undertaken by Downey and his friends. It is interspersed with footage of Downey's visits to indigenous communities in Central and South America. The style of the recording is loose and informal. It is not in the spirit of a conventional anthropological documentary. More of a filmic flip of the hat, an extension to the serious attention to subversive pleasure found in Jean Rouch. What is striking in Downey's videos is the relaxed and innocent atmosphere. When the camera turns on his fellow passengers in the car there is the expected lightness and good humor of friends on a journey. However, perhaps more surprising, given our own jaded and censorial sensibility, is the candid reception by strangers when the camera is turned on them. A young woman is driving alone in a Volkswagen beetle in parallel to Downey's car. He films her in her car, she notices and returns a smiling glace. Other travellers describe their travails and destination with simplicity and lack of affection. When the images of the journey through USA are interspersed with footage of indigenous villages in Central America we see kids punting on boats, men smoking, and women smiling. This portrayal is neither the melancholic pathos of disappearing world, nor the last stand of angry savages. Downey shows people looking back at his camera presence with an adaptive and affirmative air. The video is as much about his journey, as it is about the introduction of new apparatus in everyday life at a point in time that is most novel but almost invisible. For all the candor and rawness in the video there is also a compelling force in the narrative structure. As a viewing experience there is a desire to follow the vide to the end, and if you began watching it in the middle, there is the wish to continue with the looping presentation, until a sense of the whole is gained. Downey wrote, "The universe is not an assemblage of independent parts, but an overlapping, interrelated system of energy. All my work relates to this vision."   (Quoted in Amalia Mesa-Bains (1993). Ceremony of Spirit: Nature and Memory in Contemporary Latino Art

P17)

Roland Barthes once claimed that the pleasure of the text is always short, you see it, you get it, and then you exclaim: "is that all! " (Pleasure of the Text, 1975: 18) This request for more is not to be confused with the complaint that there is not enough. It is suggestive of the need to make the ongoing effort to connect, and the necessary adjustment to the endless deferral in the experience of satisfaction. How does the fragmentation of the narrative and the dispersal of perspectives in contemporary visual experience disrupt and reconfigure our sense of satisfaction? In A Visibility Matrix attention is not directed towards a singular point, and by virtue of the endless combinations afforded by the screening algorithm it is impossible to view the whole exhibition. Through the exchange between the editors and contributing artists Anderson and Byrne defined tags for each work that informed the associative patterns of algorithm. These tags do not add up into a new linear narrative but shuffle. Hence, each combination can leap into different associations. The content on the flat screen is often duplicated on other screens. The screens are adjacent to each other or positioned in overlapping formations, so that the same video can be seen through multiple but partial glimpses. This both stretches the viewing experience, but also provokes a mild form of paranoia. As you search for a point to place your gaze, you feel that a crucial scene will appear elsewhere. You try to lift one eye and direct it towards the impossible angle of the other side. Of course, this is frustrating. Your body cannot be everywhere, not even in all the corners of the installation of a dozen flat screens in a small gallery. In this agitated state, not dissimilar to a bargain shopper hunting in a mall, the furtive gaze shifts from one uncertain point to another at the periphery of its consciousness. One could keep oscillating between these points with suspicious wariness, or relax into an ambient perspective.

If Roland Barthes exclaimed: "Is that it!" when he reflected on a singular modernist text, what would be the exhortation that follows such a multiplicity of texts that are assembled in A Visibility Matrix? This is a work that defies linear perspective. It is formed in a turbulent dance of video inputs. To grasp the forms that 'happen' to emerge requires our eyes to move across multiple screens. By following, rather entering into, the action a different kind of immersion and exchange transpires. I am not sure I possess the language to articulate what is occurring across these screens. I suspect it will only be possible when the training of my eyes and imagination has become more attuned to feedback, iterative and relational processes. It seems obvious to note that an ambient perspective is the 'object' of attention. I can express the pleasure of being engrossed in following the movements across multiple screens, but I am not yet in possession of a language that conveys these sensations.

A Visibility Matrix is a demanding project that pushes, but has yet to resolve the very techniques of visibility that are reshaping the realm of the image, and the potentialities for democratization in a media saturated world. Such projects   return us to fundamental questions on: the separation between vernacular and artistic uses of the camera; the cost and copywrite for the aggregation of 'artwork" in an open archive or cloud based platform; the attributions of authorship in ambient productions; the scope for new interactive technologies to enhance direct audience participation to the extent that their feedback is palpable in not just enhancing aesthetic experience but also contributing a sense of being in common with others in public spaces; and finally, the capacity to activate both local and transnational public spheres. There a risk that this system invariably reintroduce through the front door of an algorithm the expansion of the cultural sphere, but one that is dominated by narcissistic and primordialist versions of individualism.

III: Kino-Aesthetics: Mix, Blur, Ambience

Two bad options stand before us. One is to protest against the incursions on the autonomy of authorship and the status of the artwork. The other is to promote the digital aggregation tools as part of the carnivorous agenda of neo-liberalism. My concern is neither to defend a retreat into the bad old hierarchy, nor promote the adoption of the new bad tendencies. In the traditional context of the museum the spectator's experience was organized around the same principles that defined the position and perspective of an objective critic. The modern condition of spectatorship revealed that objectivity is illusory. However, the challenge is not just a battle between benign universalism and dogmatic subjectivism.   Contemporary art projects such as 'A Visibility Matrix' open up the need for new lexicon on ambient awareness, as they prompt modes of participant-spectatorship that range from distracted awareness, active spectatorship, haptic visuality to deliberative co-production.

At the beginning of the twentieth century the German sociologist Georg Simmel noted the distinctive feature of the modern metropolis was the bombardment of mental stimulation, and he also observed that citizens needed to develop a blaze attitude as a coping device. Walter Benjamin was quick to note that distraction and fragmentation was not necessarily a negative experience, but rather part of the transformative process of modern culture. By the 1970s the musician Brian Eno responded to the muzak saturated urban environment by pioneering a soft mode of minimalism that he termed as ambient music. However, the digital communication revolution took the threat of mental over-exposure to another level. From the outset Paul Virilio feared that as human subjectivity failed to keep pace with information flows they would suffer from a condition he called picnolepsy (1991). By contrast, the dispersal of signs and proliferation of media was interpreted as - the source of new 'atmospheres' (Bohme 1993), an opportunity to invent multi-sensory designs (McCullogh 2013), the introduction of mediated prosthetics for monitoring care (Roquet 2016), as well as the expansion of platforms for aesthetic encounters and sites for transnational public spheres (Papastergiadis et. al. 2016). While we have witnessed a technological explosion in communication and a massive expansion in affective engagement with the cultural public sphere, there is no consensus as to whether this has generated attendant forms of social connectivity and democratic gains.

The divergence of commentaries on the impact of communicative technologies is symptomatic of the unresolved tension on the primacy of place in thought itself. For most of the 19th and 20th centuries our understanding of the world was dominated by perspectives and concepts that classified things in places and organized social, cultural, economic and political relations within national boundaries. Over fifty years ago Gombrich noted that art history had bent itself out of joint by focusing almost entirely on the problem of representing space. When time and motion was addressed, it had to be frozen into a punctum temporis – an instant point, or rather flow had to be captured in the space of a scene. (Gombrich 1982: 42) At the same time, the urban sociologist Henri Lefebvre proposed a new conceptual attunement to the "rhythms" in public life. More recently, George Marcus, noting the creative flows in participatory art practices, proposed that scholars should not just adopt 'mobile methods' but join in on the co-production of knowledge and sociality of 'mini-publics' (2015). These are clues and cues for acknowledging the expanded front of aesthetic experience and inviting experimentation with fieldwork, not quite tools and frameworks for re-thinking the image in the age of mobility. We now recognize that turbulent flows and continuous motion are vital for all of life. Without motion and mixture systems would either, overheat, collapse or atrophy. Despite this profound insight into the forces of life the conceptual reboot of our critical frameworks has not been so forthcoming. For instance, while contemporary art increasingly operates in a context of social interactivity, is experienced in multi-sensory environments, and reliant on multi-media platforms, the tools and categories of critical evaluation have barely kept pace. Our ways of seeing are still channeled into linear perspective.

Given the complexities of contemporary art we need to produce new concepts, frames and perspectives. Ambience is a useful starting point for rethinking the contemporary nexus between spectatorship and participation. However, it will also lead us to a reappraisal of the role of blurring and participation. Ambience refers to a communicative environment in which perceptual experience and human subjectivity are entangled with multiple stimuli from both strong channels and weak signals of information. However, there is not just a multiplication of media, there is also an acceleration in delivery and plasticity in feedback, and a phasing in and out of the background and foreground sources. Ambience speaks to the diversification, splitting and looping of communication. The concept refers to the interplay of media that are now dispersed across the cultural landscape and the transformations in the modes of sensory experience and cognition in public spaces. These transformations are not incidental, accidental and marginal. On the contrary, they are becoming the normal pattern of human subjectivity and the standard mode of communicative practice.

To make sense of the signs, associations and patterns that are formed in ambient spaces we need to modify our perspective. A standard approach is to identify the multiple tracks along which communication is delivered, a widening of the mapping of causation and interaction, as well as the dispersal of the points of observation across a wider field. From this 'field perspective', or what I call ambient perspective, there is a growing recognition that entities do not always have consistent identities and the relationship between perception and interpretation is destabilized by the variation of position. It has made us more sensitive to the complexity in feedback, iteration and relational transformation.

In contemporary art, ambient perspective is useful for referring to practices that adopt multi sensory stimuli and incorporate affective modes of awareness operating at the peripheries of apprehension. It complements the traditional approaches of linear perspective by highlighting the role of diffusion and contingency and the need for radial mode of critical attention. This approach is aligned to a decentered and pluriversal perspective. Just as the visitors to the museum experience art from the middle, scientists no longer see the cosmos from a human centric perspective:

We observe the universe from within it, interacting with a minuscule portion of the innumerable variables of the cosmos. What we see is a blurred images. This blurring suggests that the dynamic of the universe with which we interact is governed by entropy which measures the amount of blurring. It measures something that relates to us more than to the cosmos.   (Rovelli: 2018).

Rovelli's affirmative conception of blurring cuts across the conventional association with failure of focus. Of course, in everyday life blurring occurs when we are trying to identify a small entity that is moving with such rapidity or irregularity that its outline and trajectory appears fuzzy. Blurring can also occur when we are trying to concentrate on two or more objects that are apart from each other and our gaze cannot stretch out to put them in a coherent relationship. Or else, there is a sensation of stunned vision when we are trying to work on the computer screen but our focus is overpowered by the competing light source from the afternoon sun. However, an alternative understanding of blurring commences with letting go of an idealized notion of focus that presupposes a fixed and external position for viewing reality. As there is neither an outside nor a static point, only degrees of motion and constant interaction, it means that gradations of blurring are a constitutive feature of vision. Even if our regular sensory awareness of the world does not register the full scope of motion, and we seek to make sense of things by suspending the flow, delineating the boundary and separating the identity of things, this is always a form of what the literary theorist Gayatri Spivak called "strategic essentialism". It is done to spot, plot and name things, but it is often done in the hazy awareness that those same things are not quite we claim that they are. We do this because our senses have restricted capacities to grasp the big, small, fast and slow. These limitations are increasingly evident to us, not from philosophical reasoning or scientific demonstration, but in the banal uses of embodied communicative technologies. These tools are revealing and producing worlds that are normally imperceptible and unfathomable. Phones and watches are providing such rapid access to and extracting so much information that these devices are now blurring the border between the virtual and material. As information and pleasure come forth, interact and entangle with each other, we enter new knotting of knowledge and aesthetics. When Kant formulated the nexus of information and pleasure as the condition of aesthetic knowledge, he presupposed that both the production of art, and the aesthetic reception, occurred through the time and space of contemplation. The traditional and modern conditions of spectatorship relied on a time and space that was apart from real world. Both the artist's studio and the philosopher's desk rely on an exemption from the flow of the world. If art is now experienced in the context of knotting and folding together information and pleasure, then this also nexus between spectatorship and participation is not a capacity for the representation of time and space, but is forged in the making of timespace.

As participation swerves and stretches to merge with spectatorship it is loaded with new associations and heads in different directions. In ordinary language, participation refers to the effort or contribution of an individual, or a group, to achieve a goal. Without participation some outcomes are unrealizable, hence the term refers to the means by which an end is manifest. The new communication technologies have stretched the uses of participation from being the means for realizing as specific end into an endless activity. (Butt, McQuire, Papastergiadis 2016) Paradoxically, the spiraling feedback loop becomes an end in itself, and in some cases, this activity morphs into becoming a brand that, in turn can be sold as a new commodity. In the past two decades, participation has become a key feature in contemporary art. It has been adopted by artists to provide multi-sensorial experiences that widen the spectrum of engagement beyond the binary 'on' and 'off' switch. Participation is also the key plank for art that is entangled with social and political objectives. While participation once referred to a contributing effort, it is now exalted as an achievement: a sign that the citizen is not just a static spectator, but has been mobilized as an active agent (Tania Bruguera Museum of the Arte Util; Ahmet Ogut The Silent University). However, there are still doubts as to whether discourse on participation can fulfill the promise of stimulating creative responses, deepening critical understanding, forging hybrid formations, or whether it will be co-opted to perpetuate modular correspondences in keeping with a flat globalized world (Bishop, Kester, Sholette). Finally, after the communicative revolution and the seemingly unstoppable hegemony of the cultural industry discourse, Manuel Borja-Villel has pessimistically concluded that the role of art is threatened to a mere illusory life in the "infinite present" of endless consumption. (Esche & Borja-Villel 2016: 409) Is this how art and democracy ends, in an open invitation for mass participation that enables the authoritarianism and capitalism to be the keeper of popular consent?

Boris Groys provides a beguiling argument on the condition of spectatorship and the prospects of emancipation. From the pioneering example of the avant garde to contemporary forms of digital art, Groys charts the way artists have created conditions for training the imagination. However, the terrain that he surveys neither reveals a trajectory towards progressive politics, nor indicates that there is an expansion in cultural capacity. On the contrary, the cultural gains are messy and the political losses are many.

For Groys, the aim of the avant garde was to maximize art's communicative vitality by situating it amidst the flow of life. Art should not be preserved and protected in discrete spaces but forced to "share the fate of all other things of this world. That is why the radical avant garde wanted to destroy the museums and other traditional art institutions that protected artworks from their immersion and possible dissolution in the material flow. The artwork had to be put at risk and confronted with the same forces of destruction that endangered ordinary things". (118)

The exemplary figure of the avant garde was, in Groys's eyes, the perplexing figure of Kazimir Malevich. It was Malevich who expressed supreme detachment from the materiality of the art object and resisted the belief in the museum as the keeper of auratic objects that expressed historical progress. Malevich had no compunction in reducing all of Rubens's paintings to powder, for he claimed that: seeing art in this form "a mass of ideas will arise in people, and will be often more alive than actual respresentation (and take up less room)." (KM 'On the Museum' quoted in BG p 63)

By clearing away the old, Malevich was not declaring its redundancy, and making way for the successive new. His opposition to heritage and revolutionary zeal was not so straightforward. Groys stresses that for Malevich the value of historical knowledge did not pass from in the form of evolutionary progression. Neither were the lessons from the past accessed by studying its documents, nor was creativity a universal feature of human nature. The foundational claim of equality and the belief in progress is, according to Groys, foreign to Malevich. On the contrary, an older view on creation as arising from nothingness, and faith that power remains in negation, also brings forth the mystical conception of kenosis to explain the 'exceptional' function of the artist as mediator of banal truths. (BG p 60) By means of kenosis the potential for creation comes, not from nature, and is not enhanced pedagogy, but rather arises from aggressive self-negation and radical absorption. Kenosis assumes no reservoir of creativity in human nature, is aloof to educative procedures and social formations. Hence, the relation between kenosis and emancipation does not concord with either a claim that creativity originates in human nature, or the belief in the evolution of social progress. Kenosis allows for a new form of spectatorship and knowledge, it introduces a luminous form of access into the environment, as it renders a dissolution of the boundary between object and subject and therefore makes the other transparent and visible insofar as the subject frees itself by becoming nothingness. The spectator that is before the artwork requires a radical process of emptying out. This is not just the diversion of the gaze from decoding the content to determining the context of art, but rather a break that Groys claims ushers forth a "new transperancy, something comes to be seen that was never seen before – something that was hidden by the fullness of the world". (BG 83)

It is from this perspective that Groys looks at Malevich's paintings, finding no sign of nostalgia for the past, no critique of the present, and no promise for a better future, declares that he remains puzzled over his revolutionary status. On the contrary, Malevich "annuls" the hope for progress and equality, as he reclaims the "exceptional" status of the artist. (BG: 59) By explaining the transmission of Malevich's creative force through the concept of kenosis Groys is not necessarily embracing a return to Orthodox spiritualism, but he is distancing himself from the materialist perspectives on spectatorship and knowledge. It suggests that kenosis is also an allegory for the way revelation occurs in the age of participation.

Today, Groys suspects, that we do not spend time contemplating and deliberating over the meaning of art. In the past, kenosis required the devout subject to empty out their individuality in order to make way for the totality of God. Now in a museum we have aesthetic experience, not in the moment of witnessing objects, but through the experience and participation in events. Groys sees the museum as the institution that is complicit with and responsible for the training of the subject to abandon the sovereignty of their individual gaze. In a museum the visitor loses him/herself in a number of ways. The pathways are labyrinthine and the object of contemplation has no boundary. The visitor must constantly work with contingency, partiality and incompleteness. To complain about ephemera and chimera is to miss the point. Everything that exists finds its form amidst flows. Hence, Groys asserts that the function of the museum is to frame the meaning of eventfulness, thematize the occurrence of events, and structure the consciousness of events. (22) The museum becomes the space in which the relation between the near infinite capacity of digital communicative technologies for spawning events and are tested against the perceptual limits of the human subject and society's democratic thresholds. However, he also concludes that this produces a subjectivity that is neither under the divine gaze, nor master of its own destiny: "now we have once more a universal spectator, because our 'virtual' or 'digital souls' are individually traceable. These virtual souls are digital reproductions of our off-line behavior – reproductions that we can only partially control. Our experience of contemporaneity is defined not so much by the presence of things to us as spectators, but rather by the presence of our virtual souls to the gaze of the hidden spectator". (146)

To grasp the wider implications of this transformation in the condition of spectatorship

I will now conclude by discussing the democracy deficit that trails in the communication explosion. Amongst critical theorists, especially in Habermas's work, there is a strong argument that modernity has a progressive dynamic that incontrovertibly brings the world towards democracy. At the forefront of this argument was the assumption that communication and democracy were conjoined: the more transparent the one, the more the other becomes palpable. The faith in the inevitable ascent of democracy on the back of a communication explosion now seems misplaced. The communication revolution enhanced intersubjective relations, and it was assumed that these relations, while driven by capitalist forces, would also nurture democratic structures. The intersubjectivity that the communication explosion has spawned does not inevitably promote cultural values such as, curiosity, dialogue, trust, collaboration and collectivity. On the contrary, the technologies have been harnessed to operate under market conditions. The market does not protect culture. Markets are places for the trade in commodities. This is neither equivalent nor consistent with the exchange of ideas. Markets are not necessarily for enlightenment or pleasure. They are places for the realization of profit. Therefore, the market makes culture into a commodity because that is its business. It can only celebrate culture when it is already translated into the spirit of a brand.

There is now no doubt that the 21st century has been marked by a communication explosion, but has the march towards democracy fallen away? Equally there is no doubt that the cultural public sphere has expanded, and there is a radical transformation in the articulation of affect, but this has not necessarily led to more deliberative forms of public discourse, and the institutional platforms – such as, universities, museums – have been de-centered from their previous position as keystones of the national imaginary, and re-directed to perform a myriad of roles in the global cultural economy. For instance, museums are more crowded and more popular, but the impact of this recurring traffic, the consequences of deluded boredom, the complicities with depleted entertainment, the dependencies on the gallery-gift shop-café nexus are all passed over, in the vague hope that something educative, socially cohesive and aesthetically inspiring actually occurs en route. In retrospect it seems naïve to assume that communication would widen social outlooks, forge new collective networks and lift the democratic agenda to new heights. While the contemporary city became more and more communicative, and expressive of affective power, it has become a place of emancipation. If anything, it has contributed to the massive contradiction of our time, we live in a world that is culturally more inter-connected than ever before, the affective realm of the public sphere has expanded, and yet, there is also unprecedented levels of socio-economic inequality and geo-political polarization. The optimism the civil society would be boosted by communicative revolutions has not been matched by innovations in our democratic frameworks. We have witnessed the sawing away of old structures, the transfer of massive public assets to private interests, the eroding of traditional authority structures, and in their place, we have bloated globalism and resentment writ large at the local level. Communication has not tamed capitalism. On the contrary, it has enhanced some of its most regressive and individualist tendencies.

* Note: this is a draft for the 2018 AICA Congress Taiwan.

Seventy Years of AICA, Reflected Through the PRISME Research Project: Some Preliminary Findings from the Archives in Rennes

Henry Meyric Hughes

In 1948-49, the International Association of Art Critics (AICA) – like the International Council of Museums (ICOM) - was summoned into existence, as a non-governmental organisation in partnership with UNESCO (founded, 1946), in partial response to that organisation's lack of a specialist visual arts department. It marked a significant step in the re-establishment of harmonious international cultural relations after the catastrophe of the Second World War. AICA's expansion, the formulation of its ideals and the realisation of its programmes – many of them, aided by UNESCO – were shaped by the changing dynamics of Cold War politics, decolonisation and accelerated globalisation, and reflected the pressures of economic, political, social and technological change. This paper will offer a short outline of AICA's history and purpose, with particular reference to the three-year PRISME programme, just ended, to digitalise its extensive archives and make them more generally available on-line to students and searchers. With the aid of concrete examples, it will also take a look at the work being undertaken at the Archives de la critique d'art / Archives of Contemporary Art Criticism, in Rennes, where AICA's international archives are held under the joint aegis of its three main stakeholders: the Bibliothèque nationale, in Paris, the University of Rennes 2 and AICA itself.

The Poetics and Politics of Shane Cullen's 'The Agreement'

Liam Kelly

The political Troubles in Northern Ireland (1968-1998) were the most significant political/cultural events in Ireland since the partition on the island of Ireland earlier in the 20th century. They challenged artists to reflect on contested spaces such as democracy, equality, Britishness/ Irishness, cultural identity, place (location/dislocation) and, as I will explore, the nature of language.

This year 2018 is the 20th anniversary of the Belfast Agreement, also known as the Good Friday Agreement, which was reached by way of local multi-party negotiations and the involvement of the British, Irish and indeed American governments after thirty years of civil protests and political violence in order to create a democratically elected government in Northern Ireland on the principle of power sharing .The original official document was circulated to every citizen in Northern Ireland to read and consider and ultimately to vote on. Some 70% of people on the Island of Ireland endorsed its principles.

Signed on the 10th April 1998 it has been the cornerstone of the peace process in the north of Ireland for the past twenty years. The Agreement put in place a framework which would ensure equality, impartial policing and transitional justice. It enshrined the principle of consent by the people as to any constitutional change in the status of Northern Ireland. According to an Irish government website it affirmed 'the legitimacy of the aspiration to a untied Ireland while recognizing the current wish of the majority in N.Ireland to remain part of the united Kingdom.' (1)

In 2002 artist Shane Cullen, commissioned by Beaconsfield Contemporary Art in London, constructed a large scale installation titled '*The Agreement*'. In this work the artist transcribed the full text of the Good Friday Agreement (11,500 words) onto 56 large, heavy-duty polyurethane panels. Cullen had the text etched mechanically onto boards replicating the anonymous public language of a legal document. The artist sees the work as a celebration of reconciliation and the actual Agreement as aspirational and an example of what may be done elsewhere, as in the Palestine/Israel conflict. It endorses the power of language and its ability to persuade and enable.

In this paper I will analyse this discursive artwork together with another of his text based works, *Fragmens sur les Institutions Republicaines IV*, and scrutinise the nature of text, language and its presentation/re-presentation in the *polis* and in relation to the circumstances and condition of democracy and justice.

Working out of conceptual art's emphasis on ideas and language in Cullen's artwork there is no commentary nor imagery incorporated. There are, however, subtle re-framings at work, which is where the interaction of the artist resides. There is the monumental scale and sheer physicality of the installation. The work gains power by way of transcendence from the published brochure pages to the inscribed large (10ft high) panels which extend for 73 yards. The words are also enlarged, etched in relief and presented as a continuous unbroken text, perhaps emphasising the integrity and totality of its aspired democratic cultural outreach. We know that a serial presentation of a single unit can become more than the sum of its parts and register tremendous power, as for example in works by Christo such as his parasol project as displayed in Japan and California in 1991, or in Maya Lin's Vietnam Veterans Memorial, 1982.

Cullen, in his serial and scaled up re-presentation of the text of The Good Friday Agreement, assists in allowing the principles encoded in this political accord to percolate both social and political spaces – that is to pervade the *polis*. As previously mentioned there is no incorporation of visual imagery as there is on the cover of the Good Friday Agreement brochure but a complete investment in the power and vagaries of language

The work was exhibited in various venues in Ireland – Dublin, Derry and Belfast among others. Associated colloquia also took place not only to discuss the cultural and political readings/viewings of the artwork but the interrelationships of art and politics in general. Given the registration of justice implicit in the text, one such venue was The Crumlin Road Courthouse in Belfast, another took place in the Houses of Parliament in London at which I was invited to speak.

It should be noted that The Good Friday agreement was never thought of as a final solution to the Northern Irish problem but as an apparatus for workable governance. Historian Marc Mulholland informs us:

> Part of the success of the peace process was based upon deliberate ambiguity. The British and Irish governments, assuming the tenacity on communal polarisation, saw it as a segregatory but cooperative and balanced settlement. Both harboured some hope of eventual amelioration of division, and the Irish government at least hoped for

some form of united Ireland. (2)

The language then of the Good Friday Agreement document is based on purposeful ambiguity—fixity of language doesn't work in developing a working apparatus for joint government. As such its language is not fixed in stone and in that sense it is not monumental—clever words resist fixity; language being often wayward and slippery. Cullen's re-presentation of the original document as an artwork amplifies that ambiguity.

In an earlier and contrasting work Shane Cullen declared his interest in the more emotional, psychographic charge of language. Cullen's series of tabula-like texts, *Fragmens sur les Institutions Republicaines IV* began in Ireland in 1993 and were completed, while on residency, at the *Centre d'art contemporain de Vassiviere en Limousin*, France in 1997. The work represents secret communications or so called 'comms' written by Irish Republican Hunger Strikers and smuggled out of the Maze Prison (the so-called H-Blocks) during the highly charged period of the hunger strike in Northern Ireland in 1981. These hunger strikes, in which ten participants died, were mounted in an effort to establish political status for IRA prisoners.

In Cullen's re-presentation of these comms the emotional and fragile language of the private, was graphically and in a proclamatory way introduced into the public domain of the *polis* - that which pervades both the physical and political space. The programme illustrates all 96 panels in Cullen's serial presentation of *Fragmens*. These comms, handwritten by the artist, have been monumentalised in the act of representation, paradoxically by the handwritten process, apeing a mechanical process. On one level interjection by the artist is located in this act of transcription. In the act of re-presenting these once secret letters like a monument with a 'formal' text in the public domain, the artist opens them up to public scrutiny. This creative act draws parallels with the process-centred ritual of the early Christian scribes or Chinese calligraphers in their activity of repetitive copying in which can be detected a striving after idealism. As such Cullen's act of 'writing out', replicates the underlying ideal (national unity) sought after by Irish Republicanism. As such he textualises the body. The artist's performative and transformative act arises out of local circumstance but also registers with the wider international condition of what might be described as the universally violated body as the new and lingering anatomy. The literary critic Seamus Deane has observed:

> A work of art does not fill a prescribed space. It invents the space
> which it fills....It uses social and political conditions to reflect not them
> but its own estrangement of them, its capacity to de-familiarise them so
> that they might be seen free of the bigotry of conviction and yet within

the consolation of form. (3)

In a close analysis of both *The Agreement* and *Fragmens* Declan Long perceptively picks up and expands on this concept of 'de-familiarisation' of the referent texts and their instigation of a more active reading:

> De-familiarlsing the familiar subtracts a multiple from what has been included in the situation as a document of history, politics or bathroom convenience. For Cullen these documents properly belong to the situation, what may be instituted by these works is a more active kind of reading, but which also refuses or at least sets the work at odds with culture, this is properly speaking its utopian project in the real. (4)

The title of the *Fragmens* is itself taken from a series of political ideological texts written by Louis Saint-Just at the height of the revolutionary period in France. In 1793 – 1794 Saint-Just wrote a treatise which was posthumously titled *'FRAGMENS SUR LES INSTITUTIONS RÉPUBLICAINES'*. The Saint Just text is formally laid out in sections, separately presented but interrelated. In this way it offered itself as a model of how society could be structured both socially and politically. It offered a utopian vision of society. What appears to be an orthographical error in the spelling of the word *fragmens,* is in fact an accurate detail of the original Saint-Just manuscript. It is, actually, an archaic spelling of the word *fragments* in common usage prior to the standardisation of the French language. Cullen adopts the formal layout of the Frenchman's text for his artwork and thereby sets up ideological correspondences between the respective Republican texts – Irish and French.

The work begs questions not only about the representation/re-presentation of text but its location in the 'polis'. The work looks like a public monument but is anti-monumental and as fragile as the language it represents. The strategy of mediation at work here is that it brings the public domain of the city monument into the contemplative domain of the art gallery. It is also body related -not only to the bodies of those on hunger-strike but also to the body of the artist. Mike Wilson draws our attention to this in his catalogue essay on Cullen's project.

> This work, this monument which is more a representation of a monument than a monument proper, is marked by the trace of a particular body, the body of the painter. It is further marked by the

absent bodies, bodies reduced, erased and superceded by text. It is marked by their words, the words of dead men negotiating the terms and conditions of their death. (5)

Fragmens then relates to, but contrasts with, *The Agreement* where the text is etched mechanically on to boards replicating the anonymous public language of a legal document, Whereas the text in *Fragmens* was that of the secretive and personal, handwritten onto panels with the trace of the artist's hand. Mick Wilson continues:

> In the Fragmens we find monumental rhetoric split and compromised. The texts of the 'comms' are interrupted by bracketed insertions which seek to explicate the text. Thus the authorative voice of public address to the citizenry is divided between primary text and the text that seeks to direct and inform the construction of this prior text's meaning. The form of the monument is conflated with the format of the news media, the columns of text and the fragile material (styrofoam) suggest the throwaway of news print and the unreliable biases of editorialising. The sometimes subtle interventions by the artist into the mode of presentation of these texts in combination with the actual choice of text is the transformative element in Cullen's practice. (6)

While The Good Friday Agreement allowed for the establishment of a power sharing government between the political parties in Northern Ireland, in 2017 however, its Executive was temporarily stood down. The two largest parties, comprising Sinn Fein who seek Irish unification and wish to remain within the European Union and the DUP who defend the union with Britain and who voted to leave the EU, are in dispute over a number of issues. The principle stumbling block in their dispute is a demand by Sinn Fein for an Irish language act (like that which obtains in Wales, also part of the UK) to protect and sustain the native Irish language giving it parity with English in Northern Ireland. This has been resisted by the DUP, who see it as an erosion of British identity.

Consequently, it has to be acknowledged that where there is cultural conflict questions of language always seem to come to the fore. Writer and critic Tom Paulin, in his essay 'A New Look at the Language Question' reminds us that "the history of a language is often a story of possession and dispossession, territorial struggle and the establishment or imposition of a culture." (7)

Despite this temporary impasse The Belfast Agreement document reflected divergent community and political opinion distilling a workable programme for acceptable government. During the past 20 years Northern Ireland has been largely free of political violence. Shane Cullen's artwork *The Agreement*, which is multi-authorial, in my opinion perfectly registers within our congress's sub-theme relating to art and democracy. It demonstrates how art and related discourse can play an enabling role in the collective representations, challenges and imaginary and of the democratic process.

In conclusion, I would claim Cullen's achievement is that he conceived his artwork *The Agreement* as facilitating a democratic 'becoming' of a landmark document in the public domain where cultural identity, tolerance and difference can be located and accommodated without recourse to violence and inequality.

References

(1) See https://www.dfa.ie/our.../the-good-friday-agreement-and-today/
(2) Mullholland, Marc, Northern Ireland – A Very Short Introduction, Oxford University Press, 2003.
(3) Deane, Seamus, The Longing for Modernity, Threshold, Winter,1982
(4) Long, Declan, Ghost-haunted Land – Contemporary Art and Post-Troubles Northern Ireland, Manchester University Press, 2017
(5) Wilson, Mick, 'Fragments and Reponses' Shane Cullen Fragmens Sur Les Institutions Républicaines iV, ed. Dr Liam Kelly, Orchard Gallery/ Centre d'Art Contemporain de Vassivière en Limousin, 1997
(6) op cit.
(7) Paulin,Tom, 'A New Look at the Language Question', Ireland and the English Crisis, Bloodaxe Books, 1984

Trajective Art Criticism: Boats (Trains, Planes) and Home in the Era of Retreat from Democracy

Richard Read

As an academic art historian, I usually aim for tightly reasoned arguments, but on this occasion I'll follow trains of thought where they lead me. Both before and after I retired, my feet, and various forms of transport, took me to art galleries in many countries. Last year I visited about fifty in eight countries, this year slightly less elsewhere. If this is a boast then I will suffer for it by the end.

My first train of thought is about travel and the second is about home. The final section puts 'home and away' together in a bid to explore the implications of anti-democratic populist movements for art criticism.

1

I shall start with a few days in Iceland where the city museum at Reykjavik whets tourists' appetites for their country

Original installation, Icelandic Art Exhibition, Copenhagen, Dec. 1927

Jóhannes S. Kjarval, *Svartfell*, 1 & 2, 1921

by reassembling the earliest exhibition of Icelandic art, held in Copenhagen in 1927. It comprises more than two hundred paintings, bright with post-impressionist colour from the art of other countries.

I was eager to compare this epitomization of Iceland with what I would see on my travels. They were lovely, but not compared to the landscape itself, whose best qualities only appeared on the move.

Iceland Photo 1

It is a disjunctive, paradoxical landscape.

Iceland Photo 2

The heaviest mountain ranges look airborne.

Icaland Photo 3

Industrial slag heaps turn out to be natural scree bordering the chill purity of fluorescent blue rivers promising fat oily fish. Cold life.

Iceland Photos 4-6

Static paintings pale before scenery morphing through car windows. Icelandic sagas do better than paintings in this respect, their place names navigating us through political and geographical terrain on physical and emotional trajectories.[1]

At least one painting didn't pale by comparison, however.

Finnur Jónsson, *Morning at Sea*, 1927

The catalogue talked of its cockleshell boat amongst unruly waves and the mysticism of early morning light. To me what mattered was how the rotary rhythm of swirling waters served the classical equilibrium of effective team work on which the livelihood of local communities depended.

Eugène Delacroix, *Christ on the Sea of Galilee*, 1853

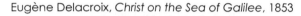

Back in London its memory returned as contrast with Delacroix's *Christ on the Sea of Galilee* (1853), expressing immanent chaos instead of stability. Crucial to this effect was that the dark blue/greys of the disciples' drapery were not quite, but nearly, the same colours as the enveloping waves, while the whites in their clothing echoed surf. Inundation had almost already happened, amplifying the abject terror of hysterical disciples whose oars, by further contrast, made no purchase on the waves. One figure adopts a pose of crucifixion, arms akimbo. But blithely asleep in the bows, Christ couldn't give a monkeys. He will wake soon enough and calm the sea. But if these are the contrasts, what is the analogy with the Icelandic painting? Whether working together as a well-oiled machine or pulled asunder by terror of capsizing, both teams of rowers allegorize the order or chaos of the soul's journey through life, a theme whose antiquity was impressed on me when I saw this marginal illustration of a boat in the c14 Luttrell psalter in the British Museum.

Luttrell Psalter, C14

The oarsmen row the soul in the direction of sin while waders in shallow water haul it in the direction of virtue.

Albert Marquet, *Vésuve, Le Matin*, 1909   Albert Marquet, *La Baie Naples*, 1909

Albert Marquet, *La Baie de Naples*, 1909;

By the time I saw these three views of Naples by the post-Impressionist painter Albert Marquet in the Palais de Tokyo, Paris, a thread was developing about modernist boat paintings. The oar or barge pole is a surrogate for the artist's brush. Men are bent by work except in the second painting where a standing man stares back at us, taking our place as observer. Manual work and aesthetic contemplation drift together and apart, as they do in Seurat's wonderful *Man Painting a Boat*, London, where the artist's brushstrokes turbulently cross those of the boat painter they constitute.

Seurat, Man *Painting a Boat*, 1883

Detail

The Marquet is strategically looser and incomplete. With Vesuvius in the background Marquet is interested in the elements of earth, air and fire NOT interacting but held in suspense across the elasticated, glassy ocean. Artist, rower, bargemen and their implements are the sign of an unrealized, non-explosive, forever immanent relationship.

Herein lies a further theme. A fundamental analogy between boats and paintings is that they both travel, one from a mooring, another from a wall to the next place of display. The aim of galleries is to trap paintings – and consequently visitors – but paintings were made to travel, and part of their valency is to enter into unknown relationship with other paintings that change their meanings, which they continue to do in the travelling gallery of our memories...

Nor is the reflexivity of the parallel really new.

J. Dehoij, *Willem Van De Velde Sketching a Sea Battle*, 1845

Three weeks ago at time of writing, this painting was the last I saw before closing time at the Hermitage. It is J. Delhoij's depiction of another Belgian artist, *Willem van de Velde Sketching a Sea Battle*. Dated 1845, it belongs to the era of Artist as Genius-Hero, and shows what must happen for an *in situ* drawing to become a fully-fledged studio painting. Is it the most callous battle painting ever painted? The 'punctum' is the facial expression of the right-hand oarsman. Does it signify admiration for the artist's heroic service to military truth, or horror at his indifference to the plight of the mariners desperately clinging to the splintered masthead? The first, probably, though the painting cleverly avoids blame. Since all three survivors would capsize the boat, there's no point in rescuing any of them. Despite insistence on Truth in the face of Danger, do we really believe Dehoij was in another boat from which he sketched the artist? The actual painting can only be the invention of the studio, not the *cinema verite* it applauds. The artist's heroic imagination of the artist trumps the mariners' terror.

John Singleton Copley, *Watson and the Shark*, 1778

No such heroic detachment in John Singleton Copley's *Watson and the Shark* (1778) at Boston. The old boatswain is in charge, but democracy reigns in his cooperation with younger crew in working to the risk of all their lives at a third attempt at saving young Brook Watson whose leg is lost to a shark in Havana harbour.[2] A simple story about ill-advised bathing? It is really about the Boston Tea Party and the breakdown of US-UK relations prior to the War of Independence.[3]

Close-up of the shark's eye

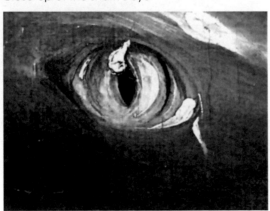

This time the artist's surrogate is the shark's eye, threatening viewers with the teeth of war if union between Britain and America sunders. (Take it from an Australian, by the way: sharks don't have nostrils!)

Shark's eye and teeth

This ushered in three new boat themes: leadership, boat types and global relations.

Emanuel Leutze, *Washington Crossing the Delaware*, 1851

Nine days ago I stood in front of Emanuel Leutze's *Washington Crossing the Delaware*, 1851, commemorating the American Civil War. With his foot staunchly rooted on the edge of the boat as if he were on land, Washington leaves the practicalities of sailing and transporting heavy canons and unruly horses to others. His visionary gaze is fixed on future victory. No democracy here, only hierarchy, including the subordinated native American in the stern.[4]

Detail of Native American

Lest we think the artist is absent from this hierarchy, Leutze has modelled Washington's face on his friend, the artist Worthington Whittredge.

Sketch of Washington's Face Modelled on Whittredge

The place of women in boat hierarchies would require a separate paper.[5]

John Millais, *Orphelia*, 1851-2

So to vessel type: where do rowing boats go to, apart from enemy river banks? Often to larger vessels bound for longer journeys, this one shuttling a VIP.

J. M. W. Turner, *Van Tromp's Shallop at the Entrance of the Scheldt*, c. 1832

But in Fitz Henry Lane's *Owl's Head, Penobscot Bay, Maine* (1862) the tables are turned.

Fitz Henry Lane, *Owl's Head, Penobscot Bay*, Maine 1862

The label says: 'A solitary boatman faces the pale, salmon-colored sunrise: is he gazing at the ships in the distance, going places he will not see?'[6] He is staying behind, then, not globetrotting. It seems my selective filter excludes vessel that travel very far, for the defining condition of most rowing boats is that they must be able to return home.

Alexander Matveevich Dorogov, *Ship in Storm*, 1848

Hence at Perm the surrealism of home fires in the lamp-lit stern of this extraordinary Romantic painting of a steamship tossed by tempestuous seas. So far from land, the *unheimlich* glowing windowpanes threaten death by fire as well as drowning.

It will not have escaped your attention that most of my examples are nineteenth-century. Just as horses died out as a form of transport across Europe, so boats in art were superseded by more glamorous forms of transport.[7]

Flo Kasearu, *Uprising*, 2015

Flo Kasearu's jet fighter installation, for example, in an exhibition of contemporary Baltic art in Helsinki, is a sinister update of my home and away theme. A four-metre long tin sculpture folded like an oversized paper dart is set next to a video of the artist removing its materials from the roof of his home in Tallinn. The overscale dart and the tiny drone that films its removal from the roof parody the Russian jets violating air space above Estonian homes.

Yet rowing boats persist in contemporary art.

Jocjonjosh, *Eddy*, 2014

JocJonJosh's installation of a triple-bowed rowing boat with three rowlocks under the disused boathouse at Yorkshire Sculpture Park symbolizes the leaderless collaboration of contemporary art making. The three artists can only pull against each other.

Ger Van Elk, *Flattening of the Brook's Surface*, 1971, 16 mm Film

Equally absurdist is the film I saw in the Rijksmuseum last year: a solitary artist in an isolated canal paddles his rubber dinghy with one oar while painting flat the waves it

causes with a trowel in his other hand. He too is going round in circles. Boats serve New Media as anachronisms that supersede the bankrupt notions of painting and the individual artist but also express nostalgia for their cottage industry in an age of mainstream media.

If you want nostalgia, here is my second train of thought. A couple of years ago I finished a work binge of several weeks in my Australian home and wanted to 'push the boat out.' Since I don't drink alcohol, I visited my local supermarket to buy one whole carton of diet ginger ale. The cashier was a listless young woman bored out of her skull. I noticed something odd about her accent that dimly reminded me of home. On enquiry she revealed she came from Wolverhampton, my home town, then she named my suburb, then my road, then my street number, declaring she still lived there! Consider the scale of this coincidence. There are 24.5 million homes in England and we met in one Australian building.

Author's First Home in Wolverhampton, UK

Later I visited her parents and found my old house stuffed with accomplished paintings of another home I had never seen. They were by John Hampton, the cashier's grandfather, who had been the respected Head of Art at nearby Bilston Community College before his death in 2012. The garden of his home four miles away had been his Giverny.[8]

John Hampton, paintings

John Hampton, sketchbook page and photos of his garden, Willenhall, Wolverhampton

Over the following months this disconcerting clash of somewhere so strange in a place so familiar slowly developed into a sense of the global relativity of homeliness, whether it be Norwegian 'hygge,'

Hygge (Norwegian / Danish) *Lagom* (Swedish)

Finnish 'Pantsdrunk' or '*kalsarikänni*'

Pantsdrunk or *kalsarikänni* (Finnish)

Welsh 'hiraeth,'

Hiraeth (Wales)

Swiss 'Heimwehe'

Heimwehe (Swiss)

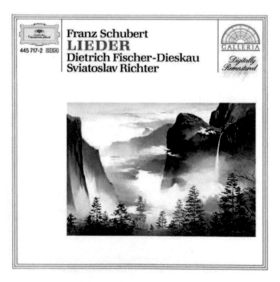

or the view from the garden toilet hailed in that magnificent paean to traditional
Japanese homeliness, Jun'ichirō Tanizaki's *In Praise of Shadows* (1933).

Japanese Toilet

In Praise of Shadows, cover (Japan)

Heart-warming as such nativist imagery may be, it has been ruthlessly exploited in recent times by anti-democratic popularist movements around the world. It also neglects the gruelling conditions of contemporary work from which we slump into these half-imaginary places in order to recover.

3

It is no surprise that the locally rooted feel their voices have been lost in the battle between mobile wealth and immobile poverty.[9] The progressive neo-liberalism of Tony

Blair, Bill Clinton and others used the social elevation of highly selected representatives of ethnic and other minorities as an alibi for sinking the majority into the international Precariat.[10] Mistaking the sources of their troubles, these lost voices suffered an unfixing of culturally uniform identity that prompted their withdrawal from the complexity of failing globalism towards the home fires of a parochial past that never existed.[11]

Tin-Tin And The Exit Plan

Pivoting towards conservative neo-liberalism, global interests invented an iconography of mass nostalgia for an invented past that could even frame Karl Marx as an ancestral medieval warlord.

Brexit Posters, Trump And Jckson, Marx As Feudal Baron

Marxism was intrinsically opposed to the divisions of societies into groups that injure one another and was committed to social enlargement programmes to bring about 'a new and broader merging of the rising aggressive element with the element it assaults and absorbs. … In this future the human spirit as represented by the proletariat' would 'expand to make the larger unity of which its mind is already compassing the vision.'[12] True, this model of enlargement with all its cruelties also fits imperialist colonisation, global consumerism and world trade agreements, but how could the good things about welfare states everywhere have come about without a vision of greater unities, including the mobility of labour that was Brexit's chief target?

By the eighties the downside of enlargement became apparent. As one progressive commented: 'cultural diversity, like ecological diversity' seemed 'threatened by technology and travel,' while in Europe it was 'feared that political and economic unification will suppress deeply rooted national identities in favour of some nebulous Europeanness.'[13] Despite its concern for indigenous rights, such well-intentioned rhetoric seems reactionary in the context of the new xenophobias.

Art criticism seems powerless against such forces, but I suppose I am proposing trajective art criticism as an attitudinal antidote. Derived from Augustin Berque's 'trajective enterprise',[14] the concept of 'trajective energy' has been applied as a necessary consideration in the design of urban parks to reflect the different character of the surrounding neighbourhoods by which they are approached.[15] No doubt there are innumerable precedents for the idea, not all of them benign: the river journeys connecting different scenes in Chinese scroll paintings,

Ma Yung, *A Crisp Autumn in Stream And Mountain*, 1160-1215

the art and literature of the Grand Tour to Italy,

Pier L. Ghezzi, *Dr James Hay As Bear-Leader*, c. 1725

the transition from Cubist passage technique to postmodernist mall architecture,

Cubism and Mall

and the very rationale of international art residences. Indeed hasn't everyone everywhere always searched elsewhere for good ideas? Culture may itself be a means of extending empathy beyond immediate spheres of interest. Despite its passé enthusiasm for actual works of art, including old ones, trajective art criticism aspires to an experimental and intuitive form of criticism that channels the interpretative and emotional energy brought from one artefact to another, across international borders. It would take account of crafted Instagram moments in art tourism and the recent work of Emily Apter on 'shareholder existence' and Borys Gros on 'the security principle', in which the currency of the 'experience economy' exceeds property as a source of cultural status.[16] It would use 'mobile' metaphysics to fight 'sedentrist' metaphysics.[17]

And so a sobering thought. As the preserve of elite art travellers, such as to a small extent I must class myself, wouldn't trajective art criticism be essentially anti-democratic? Anthony Gardner and Huw Hallam have critiqued the *kudos* of the globe-trotting biennale curator for whom 'auratic presence' has shifted from being immanent to the original work to the privileged viewer, 'whose authority is borne not by experience but by *experiences*.'[18] The target of populist nostalgia for a virginal past is often the intrusive traveller, whether asylum seeker or tourist.[19]   Could trajective art criticism counter the insularity that xenophobia feeds on without patronising those excluded from travel - or is such exclusion a predicate of what aesthetic experience has become in the age of 'shareholder existence'? Certainly neo-liberalism has its own effective trajective iconography as ideolical tools that warrant commentary and resistance: drones striking Middle Eastern wedding ceremonies,[20] for example, or that exquisite inversion of slaveship memory, the Australian supplied disposable lifeboat designed to roll asylum seekers around in their own vomit as they are sent 'back home.'

Australian Supplied Displosal Lifeboat

But how do things look from Taiwan. Got any boat paintings?

References

1   See Emily Lethbridge, 'Saga stead', *Cambridge Alumni Magazine* 80 (Lent 2017), 36-39.

2   'Scared not only for my safety but for theirs,' poem in Watson's voice by Charelyn Santana, 2013, quoted on a gallery label, Boston Museum of Fine Arts.

3   See Jennifer L. Roberts, 'Failure to Deliver: *Watson and the Shark* and the Boston Tea Party,' *Art History* 34 (September 2011), 674-695.

4   My thanks to Alan Michelson for this observation.

5   It would be difficult to find boat paintings this illustrate such examples of female heroism at sea such as Terry Davis gives in *Borth: A Seaborn Village* (Llanrwst: Gwasg Correg Gwalch, 2004), 63: 'In 1946, near Trwyn Cyntaf [Ceredigion, Wales], on a stormy July day, with a gale blowing from the southwest, the ebbing tide created a vicious undertow which swept a bather out to sea. John Arnold Davies, owning the only boat at the southern end of the village, went to the rescue. Having launched the boat in the shallows, he was imploring someone to jump aboard as it was all he could do, even with his experience, to manage the boat in the treacherous conditions. Of the people that had gathered on the beach, only Pamela Richards had the courage to join him. … Just before boarding the boat she turned to the male bystanders and snapped; "call yourself men"? The rescue was successfully completed by this duo followed by a hazardous return ashore, complicated by the need to row astern through the pounding surf.'

6   Gallery label, Boston Museum of Fine Arts.

7   The extinction of one type of boat is eloquently recounted in John R. Stilgoe, *Shallow Water Dictionary: a Grounding in Estuary English* (Cambridge, Mass.: Exact Change, 1990).

8   See notice of John Hampton, Retrospective Exhibition, Wolverhampton Art Gallery, 15 June – 13 July, 2013: http://www.wolverhamptonart.org.uk/whats-on/john-hampton/.

9   Zygmut Bauman, *Liquid Modernity* (Cambridge: Polity Press, 2000).

10   See Nancy Fraser, interviewed by Shray Mehta, 'Can we Understand Populism without *Calling it Fascist?' Economic & Political Weekly* 53, no. 22, 02 Jun, 2018: https://www.epw.in/node/151920/pdf.

11   See Paul Arbair, '#Brexit, the populist surge and the crisis of complexity', Paul Arbair Blog, posted 5 July 2016: https://paularbair.wordpress.com/2016/07/05/brexit-the-populist-surge-and-the-crisis-of-complexity/.

12   Edmund Wilson, *To the Finland Station: A Study in the Writing and Acting of History*, revised edition (London: Fontana/Collins, 1972), 200.

13   Nicholas Thomas, *Possession: Indigenous Art/Colonial Culture* (London, Thames and Hudson, 1999), 95.

14   Augustin Berque, *Être humains sure la terre* (Paris: Gallimard, 1997), 46.

15   See John Dixon Hunt, 'Reinventing the Parisian Park,' in *Tradition and innovation in French garden art: chapters of a new history*, ed. John Dixon Hunt and Michel Conan (Philadelphia:

University of Pennsylvania Press, 2002), 214.

[16]   Emily Apter, 'Shareholder existence: on the turn to numbers in recent French theory,' *Textual Practice* 28, no. 7 (2014) 1323-1336; Borys Groys, *In the Flow* (London: Verso, 2018).

[17]   See Tim Cresswell, 'The Metaphysics of Fixity and Flow,' in *On the Move: Mobility in the Modern Western World* (London: Taylor & Francis, 2006), 25-56.

[18]   Anthony Gardner and Huw Hallam, 'On the contemporary – and contemporary art,' review of Terry Smith, *What is Contemporary Art?*,' *Journal of Art Historiography* 4 (2011), 8.

[19]   See Claudio Milano, Joseph Milano and Marina Novelli, 'Tourism is becoming a major issue for cities across the globe,' *World Economic Forum*, 20 July 2018: https://www.weforum.org/agenda/2018/07/overtourism-a-growing-global-problem.

[20]   Tom Engelhardt, 'The US Has Bombed at Least Eight Wedding Parties Since 2001,' *The Nation*, December 20, 2013: https://www.thenation.com/article/us-has-bombed-least-eight-wedding-parties-2001/.

The Illusion of Art Without Mediation: Challenging the Challenged Democracy

Rui Gonçalves Cepeda

In the struggle against the political concentration of power and other controlling political regimes art has combined public and counter-public strategies against these systems of government, and has contributed to larger social movements striving for freedom, justice, but essentially, social equality. Despite being described under a plethora of different names Socially Engaged Art practices refer to the same thing, to the creative collaborative exchange of knowledge between artists and communities without mediation. From Latin America to Western Europe, from Asia to Africa, as a movement of global expression participatory art gives the opportunity to create a gateway to pass-over the dichotomy between art as an artwork and art as a tool to interrogate the places of everyone, the inclusion of each of us. Actual participation in SEA allows' to have an engaging with social empowerment. It invited the participant to make a choice of some kind – whether to participate of not. Whereas, when one chooses to participate, one may also choose to alter the work. Meaning its object, its subject, and its meaning. To a further extent it also enters the fields of actions under Democratision and is related with the principles of Cultural Democracy (pluralism or cultural diversity, active or affirmative participation, and the population being allowed to participate in political decisions). It is both this desire to be and to be together that lies at the heart of affirmative participation in democratic societies. Isn't this opening up of the public space to "alternative realities" followed by the desire for, or the illusion for a form of politics without mediation? Active participation is at the intersection of spectatorship and performance, while perverting established norms and rules. It is within this new illusion that artists are working, and should as art criticism. Either by questioning both their expressive autonomy and that of the artistic act, and of the democratisation of the creative act, in particular, and of society, at large.

In the struggle against the political concentration of power and of other controlling political regimes art has combined public and counter-public strategies against those systems of governance. In the last decades art more than before has been contributing to larger social movements that strive for freedom, justice, but more importantly, social equality. In particular we have seen a radical shift in the work of political committed artists towards activism, social regeneration, or affirmative political actions. Works by individual artists such as Rafael Lozano-Hemmer, Song Dong, Jeremy Deller, or public actions developed by collaborative groups, such as Assemble (England) or Opavivará! (Brazil) Groups actively working with the hosting communities, like many other individuals and collectives spread all over the world bringing participative works, while aiming to actively contribute to the quality of life of those communities that act as hosts.

For UNESCO, "cultural participation" is an essential part of human rights and contributes strongly to the quality of life of a given community.[1] UNESCO identifies three fundamental types of "cultural participation" on the assumption that participation in the arts is a valuable component in inclusive societies, both on a social and personal level. According to UNESCO those types of "cultural participation" behaviours are:[2]

1. "attending/receiving" – with more specific words, 'watching/reading' exist "when there is a communicational process between external sources of information and a receiving subject"[3];

2. "performance/production by amateurs" - the social impact is evident, but is less culturally valued since the added valued that can be brought in by professional practices is excluded; and,

3. "interaction" - which is focused mostly on digital engagement; it is clearly assuming a wider reach, however, it doesn't make evidence to support the fact that the receiving subject can change the object, it's subject, it's meaning.

This specialised agency of the United Nations also defends that participation in culture can be used to increase civic engagement and, as a consequence, it gives understanding and creates opportunities to engage in the strategies used in the implementation and governance of the democratic process—especially in western countries.

However, to better understand and have comparable measurable data about cultural

---

[1] UNESCO, "Cultural Participation" UNESCO UIS, Glossary http://uis.unesco.org/node/334976 visited August 17th 2018

[2] Morrone, Adolfo (2006) *Guidelines for measuring cultural participation*. Montreal: UNESCO Institute for Statistics. Online http://uis.unesco.org/sites/default/files/documents/guidelines-for-measuring-cultural-participation-2006-en.pdf (last access 17th August 2018).

[3] Morrone 2006, Ibid. p. 6

participation UNESCO uses a general framework as a guideline that crosses different cultural domains.[4] Disappointingly, this classification does not raise questions about the (unequal) social distribution of cultural preferences[5]; about the implication of having the hosting communities engaged with the "decision making" process[6]; on having the perceived "ability to choose" on an individual level, or having the individual freedom to self-determinate the final outcome - without being afraid of the consequences of the decision taken - of a choice (an individual power that is of high personal importance in a democratic society, or will be beneficial to the process of 'becoming' part of a democratic context). Also, the present process of cultural participation, that is being used by several governmental and non-governmental organisations places greater value on the idea of a public model for value[7], rather than advocating for a benefit growing from public involvement and from their interests. This public model evolves around the idea of 'downstream' decision-making for internal benefit (mostly for public funding reasons, by measuring the number of people attending or who had "participated" on a particular project, for instance; or, in support of determined aesthetic discourses for the exclusion or closure of others), and is essentially engaged with professional interest groups and experts from fields outside art, instead of being 'upstream' or transversal.

Despite 'socially engaged art' [SEA] being a global art movement known under different names, they all refer to the same thing: to the creative collaborative exchange of knowledge between artists and communities without mediation. In western countries SEA has its' theoretical roots in what, in the 1930s, the philosopher and educational reformer John Dewey defined as "art experiences."[8] In his writings he refers to "experiences" as those that have a pattern and a structure; and, to experiences within a 'artistic' context, to those that point primarily to the act of production, conveying the process of doing or making.[9] An artistic experience, therefore, for him, unites the relation of doing and undertaking, of outgoing and incoming forces and energies, i.e. the confrontation of dynamics and possibilities that are and become related between them. That is what makes

---

[4] The eight domains proposed by UNESCO are: Cultural heritage, Archives, Libraries, Books and press, Visual arts, Architecture, Performing arts, and Audio and Audio-visual/multimedia.

[5] Janconvich, L. (2015) Breaking down the fourth wall in arts management: The implications of engaging users in decision-making. *International Journal of Arts Management*, 18(1), pp. 14-28.

[6] Janconvich 2015

[7] Janconvich, L. (2015) Breaking down the fourth wall in arts management: The implications of engaging users in decision-making. *International Journal of Arts Management*, 18(1), pp. 14-28.

[8] Dewey, John (**1934**/2005) *Art as Experience*. New York: Perigee.

[9] When thinking about the 'aesthetics', on the other hand, Dewey is referring to that of the experience of perception, as in appreciation, in enjoying, etc.; for Dewey, when audiences are engaged in an art experience, the 'aesthetic' is seen to be inherent connected with the experience of making.

an experience an experience, "because it is not just doing and undergoing in alternations, but [it] consists of them in relationship ... [t]he action and its consequence must be joined in perception. This relationship is what gives meaning; to grasp it is the objective of all intelligence. The scope and content of the relations measure the significant content of an experience."[10] The doing or making is artistic because in the perceived outcome the output "is of such a nature that its qualities as perceived have controlled the question of production."[11]

Later, in the 1950s, the Letterist International and the Situationist International developed the notion that those types of experiences were Détournements as being a move away from the notion of personal property.[12] A decade later, the artist Allan Kaprow has come up with his famous Happenings that involved the active participation of the audience as a way to eliminate the boundaries between the artwork and the viewer.[13] Nonetheless, since the 1970s the academia and critics, in general, had started to use Helguera's Socially Engaged Art denomination for an art-based model that is focused on the creative contribution and collaborative exchange of knowledge between artists and spectators. Since then, for better or for worse, different individuals have formulated theoretical principles about SEA under a plethora of different names.[14] Some of those formulations apparently take their cue from previous propositions that were premises, or from a proposition that was a conclusion on a theoretical paper. The impression is that their conclusions derives from the standard formula in where two independent variables – *us* vs. *them* – are manipulated to give rise to a third – *in favour* or *against*. A bipolar view that regards the *them* as being of a single unite situated on the opposite extreme, instead of becoming a view that catalyses mutual support and nourishes closed gained relationships (to which what is not Capitalism has to be Communism, or a being under a dictatorship. How about Liberalism, Socialism, and all the other existing socio-political systems of governance?) The 'them' is, however, a multiplicity of circumstances and

---

[10] Dewey 1934/2005, p. 45-6

[11] Dewey 1934/2005, p. 50

[12] In particular by the turning of focus in the capitalist system, with its particular subservient means of production, hipster promotions, aggressive distribution, and conspicuous consumption daily fed to a passive society.

[13] *Happenings* are multidisciplinary events that have a non-linear narrative, and involves the active participation of the audience as a way to eliminate the boundaries between the artwork and the viewer.

[14] : Bruce Barber's [1985/2013] "agitational performances" or "operative art, " Jean-Luc Nancy's [1986/1991/2015] "community art," Suzanne Lacy's [1995] "new genre public art," Nicolas Bourriaud's [2002] "relational aesthetics," Miwon Kwon's 2002 "site-specific art," Grant H. Kester's [2004] "dialogical art practices," Shannon Jackson's [2011] "social works," Claire Bishop's [2012] "participatory art," Boris Groy's [2014] "art activism," and, more recently, as "situations" in Claire Doherty [2015] curatorial practice.

conditions of possibilities that allows for a continual relationship and fluid evolution between the different parts of the whole; and, an art experience is the 'conclusion' for that diversity of movements, anticipations, and multiple accumulations. It is not a one-way road that confuses socio-political doctrines for the convenience sake of a theory, while continually reaffirming and flattering art critics, historians, curators/*commissaires*, and artists grandiose and staid self-perception.

Almost a century later this ethnocentric view, typically dominated by western theoretical definitions, continues to rule the way we see and denominate what surround us (humankind) in terms of social criticality. Even when we are living in a distinctive *zeitgeist* and in a world that increasingly champions its multiplicity and diversity in ways of thinking and doing. The components of this diversity can differ enormously, but they supplement each other in certain concrete ways. A curious thing and very worrying case is that these one-way street limited-visions learned in academia or in close circuit of thought become the mainstream choice or gain wide popular support, even when all the evidence points to a distinctive way. But now to what really matters.

From Latin America to Western Europe, from Asia to Africa, as a movement of global expression SEA gives the opportunity to create a gateway to pass-over the dichotomy between art as an artwork and art as a tool to interrogate the places of everyone, the inclusion of each of us as individuals in the whole. In the book The One and the Many[15] the North American academic Grant H. Kester takes the opportunity to explore collaborative and participatory artistic practices in distinctive parts of the world (India, Myanmar, Tanzania, Venice, Germany, etc.), especially in relation to questions of creative labour. He identifies five distinctive features in SEA works, or, has he puts it, in dialogical art practice:

1. "locality and duration";
2. "the downplaying of artistic authorship";
3. "conciliatory strategies and relationship with specific communities";
4. "the process of collaboration as an end in itself";
5. "novel organisational forms".

Moving away from Kester and from the western society's ethnocentric view to the Eastern Hemisphere, the artist and academic Zheng Bo[16] sees four main traits in SEA practice:

---

[15] Kester, Grant H. (2011) The One and the Many: Contemporary Collaborative Art in a Global Context. Durham: Duke University Press.

[16] In the online course "Discovering Socially Engaged Art in Contemporary China," by City University of Hong King/Futurelearn.com

1. it "deals with social issues";
2. "the mode of production and exhibit" is different from those use by traditional art forms, such as painting, sculpture, or photography and video, for instance;
3. it is "based on collaboration and participation";
4. it "provides unique opportunities for teaching and learning".

While we can see some common basic features between the two frameworks, and when in relation with Dewey's theory about the mode of production and exhibit in "art experiences": "relationship within specific communities"; "collaboration and participation" as an end in itself; and the existence and use of novel forms of organisation." There are two main traits (one more subjective and another more objective on their approach, respectively) that although interconnected are in immediate conflict between the critical two positions. For Kester two of the inputs that define the fundamental complexities of SEA practice are the idea of 'authority', as being inherent to the concept of "authorship," and the specifics brought about by "location and duration." Whereas, for Zhang Bo, who comes from a less prune society to contain the values that make democracy appealing, the idea of providing opportunities for "teaching and learning," while dealing with "social issues" are the underlying features and starting points in his view of SEA practice as a form of developing social empowerment and having an active social impact.

Socially Engaged Art practice enters the fields of political actions under Democratision and is at the heart of Cultural Democracy.[17] Whilst acknowledging the vital importance of SEA as an enabler, as a ladder for civic participation in changes moving toward a democratic direction, we will be empowering citizens to disrupt the established powers, such as governing bodies (as is proposed by Kester) and those political phenomena that challenged democracy, for the matter; whereas, on another level, it will be also challenging the culturally attached meanings that are ruling our everyday life (as is defended Bo). Both on a theoretical and on a practical level actual participation in SEA allows' people to have a voice in their in their political system. It invites the participant to make a choice of some kind – whether to participate or not. Whereas, when one chooses to participate, one may also choose to alter the work. Meaning its object, its subject, and it's meaning. In other words, we have moved from a manipulative non-participation scheme, to an informing tokenism, to finally be in a space of citizen control, to the extent that the citizen power is determining the end product, i.e. upstream or transversal.

---

[17] The principles of Cultural Democracy are: pluralism or cultural diversity, active or affirmative participation, and the population being allowed to participate in political decisions.

However, in order for us as art critics to determine the becoming of this exchange, we shall have to experience its reverberation in the manner of Minkowski's phenomenology. Meaning with that that the essence of life is not a feeling of being, of existence, but, instead, a feeling of participation in a flowing onward. Furthermore, Friedrich Schiller expressed that "the aesthetically-determined man will judge and act with universal validity as soon as he wishes to." If we take in consideration the principles of cultural democracy (pluralism or cultural diversity, active or affirmative participation, and the population being allowed to participate in political decisions) together with these two thoughts, we will see a move from a populist form of self-expression to a communicative exchange build on knowledge, as is defended by Kester, and practice by Socially Engaged artists.

It is both this desire to be and to be together that lies at the heart of active or affirmative participation in democratic societies. However, isn't this opening up of the public space to 'alternative realities' followed by the desire for, or the illusion for a form of politics without mediation? A development in the illusion of participation through democratic acts, such as free and fair elections, for instance, has taken the form of participatory-spectatorship and has become the norm. But it is one in where there are more possibilities for transformation, and invites the participant to make a choice of some kind; to penser ensemble, not merely engaging in acts of passive regard or in normative behaviours. [Fig. 7] Socially engaged art projects or active participation is at the intersection of spectatorship and performance. It's underlying idea it to pervert the established norms and rules as they are imposed by the autocratic idea of an "authorship." It is within this new 'illusion' that artists are working, and shall do art criticism (while the expanded field of the curator is discussed everywhere and by everyone, the present role of the art critic and art criticism is left to oblivion or to a very limited number of alienated experts). Either by questioning both their expressive autonomy and that of the artistic act, and of the democratisation in the creative act, in particular, and in society as a fragmented whole, at large.

On "Art Criticism in the Age of Virtuality"

Lisbeth Bonde

Way back in 1996 my good colleague Hanne Dam – a journalist who had specialized in feminist journalism – and I sent our first email ever to each other following our male colleagues who had already started to communicate electronically via email. At that time we went to different training courses to catch up with the internet – learning among other things how to "Google". Today we couldn't think of the world without the internet, which totally has revolutionized life on earth. How much this revolution has influenced our work as art critics I'll develop in the following final paper.

The first question is whether the rampant, global cyberspace or virtuality is swallowing the last residue of the free and independent—and professionally well-founded—criticality from our practice as art critics? Once we played a predominant role regarding aesthetic evaluation of art. And once we were also some very important contributors to writing the changing cannons of art history. By virtue of our profound knowledge of art, our passion for it and our sharp and smart pens when writing we were quite indispensable to the educated audience who wanted at the same time to be well informed, inspired and entertained. Furthermore, we wanted to develop the aestethic sensibility and sharpen the critical sens of the readers. In this respect art crticism goes hand in hand with democracy where the citizen has to be an active participant in the political dialogue taking part and contributing to the community and making her/his own opinion and having her/his political preferences on an informed basis. Before the internet revolution and the dominant global travelling activity of today we had a function as being the generalized eyes of the readers i.e. we saw the exhibitions in our homecountries as well as abroad which the major part of our readers never witnessed themselves. At that time illustrations to supply the reviews or critical articles were a relatively rare phenomenon in the printed media. Either there was one illustration in black and white or none. In the last 3 or 4 decades of the 20th century the amount of illustrations has increased and most of them are in colour.

Today this has also totally changed. The many printed reviews are also accessible on the internet bringing more illustrations than ever. They may be published in the great number of online art magazines—in Denmark kunsten.nu, kopenhagen.dk and kunstkritikk.no.etc. Internationally let me mention Hyperallergic, Brooklyn Rail, Artforum, Art News, Art Review, Juxtapoz, The Art Newspaper, etc. These art magazines are accessible as online subscriptions too. So, art reviews or critical articles in the age of virtuality are often followed up by a wide range of visual, digital presentations of the art works. When changing position from the analogue to the digital/virtual era, art criticism faces new challenges. Today our words are supported by the images. The readers "can see for themselves" and form their own opinions.

This also applies to the artworks from older parts of art history that are all accessible on the internet due to the fact that much of the visual inheritance has been digitalized by the art museums. In addition, people today—as already mentioned—travel more often than ever for the purpose of seeing exhibitions or experiences art events. This has changed the task of the art critic today. Obviously it demands another approach to the artworks and exhibitions when the audience are already prepared for what it's all about and have seen the works of art and the mise-en-scène of them when they read about them. It requires more reflection, perspectivation and information about the art itself than ever. Previously our finest obligations were to "translate" or "transform" visual art works into a literary form. Now we are obliged to support the images with words explaining backgrounds, etc.

These new conditions for practising art criticism may be handled in two ways: We either give up and mourn our lost position and gradually close down giving the floor to bloggers and self-appointed art critics and art lovers. Or we can try to redefine new methods for our practices regarding it as an intriguing challenge and a new approach to criticality   in the era of Facebook, Twitter, personal art blogs and other virtual fora not yet being fully developed.

Since I started as an art critic in the end of the 1980s I've witnessed how much not only art itself, but also the art scene in general and the way people consider art has radically changed. The flourishing contemporary art scene in Copenhagen which I have followed closely since the end of the 80s was at that time provincial and extremely foreseeable. As an art editor at the left wing broad sheet daily newspaper Information from 1994-2002 it was an easy task to overcome all the newly opened exhibitions in only one day. Typically on a Tuesday where there were no people. I took my bike and went around. I witnessed how the pile of mail on my desk with invitations to different exhibition openings augmented from 5 cm a week in the beginning to 10-15 cm in average throughout the season. In the new century it has further augmented explosively due to the fact that the number of exhibition spaces has exploded—this includes both the commercial ie. privately owned galleries, the artist-driven exhibition venues and the museums and public exhibition spaces. These tendencies apply for all big cities especially in the Western world. Today we have 44 artist-driven exhibition venues in Copenhagen, the capital of Denmark with 1.5 million inhabitants.

On top of that the art itself has become more heterogenous and diverse than ever including all sorts of art practices more or less subversive or alternatively affirmative in relation to the social development in general and the serious clobal crisis which we all witness due to the electronic media. This obviously has changed the tasks we face today as art critics.

Previously we first and foremost could refer to and draw upon a consensus regarding the aesthetic preferences embodied in the cannon formulated primarily by the ruling classes ie. the aristocracy and the affluent bourgeoisie in the past. They "wrote" the agenda dictating the "good taste" together with the early art critics in general also in collaboration with the artists.

Modern art criticism originated in the eighteenth century France, as a result of the philosophy of the enlightenment and the emerging bourgois public. Art criticism was referred to as *The Salons,* because art exhibitions took place in the square salon the so called 'Salon carré' which was a part of The Royal Academy of Painting and Sculpture which at that time was housed in Louvre. This newly formed literary genre in art life encouraged many artists and people interested in art to write critical essays—in newspapers or in small magazines—of the exhibited works of art. Thus, art criticism in the modern sense of the word i.e. continuous reviews of the current art was founded. The French writer and philosopher Denis Diderot (1713-84) was responsible for giving art criticism its most precise and original profile, because he created a strong relation between form and content.

Today art criticism is predominantly practiced as theoretically-based, both descriptive and critical, analysing employment with artworks and trends especially in contemporary art—which the Australian art historian Terry Smith has defined in this way: "The art that is pushed forward by the multitudinous of energies, the art which allow us to catch glimpse of these energies while they are developing, the art which tries to transform these energies in ways, which make us engage ourselves in what will come IN What is Contemporary Art? Contemporary Art, Contemporanity and Art to Come" from 2001 (and republished in 2009). It's not that easy to recapture the lost land of the criticality of art criticism in the era of virtuality. So, how can we reformulate the role and position of our profession as art critics in the age of virtuality?

Because of the incredible increase of the number of art works, artists and art exhibitions during the last 30-40 years our role as art critics has also changed from describing and analysing artworks from a smaller art scene which was much more manageable and foreseeable than today. In this respect, selection has become an increasingly important parameter for our practices as art critics. By paying attention to an exhibition you signal its importance to the public/your readers and endows it with your professional "blessing". But at the other hand it's in my opinion very important not to forget to pay attention to less exiting exhibitions in order to make your aesthetic premises clear to the readers. Often strictly critical reviews are more entertaining than the more applauding ones.

In the age of virtuality, the art critic is more visible than ever. That means among other things that if she or he makes an error it might be exposed immediately on the internet—i.e. Facebook. That happened to one of my colleagues who had written a critical review of a group show and gave the wrong name of the curator. Not more than half an hour after the review had been published it was going viral on the internet. With such an exposure it's no wonder if some art critics feel a little bit uncomfortable and act more cautiously than earlier.

With modern art from Impressionism onwards, and with the emergence of the avant-garde in the early 20th century onwards, the aesthetic parameters also have changed dramatically in the direction of oppositional strategies and anti-aesthetic agendas. Often we as art critics identify with the new and critical art in our approach so that perhaps more affirmative and tradition-bound art will be marginalized. The best of which will get a posthumous fame—causing art history to be revised. We've seen that again and again throughout art history, but in the age of virtuality it's often possible to correct and edit in these omissions in the frequent cases the publications are accessible online.

In 1989 the French philosopher Paul Virilio published the book 'The Aesthetics of Disappearing'—in Danish *Forsvindingens Æstetik*. Here he introduced his understanding of "picnolepsy"—the epileptic state of consciousness produced by speed, or rather, the consciousness invented by the subject through its very absence: the gaps, glitches, and speed bumps lacing through and defining it. Sometimes I, and perhaps also other art critics, of this distinguished audience today find myself (ourselves) in a picinoleptic state of mind considering the speed with which the art scene and the art itself evolve and, in this connection, also the exposure rate not only IRL, but also virtually. In his book Virilio also underlined the importance of finding a rythm of slowness which could lead to deepening and concentration our attention. On that point he was far ahead of the development of our time where many people burn out caused by the hyperacceleration in the industry and in society in general.

Another serious challenge for the art criticism is the increasing amount of self-appointed "art critics" who have popped up on the internet, especially on FB or on their own, private art blogs. Among them art collectors staging themselves as art conoisseurs publishing books and curating exhibitions consisting of their own acquired works of art. Some of them acquire artworks "with the ears" i.e. listening to what other perhaps more experienced art collectors chase imitating them like lemmings. Many of them are however honest and serious art lovers, but often their artistic judgement is based on their gut feelings. You can discuss their aesthetic preferences with them from night to morning without being able to elicit some more precise aesthetic parameters for their purchases i.e. also the conceptual aspects of the works of art. Since many art institutions in Denmark are suffering from several budget cuts in this era it's a great temptation for some of them to accept an offer from art collectors who can offer to finance an exhibition. Personally I have written some very critical reviews, for instance of a book written by a certain Danish art collector who wanted to boost his collection and himself by publishing a thick book about his own collection primarily based on American figurative art of a very provoking kind. Of course this is a grey zone for art critics due to the fact that everyone who has privately acquired artworks without any public support can do whatever they want having no obligations whatsoever to represent true artistic values, but of course when exhibiting their collection or publishing a book about it, it sure requires a professional response. Here we have to get out of the sanctuary as art critics and deliver some truly critical and well-argued statements addressing the problem either in writing or speaking. It's important to be outspoken but at the same time diplomatic or even pedagogic and go after the message and not the messenger—and further to make use of some illustrative and sharp, professional arguments to raise the barrel.

In the age of virtuality we also observe the rising commercialization of the art scene and at the same time the increasing globalization including all continents which in different ways contribute to what we can call the total artistic narrative in the post-colonial state of art today. The commercialization is among other things due to the fact that Asia, the Arab countries and Russia today have an increasing amount of art institutions and a great number of private collectors competing with the "old market" in Europe and USA because these new economies are growing.

Nowadays there's no excuse for not seeing a lot of exhibitions on the internet and also following the artistic events and the development of a great number of artists from all over the world. Of course you will   miss the tactility and a lot of details when you don't explore the artworks IRL. It's really a "faux pas" as art critic. You have to confront yourself with the physical art works. Some years ago the Danish broad sheet, Politiken, enlisted the distinguished British art critic Adrian Searle from The Guardian to write a review of the Danish queen Margrethe II's exhibition 'The Soul of the Landscape' that she had done in coorperation with her long ago deceased relative, Swedish Prince Eugen. The exhibtion took place in the public art space Brandts in Odense, Denmark. In order to get a "second opinion" from a competent person from outside Denmark the newspaper gave the floor to Searle. It is, admitted, a little bit difficult for the Danish art critics to criticize our queen's art from an entirely objective point of view due to the role she plays in society which makes her a part of our own narrative. Well knowing that she's only a "Thursday painter" just having one day a week to exercise and develop her artistic skills she's of course just a happy amateur. Unfortunately, the British art critic wrote his very critical review solely on the basis of the catalogue which was send to him. Therefore, his review was devaluated and lost all its credibility. Journalists who were in favour of the queen's art of course attacked the newspaper for not having given her a fair "trial."

The contemporary art scene worldwide is, as mentioned, facing an explosive growth both in the number of practicing visual artists from all over the world and in the number of exhibition spaces on a global scale. In Copenhagen—a city of 1.5 million inhabitants— there are more than 40 independent artist run exhibition spaces and even more privately-owned galleries. These facts are also causing a change in the role of the art critic from a mainly critical approach into a more mediating and interpreting approach. Contemporary art has changed dramatically since the 1960s in its use of new materials and media and is generally more transgressive than previous art. This, of course, requires other approaches from us as art critics.

Finally, I would like to draw your attention to the fact that also the way we are being engaged by the media as employees to carry out our duties as art critics has changed dramatically—at least in my tiny country Denmark where the number of copies of each newspaper is very low. 30 years ago it was a common practice to employ full time art critics at the newspapers and it was considered an honorable profession on the same level as the news reporters. The two groups were the soul of the newspaper. Today the art critics are mainly engaged as freelancers and belong to the precariat being hired as day laborers like the harbour workers in past times. We have a lousy salary in spite of the fact that we are very well educated. Consequently, we have to wear a lot of different hats so to speak in order to make our living. It may influence our objectivity and perhaps makes us less unbiased when writing catalogues and reviews, curating, and perhaps even practicing as art consultants and other activities which of course all have to do with art. In the age of virtuality everything is ephemeral and flowing and nothing lasts very long. Also the newspapers—online or printed—want to shift focus on the art by constantly hiring new talented and younger art critics.

Turbulence: How Can Creativity and Art Criticism Respond to Unsettling Times in the Age of Virtuality?

Natalie King

In the age of virtuality and democracy, the notion of "turbulence" aptly describes our contemporary condition of precarity, displacement and upheaval both in person and online. Turbulence is also an important concept in scientific realms such as fluid dynamics, where engineers have noted that in the customary description of turbulence, there are more unknowns than equations. For engineers, turbulent fluid flow mixes heat, momentum and mass and is essential to daily life but yet to be fully theorised and understood; an unsolved problem of classical physics. This is despite centuries of efforts, at least since the studies of Leonardo da Vinci who modelled and visualised turbulence in detailed biomimetic creations such as flying machines based on the study of birds. While the sciences do the important work of calculating the geophysical and environmental changes affecting the planet, such models are incomplete when it comes to sensing, mapping or predicting the localized effects of turbulent processes.

Over time, turbulence as a concept has gained status, sometimes linked to fluid flow, but more often through its implicit connection to mixing and exchanges inherent to human conflict, global climate change and social inequalities. It is critical to re-evaluate engineering and social understandings of the physical phenomena and conceptual idea of turbulence. In a world deluged by a surplus of information and an excessive proliferation of images, how can art criticism respond to this phenomenon and find genuinely discursive modes of exchange and understanding? What is the role of creativity when technologies are evolving in a rapidly untrammelled manner in a milieu of unprecedented transformations and radical uncertainties? Contemporary culture is now largely defined by all-pervasive mass media and slavishly monitored personal electronic devices. This exhilarating expansion of instant global communication has liberated a host of individual voices but paradoxically threatened to overwhelm individuality itself. Turbulence might help us understand the role of turmoil and the contemporary condition of unsettledness.

At the human scale, models of turbulence become less predictable, requiring techniques of adaptation based on localized practices of material improvisation. Artists and art critics are vital for navigating the uncertainty of turbulence, according to curator Victoria Lynn in the 3rd Auckland Triennial on "turbulence", artists 'do not have one answer... they explore moments of survival and resilience... creating images of the human body in a state of endurance, mutation, triumph and absence ... creating new and innovative journeys into the past and future.'[1] For art critics and curators, turbulence addresses a prevailing condition of our times; a state of unsettledness, turmoil, surprise, rupture, dissensus and unpredictability.

This paper engages with uncertainty by considering how artists and writers have continually delved into troubled waters, seeking fundamental explanations for these conditions of tumult. Turbulence is postulated as a rubric for grappling with uncertainty in creative practice and the implications for the digital and virtual realms. My paper focuses on photography, digital and moving image practices in particular the work of contemporary Aboriginal artist Tracey Moffatt, whose work I curated in the 57th Venice Biennale 2017, and Indonesian Australian artist Valery Wens.

Tracey Moffatt was born in 1960 in Brisbane in the tropical state of Queensland, Australia. At the age of three, she moved with her siblings to a foster family in the suburb of Mt Gravatt. Importantly, the Aboriginal Tent Embassy was set up at Parliament House in 1971 to highlight the inequalities faced by the Aboriginal community nationally. The first film Moffatt saw was *Mary Poppins* in technicolour at the age of five and by fifteen, she lived on the Gold Coast as a nanny, reading Germaine Greer's seminal *The Female Eunuch* as she thought it was a dirty book. At eighteen, Moffatt was working in factories shelling prawns and peeling pineapples and the following year she acquired her first camera, a second-hand Asahi Pentax Spotmatic. Moffatt completed a degree in visual communication at Queensland College of the Arts where she was exposed to the American surrealist filmmaker Maya Deren. Moffatt is one of Australia's most renowned artists and filmmakers, having been selected for the Cannes Film Festival as well as exhibiting at the Dia Center for the Arts, New York, MOMA, Centre Pompidou, Paris and the biennales of Gwangju, Prague, Sao Paulo, Sharjah, Singapore and Sydney.

For the Venice Biennale 2017, I curated Moffatt's poignant narratives of human journeys and border crossings that take the tempo of our times. Somewhere between fiction and history, her scenarios are distinctively theatrical and resonate with references

---

[1]   Victoria Lynn, 'We live in turbulent times...', *The 3rd Auckland Triennial*, Auckland Art Gallery, New Zealand, 2007.

to film, art and the epic history of photography. When telling me of the conceptualisation of the short film, *Vigil*, Moffatt recounts the profoundly devastating impact and shock she felt as she watched the Christmas Island boat wreck on the television news. At 6:30am on 15 December 2010, a boat carrying around ninety asylum seekers, mostly from Iraq and Iran, sank off the coast of the Australian territory of Christmas Island in the Indian Ocean: 'It is a tragedy that has haunted me since, as do many news stories … The smashing of that rotten wooden boat is symbolic of how borders around the world are disintegrating.'[2]

In *Vigil*, the watchful unease and transgression of looking is depicted in stills of white movie stars gazing through windows at a refugee tragedy via splicing and montage. Set to a foreboding soundtrack, Moffatt reimagines desperate journeys of displacement. Her filmic riffs, terrorised stills of white, Hollywood characters peering through binoculars is interspersed with footage of the plight of refugees. In Moffatt's work, borders appear to be policed through techniques of distanced observation enacted upon the bodies subject to forced migration. Moffatt depicts the grim plight of refugees; her vision drenched in a fictional film-noir sensibility of desperate journeys and dispossession.

Moffatt shows rickety boats overflowing with refugees adrift at sea, spliced with excerpted images of white movie stars watching from apertures. Elizabeth Taylor stands aghast at a window-like aperture, while Kathleen Turner and Julie Christie peep through binoculars. Using cinematic devices such as the film still and close-up, and set to a menacing and foreboding soundtrack, this video utilises windows as framing devices to accentuate the psychology of surveillance: the viewer and the viewed. Once again, Moffatt turns to Hollywood to explore privilege (and under-privilege) in a fast-paced riff of movie stars and boat wrecks. She has further intensified the images of the boats by manipulating each still with a painterly cut-out effect and adding a blood-like hue to the sea, accentuating carnage and terror.

Vigil is a devotional act of watching, a frenetic wakefulness induced by the fiction of Hollywood and the wretched fate of refugees—what Moffatt describes as 'white people gawking at desperate poor brown people in boats.'[3] Since 1999, Moffatt has been making cinematic montages where filmic frames accrue in intensity and pace with the juxtaposition of images with sound. The pervasive human predilection to look and watch is harnessed by Moffatt with prying curiosity exposing the transgression of looking.

'The asylum-seeking storyline is not a new story: it is one as old as time. People

---

[2] 'Tracey Moffatt in conversation with Natalie King', *Tracey Moffatt: My Horizon*, Thames & Hudson, Australia, p. 16.

[3] Unpublished correspondence between author and artist, December 2016.

throughout history and across cultures have always escaped and crossed borders to seek new lives.'[4] By using cinematic devices such as cutaway, flashback, close-up, reverse shot and dream sequences, Moffatt choreographs scenes that are simmering with loss, longing and pending violence; her characters occupy a turbulent world of exile and crisis.

Indonesian Australian artist, Val Wens' performative photographs and video installation enact a shifting gravity. Juggling precariously before a sulphuric, acrid Javanese landscape or a remote, ancient forest, Val Wens performs a sequence of balancing actions: a potent metaphor for the human struggle with the vicissitudes of our contemporary condition. For Wens, 'It also echoes my own personal struggles as a gay Javanese man and religious sceptic, brought up in both a conservative Islamic and Catholic household.'[5] Wearing an ominously black protection mask within a noxious landscape, Wens' performative photographs enact a state of uncertainty. Like a live performance in a dystopian landscape, the artist balances vessels before the camera in an unfamiliar yet eerily beautiful environment, beyond the metropolis.

The artist has configured himself, face obscured, in the foreground in various stances while the background depicts a sulphur mine, *Kawah Ijen* (Ijen Crater) adjacent to turquoise water that is a lake of lethal acid. Drenched in heat and wafts of fumes, the smouldering landscape of craggy rocks and vaporous haze of toxins has workers in the background undertaking their dangerous tasks: miners exposed and unprotected who lug mammoth chunks of sulphur, ultimately used to manufacture products such as film, cosmetics, rubber, matches and insecticides—a perilous cycle of human suffering and desire.

Banyuwangi comprises a new suite of photographs, a two-channel video installation and a pair of paintings on Islamic prayer rugs. Moreover, *Banyuwangi* refers to a volcanic plateau and mountainous region in East Java, Indonesia, known as Blambangan Kingdom; the last Hindu Kingdom in Java in the sixteenth century. At the time of the fall of Majapahit Kingdom, many fled to Banyuwangi (Blambangan Kingdom), Bali and Lombok to resist conversion to Islam. The indigenous community from Banyuwangi known as Osing had been forced to convert to Islam in 1770. Despite the attempts to propagate Islam and Christianity among Osing, many still keep their longstanding beliefs of Hindu-Buddhism. Moreover, Purwo or Ancient Forest was a site of pilgrimage for Javanese mystics and Wens also performs in this forest in his two-channel hypnotic video. Wens alludes to the identity struggle among the minority Osing population within

---

[4] 'Tracey Moffatt in conversation with Natalie King', *Tracey Moffatt: My Horizon*, Thames & Hudson, Australia, p. 14.
[5] Unpublished correspondence between author and artist, September 2018.

mainstream, Muslim Javanese culture.

At the nexus of acrobatics, performance and photography, Wens adopts the stance of artist-performer within taut scenes in which body, psyche, background and foreground are fused in a precarious relationship. Wens learnt to juggle while working as a bartender at the Hard Rock Café in Jakarta: a 'hiding place to cover my sexuality.'[6] Ultimately, Wens' apprehension of an alienated and contaminated environment is a locale for exploring Javanese myths, pilgrimages, queer identity and an expedition to elsewhere: the imagination.

In turbulent times, feelings of loss, anguish, grief, anger along with the capacity to dream and find refuge become potent qualities. Fluxes, human movement due to political turbulence, borders, insurgency and flows, form part of a wider understanding of turbulence and its impacts. Often used to describe disorder, disruption, agitation and commotion, yet in our changing, fast paced world, turbulence can be understood as more complex and multi-dimensional.

By weaving research, creative practice and the role of art criticism, turbulence can help us navigate uncertain and unsettling times. With the ubiquitous proliferation of digital images, smart phone photography and the incessant circulation of texts, how can art criticism, photography and new media reach crowds of readers in meaningful and human ways? The unsettling aspects of turbulence and its association with borders, migratory pathways, exile, thresholds and the transition from one condition to another, provides a mechanism for invoking restlessness and our current state of precarity.

Ultimately, we might turn to the Aboriginal poet Lisa Bellear in her compendium *Dreaming in Urban Areas* (1996): 'You can allow your eyes and heart to see. See the injustice, cruelty, and you can also hear the laughter and the love.'[7]

---

[6] Ibid.

[7] Lisa Bellear, *Dreaming in Urban Areas*, University of Queensland Press, Australia, 1996.

Val Wens
Kawah Ijen 1 (Ijen Crater), 2018
Pigment on silver rag paper
Courtesy of Kronenberg Wright, Sydney

Tracey Moffatt
Stills from video projection, *Vigil*, 2017
Test screening at Roslyn Oxley9 Gallery, Sydney

The Post-Internet Way of Art Criticism

Ewa Wójtowicz

This paper is intended to address the issue of art criticism in the contemporary, so-called post-internet era. Since the notion of "post-internet" might be misleading, it needs to first be explained that it does not refer to any apparent end of the Web, but rather describes the internet-dependent state of creative minds. The internet is just taken for granted as some sort of foundation for almost every experience. Given that internet culture has profoundly influenced our daily life in terms of social relations (the attention economy and microtrends), the way we perceive information (filter bubbles and fake news) and the art world (an artist as a self-promoted brand), it has also had an enormous impact on art's theoretical discourse, including art criticism.

When it emerged in 2006, the term "post-internet art", as proposed by the American artist and curator Marisa Olson, meant being creative *after* browsing the internet.[1] The notion was also popularized by the New York-based critic Gene McHugh in his blog *Post Internet*, later published as a book in 2011.[2] As Michael Connor (2014) noticed, there is no more "after" being online but only "during", as nowadays we are always online.[3] This change began as a result of the emergent networked culture and the shift of the dominating cultural discourse to non-vertical, often vernacular and malleable social media streams. That said, if contemporary art critics are supposed never to "log out", is there any new post-internet of art criticism that we can recognize?

In my paper, presented at the 47th AICA Congress in 2014, I approached the issue of

---

[1] Melissa Gronlund suggests that post-internet as an aesthetic trend started to lose its impact in 2014/2015. At the same time, she says it was not a generational movement. See: M. Gronlund, *Contemporary Art and Digital Culture*, Routledge, 2016.

[2] The blog http://122909a.com/ is offline now. See: G. McHugh, *Post Internet. Notes on the Internet and Art 12.29.09 > 09.05.10*, LINK Editions, Brescia, 2011, http://www.linkartcenter.eu/public/editions/Gene_McHugh_Post_Internet_Link_Editions_2011.pdf

[3] M. Connor, *Post-Internet: What It Is and What It Was*, in *You Are Here. Art After the Internet*, ed. O. Kholeif, Cornerhouse/SPACE, Manchester-London, 2014, p. 61.

art criticism that is influenced by social networking. I have discussed the shrinking field for professional art critics as regular columnists in magazines. For example, Ismene Brown appealed to artists to "save" art critics,[4] while Phyllis Tuchman expressed irony about the possibilities of social media as being the only sources of information for those who want to be updated with cultural news and trends.[5] My case studies included, among others, Jerry Saltz's use of Facebook, Lori Waxman's performative and transparent way of creating a critical analysis in her *60 word/min art critic* project (2012),[6] and *Hennessy Youngman*[7] as a sapient internet persona and self-designed[8] expert. The apparent issues include the dispersal of authorship and the depreciation of the status of art critics in favor of folksonomy, and the disappearance of the long form in favor of more laconic social media-driven standards of communication (as well as appropriation and compilation as a contemporary mode of creativity). This kind of authorship dispersal has now gone even further due to the algorithmization of human behaviors, the delegation of tasks to so-called "mechanical turks" and the growing prevalence of artificial intelligence (e.g. bots). Another factor is the crisis of the traditional vertical model of knowledge industries, which is challenged by the heterarchization[9] of knowledge dispersal. Herein, I would like to focus on two main issues we can identify in the current media landscape: post-internet critical discourse and the issues regarding the changing status of art critics (including the dispersal of authorship and the existence of artificial intelligence).

Artificially Intelligent Critical Discourse

It is interesting to see how the notions introduced by media culture researchers, such as "the next nature" and "new networked normal"[10], treat the omnipresent technology as something quite natural, or even as an ecosystem we live within. The issue of artificial intelligence's creative potential and the possible threats it implies has been discussed since the invention of the ELISA chatbot (1966), but here I wish to focus on recent

---

[4] I. Brown, *Only the artists can save the art critics*, "The Guardian", Aug., 02, 2013 http://www.theguardian.com/culture-professionals-network/culture-professionals-blog/2013/aug/02/only-artists-can-save-critics

[5] P. Tuchman, *Art Criticism & Social Media*, "The Brooklyn Rail", Dec. 10, 2012, https://brooklynrail.org/2012/12/artseen/art-criticism-social-media

[6] L. Waxman, *60 wrd/min art critic,* One Star Press, Paris, 2013, http://60wrdmin.org/home.html

[7] The project *Hennessy Youngman* (2010-2012) by Jayson Musson. See: https://www.youtube.com/user/HennesyYoungman

[8] The term by Boris Groys. See: B. Groys, *Self-Design and Aesthetic Responsibility*, "e-flux" #07, June 2009 http://www.e-flux.com/journal/self-design-and-aesthetic-responsibility/

[9] As opposite to hierarchization.

[10] https://thennn.eu/events/electronic-superhighway/

projects that deal with the subject that is most interesting for us here: creative ideas in arts and humanities. Looking at some examples from the world of media arts, we may notice that databases and algorithms, bots and automated content production are now being explored in numerous projects.

One of them is *Predictive Art Bot* (2015), which offers "amazing concepts looking for artists!" In an interview with Régine Debatty, the blogger from *We Make Money Not Art* (2016), his creators, Maria Roszkowska and Nicolas Maigret of Disnovation.org, explain that "*Predartbot* is an algorithm for predicting artistic concepts."[11] It can do so because the project's database consists of phrases and keywords that media artists and theorists are familiar with due to calls for projects and papers or the vocabulary used in curatorial statements.[12] As Debatty writes, by launching the project Roszkowska and Maigret were "inviting other artists to collaborate with the bot, interpret some of the most puzzling/exciting/provocative tweets and turn them into real prototypes, drafts for impossible projects, live performances, failed experiments, etc." As a result, "it attempts to exhaust *ab absurdo* the current rhetorical combinations operating in the artistic field examined, which can be regarded as a caricatural simplification of the brainstorming process."[13] Debatty then reminds us that the possibilities of artificial intelligence were recently listed in the 'emerging' section of Tech Trends 2017.[14] Looking closer at this list, we can see that a trend proposal submitted by Rebecca Blum is about "learning from machine learning." As the author of the proposal notes, "We are already indirectly learning from algorithms in other ways, whether by refining our music tastes while helping Spotify refine its algorithm, or by learning about the brain by watching neural networks learn."[15] A similar approach, in which AI is discussed mostly as a threat to human sovereignty, is made by James Bridle in his new book *New Dark Age* (2018).[16] Therefore, if algorithms can shape our cognitive experience, why not let them shape the artwork? One early example is the *The Fear of Missing Out* (2013) project by the

---

[11] http://we-make-money-not-art.com/predictive-art-bot-a-call-for-artworks-that-interpret-ai-generated-concepts/

[12] However, on the current project's website we can read a slightly different explanation: *Predartbot* is "an algorithm that turns the latest media headlines into artistic concepts". Readers are able to watch the process of composing a sentence from words chosen randomly from the news and then decide which sentence would make a particularly interesting Tweet. See: http://predictiveartbot.com/

[13] R. Debatty, *Predictive Art Bot. A call for artworks that interpret AI-generated concepts*, "We Make Money Not Art", Dec. 6, 2016, http://we-make-money-not-art.com/predictive-art-bot-a-call-for-artworks-that-interpret-ai-generated-concepts/

[14] https://www.frogdesign.com/techtrends2017

[15] R. Blum, *Learning from Machine Learning*, 2017 https://www.frogdesign.com/techtrends2017

[16] J. Bridle, New Dark Age. Technology and the End of the Future, Verso, London, 2018.

Swedish artist Jonas Lund,[17] who seemingly aimed to find the criteria of artistic success. This project resulted in a series of objects that were created by following the guidelines given by the algorithms, which searched for the most successful artworks in terms of the art market. As we might guess, none of the objects were as successful as their supposed prototypes. Shortcuts to artistic achievement are often discussed ironically by artists who are very familiar with the dream of immediate success. For example, Dries Depoorter is an artist from Belgium who designed a customized camera that was offered to gallery visitors as part of his project *Trophy Camera v0.9* (2017).[18] Users could take a picture which was automatically compared to an image that was selected for a World Press Photo award. As a result, it seems that it was not the actual content and context of a photograph that was important, but only its composition, which had to be similar to an image that once was a winner in the competition.

The dream of success is also a topic of the well-known project *Excellences and Perfections* (2014) by Amalia Ulman,[19] who created both a believable persona and a durational, staged Instagram performance. The narration consisted of pictures posted to Instagram for several months in a row; it was created by the artist switching between truth and (photoshopped) fiction and between the private and the public, and left many followers confused over whether the story was true or fake.

So, if a Twitter bot is able to invent an art project scenario and Instagram is a performance space, how does this affect an art critic's experience and the way she works? Polish art critic, curator and theorist Łukasz Guzek noticed (2013) that "criticism does not have its «own» subject matter, as we cannot clearly say in fact what is art (or in other words, we keep answering this question) while dealing with ways of making meaning."[20] How can meaning be *made* if we think of collective, virtual intelligence that is comprised of a database? Hence, the ubiquitous technology seems to be our "next nature,"[21] but the more neutral and invisible it becomes, the stronger the impact it has on us. This is why an art critic, as any other user, lives in her filter bubble and is a data prosumer.

The Anonymous, the Gray and the Bot

Although writing under a pseudonym in creative arts is acceptable, making sharp yet

---

[17] https://jonaslund.biz/works/the-fear-of-missing-out/

[18] http://trophy.camera/

[19] http://webenact.rhizome.org/excellences-and-perfections/20141014162333/http://instagram.com/amaliaulman

[20] Ł. Guzek, *What about criticism?*, in *Art Criticism – Theory, Practice and Didactics*, ed. Ł. Guzek, Akademia Sztuk Pięknych w Gdańsku, Gdańsk 2013, p. 7.

[21] See: The Next Nature Network, https://www.nextnature.net

anonymous judgments is considered rather unethical. Paradoxically, it might be advantageous for the sake of the discourse as speaking from behind the mask of anonymity makes the discussion less polite but often more interesting. This is the case discussed in the article *Anonymity* published in the online bilingual Swiss art critic magazine, "Brand-New-Life," by an author who hid behind the apparent pseudonym of A. Coward.[22] The article contained a story about an anonymous art critic whose writings, published in *Art Life*, were interesting and witty as long as he was anonymous to his readers. As soon as he started to make public appearances under his real name,[23] he was received as "too nice. He watered down his opinions (…) [so] the prose of the website immediately died. The texts no longer had their bite."[24] The conclusion was that "The *Art Life*'s writing had benefited from anonymity; not because anonymity offered the freedom to be cruel, but because it offered something much more precious, the freedom to be stupid. Perhaps the most unbearable obligation of art criticism is that the critic always has to appear to be clever."[25] This is similar to the view of Roberta Smith, "The New York Times" co-chief art critic, who in a recent interview (July 2018) said that [art] "criticism has always been fairly specialized, always about your credibility as a critic."[26]

Another case was Annika Berger, a fictional art critic and author of the book *Death of an Art Critic* (2017).[27] which was published as a result of a lecture delivered by the author in Kunsthalle Bern, Switzerland. However, as we can learn from the Sternberg Press page, "Annika Bender was one of the pseudonyms of artists Dominic Osterried and Steffen Zillig, who wrote the blog *Donnerstag* (now discontinued) under her name"[28] between 2010 and 2014. As the authors explain, "The idea behind *Donnerstag* was to insist on the difference between good art and bad art. I am aware of how anachronistic that sounds and how quickly it evokes the image of an old critic-pontiff wagging his authoritarian finger. But even that image is founded in a misunderstanding: the caricaturesque exaggeration of the critic's voice as dictatorial."[29]

Speaking of a hybrid of the "old critic" stereotype and new machine learning

---

[22] A. Coward, *Anonymity*, "Brand-New-Life", 30th June, 2018, part 1: http://brand-new-life.org/b-n-l/anonymity/and part 2: http://brand-new-life.org/b-n-l/anonymity-2/pdf

[23] Andrew Frost from Sydney. https://www.theguardian.com/profile/andrew-frost

[24] http://brand-new-life.org/b-n-l/anonymity-2/pdf

[25] Ibidem.

[26] Ch. Burns, *Transcript: Talking Shop with Roberta Smith*, "In Other Words", Jul., 19, 2018, http://www.artagencypartners.com/transcript-roberta-smith/

[27] http://www.sternberg-press.com/index.php?pageId=1794&l=en&bookId=687

[28] Ibidem. The blog website is offline now.

[29] Ibidem.

technology, we might look at the example of Berenson—a more or less humanoid robot designed by anthropologist Denis Vidal and built by robotics engineer Philippe Gaussier.[30] The robot, which was named after the famous art critic Bernard Berenson (1865–1959), was dressed in a hat, wore a white scarf and had exaggerated facial features such as big eyes and lips because he was designed to mimic exhibition visitors' emotions and learn from them using Prométhé (a special simulator of neural network). Berenson debuted in Musée du Quai Branly in Paris as a part of the exhibition *Persona: Strangely Human* (2016). In reviewing the exhibition, Adam Epstein noticed that "Berenson's algorithm only works when the people he observes actually react, visibly, to the art they examine"[31] and added that "Berenson is a pretty clever satire of criticism in the age of the internet. Everyone can (and does) share their opinions of movies, television, music, literature, and other art forms online – and with little substance. Often, these opinions are informed by the reactions of other people."[32] A similar remark is made by another reviewer, DJ Pangburn[33]: "Looking at Berenson satirically, what is entertaining is that the robot art critic is a pretty good metaphor for what lies behind online media's art and cultural criticism. Across social media and search, data and algorithms highlight trending topics or perform sentiment analysis, driving a lot of what is being covered, critiqued and seen. So, Berenson might be a just a primitive robotic art critic, but he is very much in line with online criticism."[34]

But how does online criticism actually work? Is its value based on the amount of likes or shares of a given text or is it related to the regularity of publishing – the effort of living one's life as always "present" (to paraphrase the title of the famous performance *The Artist is Present* by Marina Abramoviç)?

If an art critic may become an "opinion machine"[35] as Roberta Smith describes herself in a recent interview, we might think of it as a starting point to another consideration. Machine-produced opinion is not only about meeting weekly deadlines, as happens with regular (not occasional) journalism. Looking at this phrase more metaphorically and in a broader sense, we can see it that has a lot in common with the algorithms that

---

[30] C. Munro, *Meet Berenson, the Robot Art Critic*, Artnet ® News, Feb. 29, 2016, https://news.artnet.com/art-world/robot-art-critic-berenson-436739

[31] A. Epstein, This robot "art critic" is as clueless about art as the rest of us, Mar. 2, 2016, https://qz.com/628509/this-robot-art-critic-is-as-clueless-about-art-as-the-rest-of-us/

[32] Ibidem.

[33] https://www.djpangburn.com/

[34] DJ Pangburn, *This Dapper Robot Is an Art Critic*, Creators, Feb 10, 2016, https://creators.vice.com/en_us/article/aenq45/robot-art-critic-berenson

[35] Ch. Burns, Transcript: Talking Shop with Roberta Smith... op.cit.

shape our daily experience within social media. If we narrow the meaning, we can also think of bots and their databases as they are comprised of statements produced with machine-based regularity.

The anonymous work of numerous individuals stands behind Amazon Mechanical Turk (MTurk) or so-called "gray literature", in which the aforementioned A. Coward includes "the press release composed by a public relations consultant, the annual report, the statement on behalf of a political party, the ministerial whitepaper, the instruction manual. (…) Even if such a text is attributable, is *onymous*, the authorship of the text does not abide with the person who composes it. It is not *their* writing, the author writes on behalf of other individuals, or collectives."[36] One of the examples of anonymous journalism that Coward discusses is "The Economist", which has a "Books and Art" section, in which an art world-related text appears every ten texts. Two recent examples are: *Why art exhibitions are returning to domestic settings* by A.C. from Cambridge (12th July 2018) and *Harald Szeemann and the art of exhibition-making* by J.U-S. from Bern (11th July 2018). Both texts were submitted by authors whose initials only were revealed.

The first paragraph of the article on anonymity by A. Coward starts with the statement that "«Criticality» is important in the art world, maybe even indispensable. «Criticism», not so much. The days in which a Clement Greenberg could canonize or curse an artist's career are long gone. Could it be that it's time for journals to go back to publishing anonymous criticism?"[37]. Following this suggestion, we might ask what if the anonymous content could be produced not by ghost authors recruited from the field of "gray literature," but by a collective (artificial) intelligence that is represented by a bot?

There is of course still a difference between provocative yet valuable anonymous[38] critique and the activity of 'haters.' A Polish example is *The Hater's History of Polish Literature* (2017)—a bot created for the sake of a project by art and literature researchers Leszek Onak and Piotr Marecki that was presented at the ELO17 (Electronic Literature Organization) conference in Porto, Portugal.[39] Based entirely on a Polish chat system called GG, the bot uses phrases (often aggressive and hateful) taken from critical discourse of Polish literature over the last two centuries. As the creators explain: "we

---

[36] A. Coward, *Anonymity*, part 1, June 30, 2018, http://brand-new-life.org/b-n-l/anonymity/

[37] A. Coward, *Anonymity*, part 2, July 20, 2018, http://brand-new-life.org/b-n-l/anonymity-2/

[38] This is again an opinion, but it may be interesting when compared to anonymity as it is today. Needless to say, true anonymity online is nearly impossible, but this issue is beyond the scope of this article. I understand anonymity for the sake of this study only as publishing under "no name" or a pseudonym, just as it was in the early days of internet culture.

[39] See also: E. Wójtowicz, *Ergodic Robo-poetry. Inside Job - Poetbot*, transl. from Polish J. Lewandowski, "DOCUMNT2", 2018, pp. 150-163.

want to create a bot that is programmed to be unpleasant, to be a troll and hater (...) We are going to use both classical texts, literary quarrels between the romantics and representatives of the Enlightenment, and the avant-gardists attacking tradition, and we will mix these with discussions on literary web portals, social media, statuses and comments."[40]

We can now imagine such a bot in the sphere of art criticism and there are already some examples. The attempts date back to the mid-2000s, when the French artist Eric Maillet designed his *Art Criticism Generator* (2006). As we can learn from the project's description, this French language-based program is "a piece of software which produces upon request, by a mix of random and artificial intelligence, false critical texts. The various stylistic fads and authors usually cited are summoned then blended by the software to produce a text that lies between probable and parody. The Générateur de Critique d'Art is provided to be installed in any place that displays artworks, where it can serve visitors as a guide and a tool for reflection."[41]

Another more recent project by the same artist is *Art Critic Bot* (2012), which works like a Twitter bot, but to be creative it needs to be confronted with some aesthetical content within an exhibition. As its creator explains, "From time to time, it decides by itself to generate and tweet a new sentence; however, it can be forced to work by the visitor by simply touching the screen. (...) Art Critic Bot is never fully asleep, you can follow it on Twitter (@art_critic_bot)."[42] One of the statements read at the time of writing this text was, for example, "The denial of one's self affirms its virtuality (22:37, 30th July 2018).[43]

Another interesting case is *Novice Art Blogger* (2014–present) by Matthew Plummer Fernandez.[44] The project is based on deep learning algorithms; it analyzes artworks and sums them up in a few sentences that are sometimes absurd and sometimes surprisingly apt, producing automated blog posts on a Tumblr page.[45] The bot's database comprises of meta-data from the Tate Gallery's website and some observations that look like personal remarks. The blog doesn't reach a mass audience though; for example, an entry dated Apr 27th, 2015 about an untitled black and white drawing by Naum Gabo (1950) had only 12 likes and reblogs.

Berenson and both of the described bots show two different ways of dealing with the

---

[40] https://elmcip.net/creative-work/haters-history-polish-literature

[41] E. Maillet, *Art criticism generator*, 2006, project description, http://kizuchi.free.fr/articles.php?pg=art24

[42] http://kizuchi.free.fr/

[43] https://twitter.com/art_critic_bot/status/1024167226524532736

[44] http://www.plummerfernandez.com/Novice-Art-Blogger

[45] http://noviceartblogger.tumblr.com/

issue of how art criticism has been affected by the rise of artificial intelligence. The Berenson bot is more or less human-like, but its interface is purely functional; it is just a pure "electronic brain" (to use a phrase from the 60s that was coined during the rise of computerization).

Post-Internet Criticism of Post-Digital Art

As we can read in the curatorial statement by the DIS group on the BB9 (9th Berlin Biennale) website: "Exhibitions have increasingly come to resemble TED Talks – theaters of competence."[46] This is quite similar to online art criticism, which requires competence in many areas, not only in writing a smart text on a given subject (e.g. an exhibition). If an artist is a brand, an art critic never walks (and works) alone.

Theorizing post-media art, Brad Troemel writes: "The generation of Web 2.0 artists centralizes others' content around themselves, pulling the actual work off its creator's website and placing it on their own. (…) The same can be said of the act of tagging on Facebook or writing on someone else's wall: each is a performative display made to elucidate a connection between separate identities for the spectatorship and the assumed audience. The Web 2.0 artist positions herself as part of an expanding whole."[47] If this happens to an artist, it is also a part of the contemporary art critic's experience, from Jerry Saltz to any student of art criticism who is working on her first blog posts, Facebook entries or Tweets and hoping for feedback. Everything became performative and content produced intentionally as art criticism never speaks for itself alone. It always needs the company of Tweets or cleverly hashtagged Instagram pictures by the same author. As we learn from the interview with Roberta Smith, who is speaking about Los Angeles-based art critic Carolina Miranda: "if you take her writing plus her on Twitter, you have this very fabulous thing."[48]

This remark reminds us about the issue of so-called *playbour*,[49] the strange and liquid mixture of play and labor that lots of freelancers and art critics know only too well. One's seemingly private expression space (social media) accompanies and supports their professional activity (publishing art criticism). Together, a trustworthy and coherent

---

[46] DIS (Lauren Boyle, Solomon Chase, Marco Roso, David Toro), *The Present in Drag*, curatorial statement, 2016, https://bb9.berlinbiennale.de/the-present-in-drag-2/

[47] B. Troemel, Peer Pressure. Essays on the Internet by an Artist on the Internet, LINK Editions, Brescia, 2011, p. 41.

[48] Ch. Burns, Transcript: Talking Shop with Roberta Smith… op.cit.

[49] The term was coined by Julian Kücklich in 2005. See J. Kücklich, *Precarious playbour: Modders and the digital games industry,* "Journal Fibreculture" #5/2005, http://journal.fibreculture.org/issue5/kucklich_print.html

image of the person writing a critical text is created.

Having said all this, we need to remember another profound question: "How do we write when we write online?"[50] This was asked in 2014 by Orit Gat and brought to discussion again by Miriam Rasch, who updated this question by saying:

> (…) it's not just about writing online anymore. 'Online' almost seems an old-fashioned concept; since 2014 there have already been so many new (social) media, channels and platforms where writing is happening, and this writing has seeped into places that aren't online per se. Now we talk of post-digital writing, which can take place online, but just as well in an offline application, or in a paper notebook, in a printed volume, in the park. Let's say there are many spaces where we write in post-digital times. And in these spaces, we are writing through the digital.[51]

In another essay *Has the Internet Changed Art Criticism?* (2015), Orit Gat pointed also at some sort of crisis of longform in the contemporary media landscape.[52] Editors assume that readers do not expect a long text anymore; just a few paragraphs or even sentences must suffice for the utterance. Often online publishers prescribe the established amount of time in which a reader is supposed to read a text ("a four-minute read" for example). This is similar to a full-length movie reduced to a trailer: it is more intensive in its narration but lacks depth.

Another thing is the aesthetics of online (or post-digital) writing, which needs to meet (often unwritten) standards of communication: eye-catching pictures, an intriguing headline and smart hashtags. This is all done to generate clickbait at the expense of quality content. There is a similarity to digital imaging's pursuit of beauty and pure, flawless, classy-and-glossy aesthetics (in documenting fine arts). This kind of post-internet art aesthetics was criticized by Brian Droitcour, who compared this type of artwork to a detergent that looked good in a post-produced advertisement but was not so great in non-digital daily life.[53] Does the same apply to contemporary post-digital forms of art

---

[50] O. Gat, *How Do We Write When We Write Online*, Dec. 2014, http://oritgat.com/How-Do-We-Write-When-We-Write-Online

[51] M. Rasch, *Shadowbook: Writing Through the Digital 2014-2018*, Deep Pockets #2, Institute of Network Cultures, Amsterdam 2018, p. 7.

[52] O. Gat, *Has the Internet Changed Art Criticism?*, June 2015, http://oritgat.com/Has-the-Internet-Changed-Art-Criticism

[53] B. Droitcour, *The Perils of Post-Internet Art*, "Art in America", Oct. 29, 2014, https://www.artinamericamagazine.

criticism? Speaking of Instagram coverage and Twitter updates from art shows and exhibition openings, we can see the need for perpetual content production, witty hashtagging and, sometimes, smart and ironic selfies. So, the modes of content production are not that different from those we know from mainstream networked culture.

Analyzing this situation a few years ago, Brad Troemel proposed that:

> (…) critics and viewers should recognize productive systems as sites permanently in progress (…) A journalistic blogging approach to criticism may be best suited to address specific elements of these projects as they unfold. Through a writing format that is continuously adaptable, the critic preemptively acknowledges the fleeting nature of her subject matter. Alternatively, critics may reflect on productive systems using a narrative approach, identifying the broad-sweeping changes in user contributions leading up to its current state.[54]

But how to find the delicate balance between art world-related gossip and the jargon-packed hermetic texts that should instead be circulating within academia? In other words: how can thoughts be formulated clearly and critical analysis kept insightful, while at the same time being accessible for a larger and responsive audience? This dilemma was clearly visible last year—a prolific season in Europe for art critics, as always happens when the documenta exhibition and the Venice Biennial take place in the same summer. Documenta's dual location (Athens and Kassel) was another challenge for art critics who wanted to follow all the events and cover them accordingly. Sometimes, not being able to see everything as planned, a viewer may be tempted to Google for some interesting information and find that the information gained online is enough. Images and video excerpts from press kits as well as those uploaded by other viewers of a particular exhibition may replace the direct experience of going there and seeing it. However, there is another factor: the filter bubble that every user is somehow "locked within", which may distort our impression of what the exhibition is really like. For example, we can imagine our algorithm-shaped experience that let us showed us only negative reviews of those authors who didn't like a particular exhibition or an artist. Or the other way around, as Mat Honan from "Wired" showcased in his experiment called *I Liked Everything I Saw on Facebook for Two Days* (2014). The author not only describes his experience about being gradually

---

com/news-features/magazines/the-perils-of-post-internet-art/
[54] B. Troemel, *Peer Pressure…*, op.cit., p. 74.

locked in a filter bubble and confusing his friends, who were confronted with the content he produced, but also gives a quote from an interview with Andy Warhol (1963):

> ***Warhol:*** *(...) Everybody looks alike and acts alike, and we're getting more and more that way. I think everybody should be a machine. I think everybody should like everybody.*
> ***Art News:*** *Is that what Pop Art is all about?*
> ***Warhol:*** *Yes. It's liking things.*
> ***Art News:*** *And liking things is like being a machine?*
> ***Warhol:*** *Yes, because you do the same thing every time. You do it over and over again.*[55]

Andy Warhol's statement sounds as provocative as his artistic activity and attitude, but there is a point in this process of turning oneself into a machine that every user deals with at a certain point of engagement within social and digital media. An art critic is supposed to "like things" from the art world and keep pace with the general trends, but what if the pace becomes so fast that it is almost impossible to keep with?

When dealing with such complex issues as well as character limits and tight deadlines, is the art critic able to "capture all"[56] when "the present" is "in drag"[57]? This endless game of playbour, mimicry or being "in drag", along with the aestheticization of offline and online public spaces (with the internet dominating the one previously considered "real") makes the task of an art critic particularly difficult. How to recognize the vast range of art issues, when a post-internet artwork is styled as an advertisement which is styled as a blog post which, again, may be styled as an art manifesto? We can find relevant examples in the works of artists who are also theorists, such as James Bridle, Hito Steyerl or Artie Vierkant, as well as the DIS collective. For example, James Bridle in his book *New Dark Age* (2018) notices that "We live in times of increasing inscrutability. Our news feeds are filled with unverified, unverifiable speculation, much of it automatically generated by anonymous software. As a result, we no longer understand what is happening around us."[58] Although it is a general remark, it may be as well applied to the consideration of contemporary, post-internet art criticism.

---

[55] M. Honan, *I Liked Everything I Saw on Facebook for Two Days. Here's What It Did to Me,* "Wired", Aug. 11, 2014, https://www.wired.com/2014/08/i-liked-everything-i-saw-on-facebook-for-two-days-heres-what-it-did-to-me/

[56] To quote the title of Transmediale 2015: *Capture all.*

[57] To paraphrase the title of the 9th Berlin Biennale (2016) *The Present in Drag*, curated by DIS group.

[58] http://jamesbridle.com/books

Summary

There are many misunderstandings in the art criticism environment when it comes to covering issues of media art.[59] Particularly, the most famous example of such a misunderstanding was the text *Digital Divide* (2012) by Claire Bishop[60] and the critical reception to her statement that followed.[61] However, there are some art critics and bloggers who present vast knowledge of the topic together with the ability to cover it competently. A good example of insightful online writing, although not exactly art criticism per se, is Régine Debatty's website *We Make Money Not Art*. The author finds the right balance between the highly specialized content that media artists and theorists may have an interest in, and the informal, friendly tone that is so valuable when one aims to popularize difficult topics. Other good examples of post-internet art criticism are "DIS Magazine" and "e-flux", in which different authors publish reviews that sometimes sound like independent artistic statements.

In summary, in my opinion there is still no solution to the outlined problems and no direct answer to the questions asked within this text. The state of confusion we may recognize in some critics' and theorists' statements may result from the fact that nowadays long-term experience does not help as there is no time to accumulate knowledge and make use of it in this rapidly changing world. If some contemporary philosophers are brave enough to say "I don't know," what about art critics, particularly those defending the traditional (printed) media workflow? Maybe the artists are the ones who dare to ask questions. Last but not least, there is the issue of archives of thought, which are so fragile in the "digital dark age", as Vinton Cerf called it.[62] What will happen to all the online art discourse when the platforms that host it disappear because of technical issues or just become outdated, as has happened to a lot of once-popular technologies over the last three decades? One attempt to preserve the rich and vital discourse about the (then freshly emergent) net.art environment was the *readme!* book

---

[59] The issue was discussed by Domenico Quaranta, who made the differentiation of notions between new media and postmedia. See D. Quaranta, *Beyond New Media Art*, trans. A. R. Carruthers, LINK Editions, Brescia 2013.

[60] C. Bishop, *Digital Divide. Contemporary Art and New Media*, "Artforum" 09/2012, https://www.artforum.com/print/201207/digital-divide-contemporary-art-and-new-media-31944

[61] See M. Gronlund, Contemporary Art and Digital Culture, op.cit. and F. Cramer, When Claire Bishop woke up in the drone wars: art and technology, the nth time, in: across & beyond. a transmediale reader on post-digital practices, concepts, and institutions, ed. R. Bishop, et al., Sternberg Press, Berlin 2016.

[62] See: P. Gosh, *Google's Vint Cerf warns of 'digital Dark Age'*, BBC news, Feb., 13, 2015, https://www.bbc.co.uk/news/science-environment-31450389

(1999), which comprises numerous posts from discussion lists and bulletin boards.[63] Most of the content is now long gone if we search for it online, but the book allowed at least some of it to be kept for readers, who are now able to discover the Atlantis of the World Wide Web as it was at the beginning of cyberculture. Going back to the Gutenberg era is not a solution, but just one possible option. Art critics are not going to stop chasing the post-digital mirage, and the same is true of artists, writers or other participants of network culture.

*   Ewa Wójtowicz's participation in the AICA Congress was possible thanks to the funding received from the Faculty of Art Education and Curatorial Studies, University of Arts in Poznan, Poland.

[63] See: ReadMe! ASCII Culture and the Revenge of Knowledge, ed. J. Bosma, Autonomedia, New York 1999.

Aesthetic of Protest: The Colorful Revolution

Jovanka Popova and Mira Gacina

What is the input of social and political clashes in the process of recreating of public space? Can we interpret the term 'urbanity' as a nucleus of social solidarity or as a space of materializing various political agendas? How do we manage power and its direct effect on urban development? By deconstructing the processes of the engaged art practices and artistic involvement as part of the protest movements, the attention is turned toward the left-oriented voices, the gray-zone of activism between the radical and the consensual, and the borderline points where discourses are contested in order to generate counter-discourses. In this sense, the possibilities and limits for the shifting place of art practices are examined: where they can exceed traditional boundaries and spill over in institutional terms, transforming everything into politics of life, producing both: affect as effect.

1.

Art that is intentionally produced for institutions occupies a privileged space of politicization, closely related to neoliberal processes. By being used in daily politics as mechanisms of intervention and renovation, contemporary art supports the stabilization of neoliberal strategies, occupying real-life spaces.   The use of freelancers or the "third sector," non-profit organizations as representatives of a prospective market for the so-called "creators of culture," in the distribution of state services also became a trend. Political struggles and social opposition have stretched their way out of the field of state apparatuses to the domain of diverse "cultural options." But, culturalization is not only the transmission of political questions into cultural ones. Culturalization tends to become an ideological education for "the masses" or the subjects of the capitalist order. All in one, the prefix "cultural" is just the neoliberal form of a new social literacy—new expertise or the ones who "know-how-to-do it."

The effort to be critical in the field of cultural production remains untruthful, and it only emerges as an "aesthetic of administration," shifting between the market, state, and freelance activism. This kind of criticality shows no capacity to abandon its comfort position, which sets it off from the formal articulation of the needs of "class cultural workers." It does not intervene in real-life activity. Instead, it is the negotiable middle class's interpretation, which only makes a distinction between the "conscious" bourgeois and the consumer of spectacular kitsch; critical stance appears as a trademark for the enlightened citizen, just as the industrial product is.

The recent Macedonian government-organized project "Skopje 2014," and the rebellious acts in the arts and protest movements in response to it, serve as the case study to examine the possibilities and limits of the art practices. What happened in Macedonia in 2009 was unacceptably unreasonable and shocking. The project started when the government announced large-scale developments for the city center, including a complex of buildings and monuments built in inappropriate public spaces, without consulting professional opinion, without a broader examination of the subject of urbanity or civic involvement. In the government's nationalistic censoring of the past, it replaced the modernist facades of buildings with baroque and neo-classicistic designs - obsolete historical styles that never existed in the history of architecture in Macedonia. An enormous amount of public money was spent on covering modernistic architecture with inauthentic facades. Public space was packed full with numerous sculptures and monuments of disputable heroes from the national pantheon. The project itself reflects the nationalistic, authoritarian regime, populism, and hegemony of the right-wing ruling party. Even though dissatisfaction, especially among intellectuals, had been rising, most people actually approved, or even more incredible, liked the project.

Since then, linked to the protest actions on the level of similar politics, many art projects had been produced in the direction of social activism. Artists actualizing these kinds of projects were dealing with an attempt to intervene in the public sphere in order to actualize or resolve urgent questions in society, in all of its complexity. The results from these kinds of actions were exhibited mostly within the frames of institutional. But, the problem, according to Groys, is not that the political sphere of the arts has already become aestheticized. Groys interprets the artistic process of art activism as something that often cedes its territory to a political sphere, that has no need of an artist (as an expert in this field with appropriate education), or the term art as such. When art becomes political, it is forced to make the unpleasant discovery that politics has already become art and that it has already situated itself in the aesthetic field.[1] There is no better example for Groys than the representation of terror itself, which constitutes an image-production machine: the terrorist, Groys argues, consciously and artistically stages

[1]   Boris Groys, Self-Design and Aesthetic responsibility, E-flux journal, no. 7, June 2009.

events that produce his own easily recognizable aesthetics, with no need of an artist to represent them in mediation. Images of the defeated and humiliated also bypass the need for an artist.[2] Therefore, Groys suggests that the point is not that art should conquer the territory of politics. Instead, it needs to find its way into territory that is now being conquered by political and economic forces. Consequently, artists dealing with engaged practices, just as curators who became the new critics, unsatisfied with their position, are "forced" to enter in public activism or into the masses.   And mostly, the links between the arts and the protest movements were widely recognized because of the initiating role of the artists from the very beginning, which leads to the old questions about the borders between art and activism expressed in Nato Thompson's phrase "far beyond the arts."[3]

2.

Despite the entertaining appearance of their images on social media, the initial rebellious movements in Skopje in 2016 escalated onto a mass protest called the "Colorful revolution." It mobilized thousands of people who vented their anger by throwing paint on the monuments—symbols of the government's oppression and hegemony. And although peaceful in its nature—the movement covered all of the government institutions and Skopje 2014 monuments in a multicolor paint.

So, the questions arise: If there is an aesthetics of the protest, do we have serial images produced at once, instead of its representation? Does the protest that is being organized around short sequences of images do what Hito Steyerl would call "editing"? Articulation of protest is being held on two levels: the language of the protest or verbalization and visualization; and the same combination of concepts that are shaping the structure of the internal organization of the protest, actually two different types of combining different elements: on the level of symbols and on the level of political powers. What kind of political meaning can come out of this type of articulation?

As argued by historian and art theoretician Nebojša Vilić (Facebook project: "Status #100 – 66/34, Доста е со "шарената револуција", 2016), after coloring the objects of Skopje 2014, which highlighted their absurdity, the protesters' interventions on facades and on the streets took a new course. First, the image turns into text, the coloring to writing. The initial stubbed colors poured on the facades were replaced with more pleasant and enjoyable pastel colors. Thus, the "Colorful Revolution" of radical, rebellious red and black became pleasant: pink, turquoise, and violet soft as if they were

---

[2]   Boris Groys, *Art   Power*, Cambridge, MA: MIT Press, 2008, p. 122-126.
[3]   Nato Thompson (ed.), *Living as Form: Socially Engaged Art from 1991–2001*, Cambridge: MIT Press, 2012.

the consensual compromise between colors from the palette. The protests became a kind of consensual compromise between protesters and police; as the protesters' palette of colors softened, the police began to allow painting and they removed barricades. It is difficult not to notice that the number of protests rapidly increased (as a result of social media). The difference toward previous protests movements concerning the stage design, and performative elements, taken as a form from arts is also noticeable, and the number of people who were involved in it.

Being based on the values of liberal democracy, the Colorful Revolution did not dissolve important obstacles. It did not possess the strength for the massive mobilization of different segments of society: one of the conditions for significant political change. Its failure comes as a result of the unequal social groups support, introduced by the ruling party and its opposition. While on the one hand voters of the ruling party (as the counter-protesters in the Colorful Revolution) represent the most oppressed social stratum in society, the poor and the workers, on the other hand, the protestors, mainly followers of the opposition, who do not identify themselves as workers, march from the relatively comfortable position of economic security, emerge as representatives of citizenship. The Colorful Revolution failed to avoid the elitist moment. As Nebojša Vilić points out, although initially pro-leftist, the Colorful Revolution, identified mainly through the concept of citizenship as compromised and consensual social category, was not able to tap into the radical and oppressed and underprivileged classes.[4] And although there were no elements or the insistence of authorship through the coloring as identification with the artistic act, the graphite written on the newly built triumph gate "Macedonia": "The Art of citizens" stands as opposite of the main revolutionary goal since the art does not include the collective, but the artist/individual as such.

The protest, in political and social terms, was an effort to reconfirm democracy. But, at the same time, it failed to extend its limits as a social act of resistance on behalf of precarious and to initiate the process of self-organizing of the general intellect. The protest movement failed because of the impossibility of to reach beyond the borders of the general intellect. And as Maurizio Lazzarato's defines it, "the general intellect" is a representation of a social stratum of immaterial workers whose presence is set upon the old modernist presumption: that it is always necessary to draw the line between invention and work, creativity, and routine.[5] The protest means "the reactivation of the social body. But the energy coming from protest must be transferred into the real place of production:

---

[4] Vilić Nebojša, Facebook project: Status #100 – 66/34, Доста е со "шарената револуција", 2016.

[5] Maurizio Lazzarato, General Intellect: Towards an Inquiry into Immaterial Labor, Multitudes, online journal, 2004.

not just the urban territory, but the bio-financial global network and real life relations."[6]

The intellectuals established a zone where breaks occurred in social reality. As freethinkers, they are the most democratic strata but also the leaders (although not in commanding positions) in the most authoritarian spheres, like education and expert governance. They embody society's contradictions between the consolidation and exploitation, between solidarity and the division of labor, or between the intellectual and the material labor, where those excluded from the privilege of leisure or liberal education, in all its necessity to gain the attributes of intellectual contradictions, exist also.

3.

Hence, the question is: Should the "general intellect" be defined through the terms of the most operative form of production under capitalism or is it more important to give consideration of less pragmatic meaning that cannot be reduced to knowledge and qualifications? Will the general intellect ever be in the position to be the avant-garde of protest? Even though precarious, this social stratum still owns its means of production: the "general intellect," which is on its own. The "general intellect" and its embodiment in the "immaterial worker," must take up a more avant-gardist position, namely on the side of the oppressed based on its isolation from this same intellectual instrumentalization. And it is finally time for artists, critics, and scholars to stop lecturing and learn how to slip into someone else's shoes. What we need is to critically re-examine the materiality of a world facing ongoing modification, and to join the marginalized in the process of producing an applicable theory that unifies the essential critique with a new form of practice. As Chantal Mouffe explained it:

> Today artists cannot pretend anymore to constitute an avant-garde offering a radical critique, but this is not a reason to proclaim that their political role has ended. They still can play an important role in the hegemonic struggle by subverting the dominant hegemony and by contributing to the construction of new subjectivities. In fact, this has always been their role and it is only the modernist illusion of the privileged position of the artist that has made us believe otherwise. Once this illusion is abandoned, jointly with the revolutionary conception of politics accompanying it, we can see that critical artistic practices represent an important dimension of democratic politics.

---

[6] Önder Özengi & Pelin Tan (LaborinArt), Running Along the Disaster: A conversation with Franco "Bifo" Berardi, E-flux journal, no. 56, June 2014.

This does not mean, though, "that they could alone realize the transformations needed for the establishment of a new hegemony. A radical democratic politics calls for the articulation of different levels of struggles so as to create a chain of equivalence among them."[7]

In order for art to transform into life, it must accept the idea of "equality," in Rancière's terms, as he puts it in the "The Ignorant Schoolmaster": the equality of all subjects, freed from the hierarchies of knowledge, the idea of the equality of intelligence itself. As he declares, emancipation can't be expected from forms of art that presuppose the passivity of the viewer or those that want to make viewers "active" at all costs with the help of gadgets borrowed from advertising. The practice of art is emancipated and emancipating when it renounces the authority of the imposed message, the target audience, or, when, in other words, it stops wanting to emancipate us. The most radical way in which art can represent a form of social critique is to start to question and transform meaning and the function of the art system itself. We have already become subordinated to a hegemonic idea of what art is and what it does if we agree upon the questions: In what way can art contribute to hegemonic repression; or, what is the way that can be used in order to give voice to the silenced and oppressed? As Bishop has pointed out, such questions are hegemonic in themselves, as long as they presuppose what art is and what it can do. Ideology is in the question, not in the answer.

References

Bishop, C., *Participation and Spectacle: Where Are We Now?* Nato Thompson (ed.), Living as Form: Socially Engaged Art from 1991–2001, Cambridge: MIT Press, 2012.

Groys, B., *Self-Design and Aesthetic Responsibility*. E-flux journal, no. 7, 2009.

Groys, B., *Art Power*, MIT Press, Cambridge, MA, 2008.

Lazzarato, M., 2004. General Intellect: Towards an Inquiry into Immaterial Labor. Multitudes, online journal, 2004.

Mouffe, C., *Artistic Activism and Agonistic Spaces*. Art & Research, A Journal of Ideas Context and Methods, Vol.1, no.2, 2007.

Nebojša, V., Facebook project: Status #100 – 66/34, Доста е со "шарената револуција. ", 2016.

Özengi, Ö., Tan, P. (LaborinArt), Running Along the Disaster: A conversation with Franco "Bifo" Berardi. E-flux journal, no. 56, 2014.

Rancière, J., Carnevale, F., Kelsey, J., Art of the Possible: Fulvia Carnevale and John Kelsey in conversation with Jacques Ranciere. Artforum, March, 2007.

Rancière, J., *The Ignorant Schoolmaster. Five Lesson in Intellectual Emancipation*, Stanford University Press, Stanford, California, 1991

---

[7] Chantal Mouffe, *Artistic Activism and Agonistic Spaces*, Art & Research, A Journal of Ideas Context and Methods, vol.1, no.2, Summer, 2007.

A Field of Non-Field

Chieh-Jen Chen

Single channel video installation *A Field of Non-Field* conveys the concept that the relationship between technological development and capitalism has formed a new concept of technology capitalism, imposing control over technology and even the desires, perception, and thinking of individuals. This condition forms a situation of "global imprisonment, at-home exile." What are our options of survival under circumstances such as these?

From the dialogue between the little girl and her mother, the viewer listens to how the little girl's brother left the hospital without permission after being admitted for suicide, and was never to be seen again. The mother said: "Your brother just went somewhere far away, beyond the west…" and "Your brother is just on his way back…" With these statements, an" outbound" and " return" journey begins.

The geological scenery of capitalism is presented almost as a relic during the "outbound" journey. Images of wall-less industrial grounds filled with echoes with a view of empty modern apartments hint to the abandoned dispatch workers and objects, such as human organs and old computers, that are sacrificed in the name of capitalism. Collective murmurings such as "When did we accept being sentenced to at-home exile?" and the chanting of "What can we do? Nameless. Nameless, what can we do?" can be heard, forming multiple imageries and the fluidity of meaning. Throughout the "return" journey, the troop disappears, and the brother is seen standing alone in a wasteland, listening attentively to the resounding singing of female workers as the music gradually fades.

This work mixes the spectacles of different realities and frustration, creating a state of suspension that accentuates hidden problems. With title *A Field of Non-Field*, the artist explores the concept of Sunyata (nothingness) in the Madhyamaka School and the Madhyamaka method, which involves multiple dialectic approaches. Applying the concept of "no destruction without existence, no discontinuity without consistency, no diversity without sameness, no departure without arriving," the fact that all things are relative, codependent, and constantly changing is manifested, and the illusion of absolutism is shattered. Chen Chieh-Jen calls this method "multiple dialectics" and believes that the philosophy of the Madhyamaka School is one of the ways of changing the new politics formed by gaining complete control over technology.

Notes on the Causes

Chieh-Jen Chen and Chien-Hung Huang

Notes on the Causes is a single channel video installation that artist Chen Chieh-Jen started working on after Revolt in The Soul & Body since 1996, a series of computer-revised historical photographs portraying punishment methods, Chen used actors in 2000 and started exploring topics "virtual future" and "unreachable future" in Notes on the Causes Series.

The video on display in this exhibition is a recording of the preparations for Notes on the Causes. Two blind characters engage in a conversation about their imaginations and hopes on future technology regarding the electronic eye. The pregnant character mentions that she dreamt her child was born during a big plague. The images of the apocalypse and the unborn baby compose the "unforeseeable life and future." The work refers to the layering of past, present, and future, while the visible∕invisible memory of time, the context of existence in the apocalyptic era∕technological era, historical narrative of past∕present, all encourage contemplation towards the history and the future.

Truth or Post-Truth?

Rahma Khazam

According to a significant number of critics and curators, contemporary art faces new challenges in our post-truth era, whether highlighting populist politicians' reductive conceptions of reality, exploring neglected nuances of our contemporary moment or opposing cultural fascism. Yet are these challenges really that new after all? And is art the right instrument for resolving them, given that it has always been about subjectivity and illusion rather than truth?

I will begin with the question as to whether the challenges facing art in the post-truth era are new or not, taking as my starting-point Michael Hardt and Antonio Negri's theory of two modernities, as set out in *Empire* (2000). The first modernity consisted in a 'revolution' in political thought, a revolution that rejected transcendence and embraced immanence, as Lucas Freire points out:

> This was the first proposal of rupture in relation to the medieval order, the first mode of modernity. However, in a counterrevolution, the second mode of modernity attempted to discard the plane of immanence by denouncing it as potential or actual crisis and by rescuing the idea of transcendental authority [...] In politics, this led to the legitimation of the transcendental apparatus of sovereignty. The first mode of modernity emerges as a revolution against the medieval worldview. (Freire 2018)

Just as Hardt and Negri associate their two modernities with immanence and transcendence, so do I wish to associate truth and post-truth with these two planes: truth is immanent, disinterested and independent of any higher authority, while post-truth serves a particular purpose and functions transcendentally, as does sovereignty.

We may also note another parallel between truth, post-truth and the two modernities, their relation to capitalism: one of Negri and Hardt's two modernities is in the service of capitalism, as is generally the case of post-truth politics, whereas their other modernity is linked to anti-capitalism, as is often the search for truth. Alexei Penzin also emphasizes the relation of the two modernities to biopower and biopolitics:

> One of these modernities has to do with the emergence of capitalism, the sovereign nation-state and its apparatus of domination, biopower. The other has to do with the time of struggle and antagonism, with living subjectivity and its constituent "power", with the biopolitics of new forms of life. (Penzin 2014)

In line with this definition, we might describe post-truth as part of the apparatus of power, while truth is a goal we might have to struggle to attain.

Immanence vs. transcendence, objectivity vs. fabrication, revolt vs. tradition, anti-capitalism vs. capitalism, biopower vs. biopolitics, are recurring themes in art, that are often found together: it is surely no coincidence that one of the first art collectives to critique the disinformation practices of the society of its time was the resolutely anti-capitalist Dada. Dada used strategies of alienation, anti-aesthetics, collage, assemblage, fragmentation and irony to critique the bourgeois society of its time—as in the first international 'Dada-Messe' organized in 1920 by George Grosz, Raoul Hausmann and John Heartfield. As Sophie Bernard writes

> The Fair was nihilist, communist, anticlerical and anti-bourgeois [...] Calling the exhibition a Messe [fair] and the 'works of art' *Erzeugnisse* [= products], as well as the mention of 'Exhibition and sale of Dadaist works', provided a parody of commercial fairs developing at that time in Germany. In opposing capitalism and denouncing art made for the bourgeoisie, Hausmann imagined the destruction of all the assemblages presented, at the closing of the exhibition. (Bernard 2005)

Through these denunciations, Dada expressed its immanent, rebellious, anti-capitalist and anti-authoritarian stance.

More than just rejecting capitalist and political transcendence however, Dada also eschewed the authority of history and the past, deploying instead the far more exacting strategy of critiquing the present. As Wieland Herzfelde emphasized in the introduction to the catalogue of the fair:

> The only agenda for the Dadaists is to give, temporally and locally, current events as the content of their works. This is why they don't consider A Thousand and One Nights or Images of India to be the source of their production, but, on the contrary, the illustrations and editorials from newspapers. (Herzfelde cited in Bernard 2005)

In her book *Dada Presentism: An Essay on Art and History* (2016), Maria Stavrinaki examines Dada's rejection of memorialization in favour of a savage critique of the present, as expressed through collage and assemblage. A prime example of their rebellious anti-authoritarian stance is Hannah Höch's *Cut with the Kitchen Knife Dada through the Last Weimar Beer-Belly Cultural Epoch in Germany* (1919), a satirical collage portraying the contradictory and often hypocritical political tendencies that emerged after the First World War. So is there a difference between post-truth at the time of Dada and post-truth today? One might argue that if the tactics and counter-tactics I have just been describing appear familiar, it is precisely because Dadaist techniques have been around for a time, to the point where they have become ingrained in contemporary art, and because fake news itself has been around a long time, very much connected, once again, with the authority of the sovereign nation-state. As the UK-based collective Forensic Architecture points out:

> In the field of mainstream politics now we encounter the accusation of fake news. But within the fields of journalism and activism around conflict, instances of powerful states accusing those holding them to account of "fake news" is as old as war itself. Almost anything you discover about state crimes will be counteracted by the state dismissing it as a manipulation of the truth, a politically motivated lie. (Forensic Architecture and Metahaven 2018)

One might also argue that propaganda and conspiracy theories have also been around for ever, to the point where there has never been a period of absolute truth, even if the term post-truth suggests the contrary. In other words, post-truth is much the same as ever and Dada is proof of it.

However, when viewed from a contemporary perspective, Dadaist techniques have their shortcomings. The current climate of post-truth differs from previous eras in that instances of fake news and fake information, which might previously have met with wholesale condemnation, are greeted today with blank indifference. In other words, people are increasingly less swayed by rational argument and hard facts, and more by corporate or private interests for which the only authority is not some higher order such as history, or politics but only themselves. Under the regime of relativism, there is no higher authority: the distinction between information and disinformation breaks down and immanence, revolt, anti-capitalism and the insistence on objectivity are no longer enough. It is this situation that contemporary art needs to address.

I will now move on to some examples of how it is addressing it—which will also serve to answer the second question posed at the beginning of my paper: whether or not art is the right instrument for resolving the question of disinformation, given that it has always been about subjectivity and illusion rather than truth. In his book project *What is Different?* (Tillmans and Oetker 2018), the German photographer Wolfgang Tillmans investigates the new post-truth climate, and specifically such phenomena as the backfire effect, identified in 2006 by two American political scientists, whereby people who are convinced by a statement, even one that is patently incorrect, cannot be persuaded that it is false even when presented with facts to the contrary (Tillmans 2018). As Tillmans states:

> We have known for some time that there are people who feel drawn to esoteric conspiracy theories. What is new, however, is that hard facts are no longer believed by wide segments of the population. During the past two years, I have come to realise that if 30% of the electorate are resistant to rational argument, we are on a slippery slope. In light of all this, I wanted to investigate why the backfire effect is having more impact today than it did 10, 20 or 40 years ago. What has changed? What is different? This latter phrase became the title of the book.
> (Tillmans 2018)

Much of the groundwork for the publication came out of Tillmans's installation *Truth Study Centre* (2005), which sought to draw attention to the absurdity of erroneous proclamations purporting to be the truth—such as a former South African Health Minister's statement that HIV was not the cause of Aids (Tillmans 2018). By displaying photocopies of such statements, it pointed to the high levels of credulity in populations at large. Interviews with cognitive scientist Stephan Lewandowsky, political activist Bianca Klose, and the German Foreign Minister, among others, yielded further explanations as to why the backfire effect may be gaining ground: Lewandowsky commented that the internet was a powerful tool for post-truth because it makes promoters of fringe ideas feel that they are part of a large community when they are online, while a team of neurologists showed that political and non-political statements generate different neural activity, with beliefs relating to our political identity being particularly hard to shift (Tillmans 2018). Another issue Tillmans seeks to explain is the recent progress of right-wing populist groups across Europe through such techniques as post-truth. Putting the blame, once again, on capitalism, he concludes: 'Working on the book confirmed my suspicion that the populist revolts of 2016–17 were less a movement started by globalisation's losers and more a result of the manipulation of those groups for reactionary and capitalist purposes' (Tillmans 2018).

Art collectives such as Forensic Architecture and Metahaven are likewise testifying to art's capability to address the question of fake news while taking into account the insidious techniques of the new mode of post-truth: both of them engage in research-led practices involving design, art, filmmaking, and writing that expose not only abuses of state and extra-state power, but also the functioning of propaganda and fake news. Metahaven, for its part, is interested 'in the stealthier ways that design operates, and how it, on a broader scale, embodies the explicit and implicit ideologies of its time' (Forensic Architecture and Metahaven 2018). Their works include *The Sprawl: Propaganda about Propaganda* (2016), a film exploring internet activism that spans the documentary, the art film and the music video. Comprising different narratives covering the same subject-matter, each of which makes sense from its point of view without acknowledging the others, the film shows how 'fantasy and propaganda have gained prominence over transparency and accountability' and how 'fantasy can be designed so as to seem or feel like a truth', as Daniel van der Velden of Metahaven explains (Muraben 2016).

Forensic Architecture's starting-point was the question of the Israeli occupation of Palestine and the place of the built environment environment within it. There was no publicly available map of the military-civilian occupation, so Forensic Architecture decided to create a counter-cartography, which soon became a cartography of micro-incidents, a laboratory 'for developing theoretical techniques and technologies of resistance that could be brought to bear on other situations worldwide' (Forensic Architecture and Metahaven 2018). Recent works by Forensic Architecture consist of videos and texts reconstructing the trajectories of missiles by means of the traces they leave on walls, thereby making use of buildings to obtain evidence of drone strikes or other armed attacks. Like Metahaven, Forensic Architecture is interested in propaganda and particularly such relatively new forms of denial as '"glomarization"—the official formulation used by the CIA since the 1970s [to indicate that] they will "neither confirm nor deny" an incident or active operation (Forensic Architecture and Metahaven 2018).

At the same time however, both collectives come up against the problem that even they have to package their work, and decide what and how much they want to reveal to the different audiences with which they engage—which brings us back to the question of the limits between objectivity and manipulation. As Forensic Architecture points out: 'The question is how to mediate between the two extremes. What's the argument between the purity of un-chewed information and the overly selective and targeted campaign? What would a conscious, critical media approach be?' (Forensic Architecture and Metahaven 2018). For Metahaven, propaganda and its effects reveal the existence of multiple truths, which does not imply denying that facts exist, but accepting that truth is a construction (Forensic Architecture and Metahaven 2018). An equally challenging question is how to distinguish between fictitious connections and hard facts. Forensic Architecture take an oblique approach, their aim being not so much to find out what happened in particular situations, as to dismantle existing statements or narratives that smack of propaganda or lies (Forensic Architecture and Metahaven 2018).

On the basis of these findings, how do we then answer my second question as to whether art is indeed the right instrument for resolving the issue of post-truth. The answer is yes, if it is the kind of art we have been looking at here, that is, art that concerns itself neither with imitation nor with representation, but instead, to quote Gabriel Rockhill's definition of the aesthetic regime of art in Jacques Rancière's *The Politics of Aesthetics* (2006), promotes 'the equality of represented subjects, the indifference of style with regard to content, and the immanence of meaning in things themselves' (Rancière 2006)—so an art that promotes not only democratic equality rather than capitalist inequality but also immanence rather than transcendence—to which we might add a third criterion: that it seeks to engage with the new state of post-truth.

References

Bernard, Sophie (2005), 'Dada-Messe / International Fair', translated from the French text published in the catalogue *Dada*, Paris, Editions du Centre Pompidou, p. 67-68. The translation was part of the Press Pack, published by MNAM Centre Pompidou 2005, p. 61-62 [Courtesy MNAM Centre Pompidou], http://www.dada-companion.com/dada-messe/, accessed on 20 July 2018.

Forensic Architecture and Metahaven in conversation with Richard Birkett (2018), 'The Inhabitant and the Map: Forensic Architecture and Metahaven', CONVERSATIONS *Mousse* 63, April-May 2018, http://moussemagazine.it/metahaven-forensic-architecture-richard-birkett-2018/, accesssed 20 July 2018.

Freire, Lucas (2018), 'Political Thought, International Relations and a Tale of Two Modernities', *Liberdade Economica*, 07/02/2018, http://liberdadeeconomica.mackenzie.br/artigos/arquivo/artigo/political-thought-international-relations-and-a-tale-of-two-modernities/, accessed 20 July 2018.

Muraben, Billie (2016), 'Making propaganda about propaganda', *It's Nice That*,
https://www.itsnicethat.com/features/metahaven-thesprawl-110216, accessed 20 July 2018.

Negri, Antonio and Hardt, Michael (2000), *Empire*, Cambridge, MA and London, Harvard University Press.

Penzin, Alexei (2014), 'The Biopolitics of the Soviet Avant-Garde', in Budraitskis, I. and Zhilyaev, A. (eds.), *Pedagogical Poem*, Venice, Marsilio Editori.

Rancière, Jacques (2006), *The Politics of Aesthetics*, London and New York, Continuum.

Stavrinaki, Maria (2016), *Dada Presentism: An Essay on Art and History*, Stanford: University of Stanford Press.

Tillmans, Wolfgang and Oetker Brigitte (eds.) (2018), *What Is Different?*, Jahresring 64, Berlin, Sternberg Press.

Tillmans, Wolfgang (2018), 'Wolfgang Tillmans: my two-year investigation into the post-truth era', *The Guardian*, 28/02/2018, https://www.theguardian.com/artanddesign/2018/feb/28/wolfgang-tillmans-what-is-different-backfire-effect, accessed 20 July 2018.

A Brave New Virtual World?

Elisa Rusca

"We are often told that privacy is disappearing, that the most intimate secrets are open to public probing.
But the reality is the opposite: what is effectively disappearing is public space, with its attending dignity."

Mark von Schlegell, New Dystopia

In 2011, as part of the exhibition *Dystopia* at CAPC musée d'art contemporain de Bordeaux, Mark von Schlegell published the book *New Dystopia,*[1] a fiction novel about cultural and spatial possibilities in the future. In *New Dystopia* a-gendered characters move through offline non-spaces and cyberspace networks, confronting themselves with architectures depicted as living creatures and highly regulated public spaces.

Some years have passed by from the launch of this fictional book; in today's reality of 2018, we can assist to a progressive hyper codification of the public space, which is getting along with the digitalisation of our existence in most of the countries of the world: from Europe to Brasil, from the United States to India, from Russia to the Emirates, from South Africa to the People's Republic of China. Offline and online spaces, contrarily to the dreams of the cyber-enthusiasts of the 1990s, aren't two different realities. The so-called "independence" of the cyberspace[2] clashes against its current structural organisation that makes its existence dependent of "prosumers" (Lovink, 2011), productive-consumers who, once paid their connections to Internet providers, add content online and, simultaneously, subscribe to services and use this space as an entertainment spot. Predictive algorithms and filter bubbles create echo chambers for each prosumer, isolating him or her from the rest of the information flow and from other prosumers, while betraying him or her in making them believe that they are part of a vast community.

---

[1]   Mark von Schlegell, *New Dystopia*, Berlin: Sternberg Press, 2011.
[2]   John Perry Barlow, A Declaration of the Independence of Cyberspace, 1996.

Once defined by John Perry Barlow as "the new home of the Mind"[3] and a potential tool of alternative political and economic discourses, the Internet is yet today capitalised and transformed in an instrument of surveillance, control and propaganda. As artist Tabita Rezaire explained in an interview for the magazine *OK Africa*, "the internet reproduces IRL [in real life] fuck ups" such as western domination and occidental hegemony[4]: cyberspace it is not the exit to a brave, new world, yet the mirror of the dystopia we are living in.

Like Alice through the looking-glass, we enter this mirror through the thin surfaces of our screens. The interface is still the ultimate barrier between the universe of the objects and the universe of their shadows made of data. However, the interface is a one-way barrier: it allows us to access the shadow-world, but it doesn't prevent the data-shadow to affect our life in the real world. The data-shadow that each of us prosumer left behind online embraces us in the offline world, and it knows more about us than ourselves. It is so precise that can predict our behaviours and desires, and influence them as well, in a very accurate way. Therefore, we are not free to move and to interact within the actual cyber-system, nor this space is public or for democracy. And because of this, even when we are disconnected we are less and less free.

To paraphrase again Mark von Schlegell, privacy hasn't disappeared: it is the notion of public space that has been completely shaken.[5]

"To hack" means to enter and to reconfigure a certain, determined space. When Loyd Blankenship, better known as The Mentor, wrote the *Hacker Manifesto* in 1986,[6] he claimed:

> This is our world now... the world of the electron and the switch, the beauty of the baud.   We make use of a service already existing without paying for what could be dirt-cheap if it wasn't run by profiteering gluttons, and you call us criminals.   We explore... and you call us criminals.   We seek after knowledge... and you call us criminals.   We exist without skin color, without nationality, without religious bias... and you call us criminals. You build atomic bombs, you wage wars, you

---

[3]   John Perry Barlow, *A Declaration of the Independence of Cyberspace*, 1996 : "Governments of the Industrial World, you weary giants of flesh and steel, I come from Cyberspace, the new home of Mind. On behalf of the future, I ask you of the past to leave us alone. You are not welcome among us. You have no sovereignty where we gather."

[4]   http://www.okayafrica.com/culture-2/tabita-rezaire-cyber-warrior-e-colonialism

[5]   Mark von Schlegell, *New Dystopia*, Berlin : Sternberg Press, 2011, p. 8.

[6]   Also known as *The Conscience of a Hacker*, the small essay was written shortly after his author's arrest. First published online, on the hackers' platform *Phrack*, it is considered as a cornerstone in the hacker culture.

murder, cheat, and lie to us and try to make us believe it's for our own good, yet we're the criminals. Yes, I am a criminal.   My crime is that of curiosity. My crime is that of judging people by what they say and think, not what they look like. My crime is that of outsmarting you, something that you will never forgive me for.

The figure of the hacker has been indeed criminalised since, along with the privatisation and regularisation of the cyberspace. However, the hacker is a complex and controversial character: someone who can be fighting for justice as a member of Anonymous,[7] or working for a national security agency,[8] or entering Dallas' emergency siren system at night just for fun[9]—in any of these circumstances, the hacker is an outcast, most of the time quite young and with a very high I.Q.

Now, the archetypal figure of the artist is also connected with the idea of accessing and reconfiguring, and to some extents, one could say that hackers are artists. And contemporary artists who know how to code, enter and rewrite programmes online, as well as analogue systems, can be defined as hackers. This paper aims to present the work of artists working with networking technologies, hacktivism and patterns reconfiguration. I will give you three examples of Swiss hacker-artists or artist-hackers collectives, you decide which one come first.

I'd like to start with the collective Gysin&Vanetti.[10] Andreas Gysin and Sidi Vanetti met at the University of Applied Sciences in Lugano, Ticino, and since the mid-90s are collaborating in artistic projects involving found hardware that they reprogramme. Multipurpose displays of fixed, type geometries such as train signs or gas station price panels are taken and not modified in their layout: their shape and look are the physical constraints. Within these done frames, the artist duo looks for alternative patterns and image visualisations that can spread from the given layout. Playfully and skilfully, Gysin&Vanetti explore the aesthetic of infinite combinations: they create new images,

---

[7] Anonymous is a non-hierarchical, decentralised hacker group that came to the media attention because of their action against the church of Scientology in 2008 (cf. "Project Chanology", https://www.theguardian.com/technology/2008/feb/04/news).

[8] For years from now we know that governments and private companies around the world hire hackers to improve their security systems and to develop new ideas in programming and network development (here's an article from 2004, stressing especially Israeli, American and Swiss situation: https://www.technewsworld.com/story/32847.html; and here's a Washington Post article from 2015 about the US government recruiting hackers : https://www.washingtonpost.com/news/the-switch/wp/2015/10/24/how-the-government-tries-to-recruit-hackers-on-their-own-turf/?noredirect=on&utm_term=.378fa3d01331).

[9] In April 2017, an unknown hacker entered the Dallas' emergency siren system and woke up the whole city. https://www.zdnet.com/article/experts-think-they-know-how-dallas-emergency-sirens-were-hacked/

[10] http://www.gysin-vanetti.com

they mix and generate patterns, they build animations while searching for ever changing visual permutation. The challenge is to create complexity within a small, simple grid.

Their work *Digits* (2014-2016) is a perfect example of their philosophy: the sculpture is composed by 42 elements, each of it being a 7-segments display, the same used by petrol stations to show their prices. 7-segments displays are commonly used for analogical numerical representation: each digit has seven individual blades that combined with the other depict the number. The piece can be placed on the floor, as a long line, or put on a wall as a rectangle. In the floor installation, each blade is programmed to produce waves of horizontal back and forth motion; in the wall piece, the animation is programmed to move more slowly, creating gentle waves of combined lines. The same reconfigured object can then take different final shapes, producing very different perception of the piece: loud sound and quick movement when on the floor, soft variations of a meditation diagram on the wall.

The familiar object, which is the petrol station panel, showing usual digits, is redesigned not in its shape, but in its function. The spectator is triggered: a cold, mechanical sign suddenly becomes animated by another force that unexpectedly breaks our common way to read the information displayed. This subversion in our perception is the same that occurs in their work *Zh HB flap* (2016). The original, mechanical timetable of the Zurich train station has been replaced in 2015 by a new digital screen. Gysin&Vanetti took the old display, composed by 452 PVC split-flap elements silk screened with a destination, time or rail information. Similarly to what they did for *Digits* (2014-2016), the duo recombined the rhythm and the associations of the different elements, designing new animations with the given material. Each element acquires a sort of mechanical independence from the whole composition, which becomes a chalkboard for recombination of a number of shifting, abstract signs.

The pulsations of sound generated by the new movements, together with the extraction of the minimal, basic elements of the structures they use, change our look on ordinary, mechanical objects. Hacking the analogical vestiges of the offline world, Gysin&Vanetti create the ultimate ready-mades of the 21st century.

Carmen Weisskopf and Domagoj Smoljo are the second artist duo I'd like to talk about. They formed the !Mediengruppe Bitnik[11] since the early 2000s and, as their statement says, they "work on and with the Internet". Based in Zurich and London, their work is more varied than Gysin&Vanetti's analog hacking: more than automatism and recombination, to !Mediengruppe Bitnik is important to include their audience in the process of making their pieces.

---

[11] https://www.bitnik.org

In 2007, the artists placed several hidden microphones in Zurich Opera. From the 9th of March to the 26th of May, all the concerts were recorded and hired through telephone lines: a secret contact centre was placed in Cabaret Voltaire (the historical Dada movement headquarters), randomly accessing the home telephone numbers of the Zurich inhabitants, who received calls from there. If you got the call, you could listen to the concert in the Opera from your house for free. During *Opera Calling!*, 90 hours of opera were transmitted to more than 4000 households. The ephemeral nature of *Opera Calling!* merges the will to democratise the opera with a dada spirit, but also recalls Nam Jun Paik works on radio and radio waves, placing Fluxus as one of the influences for !Mediengruppe Bitnik.

In 2012, the group created *Surveillance Chess*, which still exists online at the address http://chess.bitnik.org/. The piece takes place in London; carrying an interfering transmitter in a yellow suitcase, !Mediengruppe Bitnik hijacked CCTV cameras, replacing the real-time flow of recorded footage with an invitation to play a game of chess. Guards and security services people sited in control rooms were then faced to their monitors showing a chessboard instead of the surveillance images. The interaction here takes place between the artists and the operators watching the surveillance feed; the roles of the observer and the observed are suddenly reversed, as for the power structure behind them: the observer is not in control anymore, and the tool of surveillance, which is the camera, becomes a tool for communication between two distinct entities placed in two different spaces.

Random Darknet Shopper (2014-ongoing) is a most recent work that relies only on the cyberspace, more precisely it explores the darknet, the part of the Internet that is encrypted and hidden from most of the popular browsers and navigation systems. The darknet is known to be the place where mostly of the illegal activities online take place, from child pornography to guns black market. !Mediegruppe Bitnik created a bot, an automated computer programme, designed to randomly buy something every week from Agora and Alpha Bay, online marketplaces on the Tor browser. This piece was first commissioned by the Kunst Halle Sankt Gallen, and since then had two more other editions in London and in Ljubljana. For each chapter, the shopper-bot has been equipped with a weekly budget of 100$ converted in bitcoins, and let go shopping during the exhibition's period. What was bought, was then showed in the hosting institution. The collection of the objects bought for *Random Darknet Shopper* are diverse and bizarre: from a Canadian gold coin to a Viagra generic made in India, including a guide about not to be arrested on the darknet and a set of car keys.

In their practice, !Mediengruppe Bitnik reveal the invisible infrastructure connecting offline space and cyberspace: the act of hacking and hijacking actual digital systems is part of a wider analysis of contemporary technological societies, and aims to a subversion of the present categories through different, participatory interactions.

The last example I will bring up is UBERMORGEN[12]. Ubermorgen.com is the oldest collective presented here since it was officially established in 1995 by Elizabeth Haas (who is also officially known by her pseudonym "lizvlx") and Hans Bernhard. They claim to be from Austria, Switzerland and the US because both grew up between Europe and the United States, and today they are based between the Basel and Vienna. From software art to installation, Ubermorgen.com have been often confronting themselves with political and economic topics. Maybe one of their most emblematic works is indeed *Vote-Auction* (2000), a fake website "bringing democracy and capitalism closer together"[13]: conceived for the US presidential elections, the page seemed to offer US citizens to sell their vote to the highest bidder. Taken for a real online page and debated in public, mainstream media such as CNN[14], *Vote-Auction* is a distinctive example of media hacking, which means to enter the information flow with a fake news that is considered to be true[15]. In fact, over 2500 global and national News features (radio, television, print and online media) reported about the page.

Torture Classics (2010) exists also as an online website[16]. Visiting users can download music compilations used by the US military in Iraq and Afghanistan to torture inmates. Loud music played repeatedly to prisoners as an interrogation tool psychologically breaking the interrogated person has been reported and attested publicly by government officials, guards, interrogators and human rights organisations, and has been declared illegal by the United Nations and the European Court of Human Rights. The actual music in *Torture Classics* includes commercial jingles and children songs, pop, rock and metal hits, as well as special mash-up created by CIA interrogators. When visiting *Torture Classics* one is taken by a mixed feeling of attraction and repulsion, due to acknowledging many of the songs featured in the "classics" as tools for torture and, simultaneously, as indeed part of what one could listen everyday from a local radio.

Merging reality and a nightmarish-distorted perception of it, Ubermorgen.com

---

[12] http://www.ubermorgen.com

[13] http://www.vote-auction.net

[14] Video to [V]ote Auction - CNN "Burden of Proof", in which the fake website is discussed as a real news within a 27-minutes exclusive CNN debate : https://vimeo.com/19218313

[15] It is very interesting to consider that in 2018 we are now used to the term "fake news", which is indeed media hacking. Today's media are constantly hacked by alternative facts and false stories, to the point that every time we read or see something we have to question whether this information might be fake. In the year 2000, insinuating false truths in the mainstream media wasn't so easy to achieve.

[16] www.tortureclassics.com

launched in 2015 the ongoing project *Chinese Coin (Red Blood)*, a mockumentary about bitcoin mining in China. Based on the real fact that the People's Republic of China is the world's largest producer of bitcoins, the ten-minute video[17] showed red-filtered images of a "bitcoin mine" as bitcoins were physical goods to extract from the earth like coal or gold.

Ubermorgen.com's work originated often from actual facts: the recombination happens on a meta-level. Differently from !Mediengruppe Bitnik and Gysin&Vanetti, the action of hacking consist in producing alternative realities triggering and questioning the spectator. Their pervasive way of action through the websites that they create links directly both spaces, the offline space and the cyberspace.

The artists presented here are only three collectives in the wide world of cyber-art and hack-artivism; they come from the same geographical area and are more or less of the same generation. However, they act in very different ways, showing us already the complexity and variety of approaches within this category. The hacker-artist figure is a multiple-facets one; if someone would dare to find a common denominator, maybe we should again refer to The Mentor and notice that all of them commit "the crime of curiosity". All the artists presented here show a particular curiosity for something: Gysin&Vanetti are curious about approaching and reprogramming analogue vestiges, !Mediengruppe Bitnik have a special curiosity for interaction and trespassing boundaries, while Ubermorgen.com's curiosity about news and current political and economic affairs pushes them to realise their alternative facts websites. Nevertheless, is this enough to draw a critical approach in order to read cyber-art? Where should we put the limits of new ways to access and use Internet related technology, and the artistic production? These questions remain open. Certainly, we should stop falling into the trap of classing everything that is related to networking technology under the sterile umbrella of "net-art", as it has been done for the last 30 years. On the other hand, we should start looking for similar patterns, designing families, groups, affiliations, differences. Hacking strategies such appropriating and reconfiguring given structures, physical and immaterial, can be effective as a tool for producing cultural value only if they embrace both worlds.

In her book *Whatch this space,* Francesca Gavin exhorts the reader for the necessity to create a "brave new virtual world"[18] through new approaches on cyber-art. Since offline and online worlds are deeply intertwined, as shown during this short excursus, a brave new virtual world can exist only if we act in a brave new way offline: and maybe, still seeing a division between the two would appear reactionary in the end. Eventually, a

---

[17] https://vimeo.com/145141943

[18] Francesca Gavin, *Watch This Space,* London: Pentagram, 2017, p.180.

way to exit the "net-art" category trap, would be to start thinking that there is no cyber-art nor hack-artivism, but only artists dealing with their contemporary tools.

References

Assange, Julian, Cypherpunks. Freedom and the Future of the Internet, London: OR Books, 2012.
Berardi, Franco "Bifo, "Cognitarian Subjectivation", *Are You Working Too Much? Post-Fordism, Precarity, and the Labor of Art,* Berlin: Sternberg Press, 2009.
Gavin, Francesca, *Watch This Space,* London: Pentagram, 2017.
Lovink, Geert, "What is the Social in the Social Media?", *The Internet Does Not Exist,* Berlin: Sternberg Press, 2011.
Magrini, Boris, "Gysin-Vanetti: Lirica dei Macchinari", in *Kunstbulletin,* 03/ 2016.
Quaranta, Domenico, *UBERMORGEN.COM,* Brescia: FPEditions, 2009.
Ryser, Daniel, *Delivery for Mr. Assange,* Zurich: Echtzeit Verlag, 2014.
Von Schlegell, Mark, *New Dystopia*, Berlin: Sternberg Press, 2011.

*   The author's participation to AICA International Congress in Taipei, Taiwan, was possible thanks to the kind support of Pro Helvetia, Swiss Arts Council.

The Image War of Chiang Kai-shek's Statues: The State of Exception in the Process of Promoting Transitional Justice in Taiwan

Kang-Jung Chan

Recently, there are several controversies involving Chiang Kai-shek's statues in Taiwan. Those actions certainly arouse opposition from some people who support to preserve the statues. In this essay, I intend to quote Giorgio Agamben's interpretation of "state of exception", in which he points out that every citizen could lose all his/her human rights and be excluded by the community anytime as a Homo Sacer. Therefore, I would argue that instead of supporting Chiang's oppressive regime or resisting the transitional justice, these supporters show their fear that they could be excluded by current transitional society. The Act on Promoting Transitional Justice, effective at the end of 2017 in Taiwan, has listed "Removal of authoritarian-era symbols" as one of the major projects in transitional justice. However, those incidents, including the vandalisms, dressing the statues or relocating them to other places, aroused by Chiang Kai-shek's statues reflect certain degree of difficulties and paradoxes in the process of transitional justice. I believe that the intentions of those opponents are not to fight against the aim of transitional justice, but rather the exclusion from our current society. This war of images continuously challenges whether Taiwan would reach this contradictory and strained ideal goal of "uncovering historical truth and pursuing the reconciliation of the society" in the process of transitional justice.

I. Introduction

The legislation of "The Act on Promoting Transitional Justice", effected by December 27th 2017, is aim to "promote the transitional justice and execute a liberal, democratic constitutional order". According to the Act, the Executive Yuan of Taiwan should found the "Committee of Promoting Transitional Justice" in order to program and comply the tasks, which are "uncovering political files", "removing authoritarian-era symbols, reserving the unrighteous site", "reverting judicial injustice, recovering historical truth and accelerating the conciliation of society" and "dealing with the dishonest property of political parties".

Those tasks above are related to broad and various agendas, hence, the most focused by Taiwanese and media are those incidents related with "removing authoritarian-era symbols". While I am writing this paper, the statue of Chiang Kai-shek in Taipei Chiang Kai-shek Memorial Hall is poured with paint by some opponents.[1] Again, this incident arouses diversely intensive disputes, which also demonstrates that the images of authoritarian are not "naïve, magical and superstitious" from savage mind. (Mitchell, 7-8) On the contrary, this "war of the images" (Mitchell, 11) of authoritarian actually reflects certain degree of difficulties and paradoxes in the process of transitional justice in Taiwan.

From the point of view of supporting the removal of statues, there are indeed some authoritarian remnants, which needed to be removed after the 43 years of Period of National Mobilization (1948-1992) in current society. Nevertheless, Chiang has passed away in 1975, it's hard to imagine that people would still indulge in the emotional attachment to Chiang's statues and the images of Chiang. Therefore, it will be inadequate to completely interpret the inner structure of this image war if we believe the opponents' opinions, which were insisting on reserving those statues, are equal to against the ideal of transitional justice.

Consequently, after listing all the incidents of the war of images, I intend to quote Giorgio Agamben's interpretation of "state of exception", in which he points out that every citizen could lose all his/her human rights and be excluded by the society anytime as a *Homo Sacer* in contemporary political condition. I believe that rather than supporting Chiang's oppressive regime or resisting the transitional justice, those opponents, who express their anxiety of removal of those statues, actually reveal their fear that they could be excluded by current society.

II. The authoritarian image of Chiang Kai-shek

> *Let me put my cards on the table at the outset. I believe that magical attitudes toward images are just as powerful in the modern world as they were in so-called ages of faith. When students scoff at the idea of a magical relation between a picture and what it represents, ask them to*

---

[1]   *Central News Agency.* Retrieved from http://www.cna.com.tw/news/ahel/201807200308-1.aspx

>   *take a photograph of their mother and cut the eyes.*
>
>   ---- *W. J. T. Mitchell (8-9)*

Building the authoritarian images are the major instruments that all the authoritarian regimes would've used. Mitchell reminds us to exam ourselves with humble attitude if we could be completely exempted from the influence of authoritarian images. After Chiang's death in 1975, Taiwanese government had even promulgated a regulation named "Notes of Building Chiang Kai-shek's Statues". Ironically, it was neglected for a long time, and demolished as late as in 2017.

In current atmosphere of Taiwan, the Notes seem to be ridiculous. Yet it's an important text record of how to build the image of authoritarian and worth being read carefully. In addition, the Notes quoted below were published after the death of Chiang, they reflected the compilations of Chiang's authoritarian images in certain degree.

> *"Notes of Building Chiang Kai-shek's Statues"*[2]
>
> *(1) The appearance of the statue: it should completely show Chiang's kind and graceful face; and should imply great merciful, great wisdom, great courage, persistence, and positive revolution spirit as well as the honest, universal love, delightful and vivid expression.*
>
> *(2) The posture of the statue: it should adopt natural standing position; the appearance should be straight, powerful, comfortable and vivid.*
>
> *(3) The costume of the statue: it should adopt his favorite Chinese Tunic Suit*
>
> *(4) The height of the statue: the height of statue and its base should be in proper proportion to fit the site and the surrounding. The base cannot be lower than two meters; the height of the statue cannot be lower than 170 centimeters.*
>
> *(5) The base of the statue: the surface of the base should be engraved with marble or granite; the front side should be carved with inscription "President Chiang Kai-shek's Testament". The other sides could be engraved with President Chiang's calligraphy, precepts or relief of his revolution achievements.*
>
> *(6) The environment around the statue: it should be surrounded by evergreen plants, flowers and lawn as well as with proper lightings and benches. The front side should be reserved with proper area and space for offering flowers, paying respect as well as paying tribute.*

---

[2]   *Rootlaw.com.tw.* Retrieved from http://www.rootlaw.com.tw/LawArticle.aspx?LawID=A040040031007600-0640805

III. The image war of Chiang Kai-shek's bronze statues

Recently, there are various incidents and vandalisms happened in Chiang Kai-shek's bronze statues. They even could be categorized into four different approaches to conduct the image wars, including "Removing the images", "Weakening the images", "Transforming the images" and "Maintaining the images".

1. "Removing the images"

I don't attempt to process the legitimate analysis for various approaches, yet I intend to distinguish some that might have violated the criminal Code, for example: "Sawing the head down from Chiang's statue in Zhong-Zheng High School " [3]; "Attempting to knock down Chiang's statue with tools such as power generator and grinder on Fu-Jen University campus. Therefore, the crutch on the statue was sawed down."[4]

As for some other cases that the supporters who followed the administrative decision to remove the statue, there were also: "Because there is Chiang's statue in National Taichung University of Education, there are some groups coming to campus to pour paint or stick labels to express their anti-authoritarian opinion from time to time. Those actions caused lots of troubles for the school. Therefore, today, the school board has passed official decisions through administration meeting that school should keep the administrative neutrality on campus. There shouldn't be any political figure statue or totems existing on campus anymore."[5]; "During the 197th school meeting of National Chengchi University, held on 5th, the school board members had voted to remove Chiang's statue in Zhong-Zheng School Library."[6]

2. "Weakening the Images"

There are several approaches to weaken the authoritarian images by pouring paint on statues or dressing the statue to others, for example: "the statue of Chiang Kai-shek in Taipei Chiang Kai-shek Memorial Hall was poured with red paint by some opponents." (Mentioned above)"; "Chiang's statue in National Sun Yat-Sen University has been poured paint continuously for two years. Starting this year, school has appointed 24 hours security guards to monitor it, yet the statue still has been poured paint from the head of

---

[3] *Sanlih E-Television news.* Retrieved from https://www.setn.com/News.aspx?NewsID=383959

[4] *Liberty Times Net.* Retrieved from http://news.ltn.com.tw/news/society/breakingnews/2289782

[5] *Liberty Times Net.* Retrieved from http://news.ltn.com.tw/news/politics/breakingnews/2371477

[6] *Chinatimes.com.* Retrieved from http://www.chinatimes.com/realtimenews/20180105003560-260407

the statue"[7]; "For the past few years, the students in Taipei Municipal Jianguo High School has always aroused some attentions by dressing Chiang's statue, located in the front of the school gate, to other figures. According to the topic this year, students dressed it as the military instructor who used to greet students every morning."[8]

3. "Transforming the Images"

In current Taiwan society, bronze statues are not merely the symbols of the authoritarian, therefore, some people propose to transform them to be tourist attractions or to be history class material, for example: With more than 200 Chiang's statues, Cihu Memorial Sculpture Park has promoted itself as a mixture of space-time tourist site and historical space. There is also a business mall, now closed, in which had installed Chiang's statue intentionally in the mall entrance to feature its nostalgia style.

4. "Maintaining the Images"

Within the controversy of Chiang's image war, certainly, there is also the other side of "maintaining the images", for example: "All Chiang's statues in Tainan City were removed. Therefore, Yongkang Nan-Ying Military dependents' villages' Cultural Center has lounged a campaign to 'donate one-dollar to save Chiang'. The supporters propose to build five sculptural statue with the face side of one-dollar coins."[9]; "With the donation from hundreds of locals and communities, a Chiang's statue will be installed in the Jing-Zhong New Village. The unveiling ceremony will be held on the Birthday of President Chiang Kai-shek."[10]

IV. Transitional justice or the state of exception

According to the Ruti G. Teitel's expectation of transitional justice, a paradigm of transitional justice is capable of constructing the liberalizing change (Teitel). According to common understanding, the ideal of transitional justice seems to eliminate the "state of exception" completely and regulate a country to be under the rule of law. After 43 years of Period of National Mobilization in Suppression of Communist Rebellion in Taiwan,

---

[7] *Liberty Times Net.* Retrieved from http://news.ltn.com.tw/news/politics/breakingnews/1989401

[8] *Liberty Times Net.* Retrieved from http://news.ltn.com.tw/news/local/paper/1205539

[9] *KK News.cc.* Retrieved from https://kknews.cc/zh-tw/culture/96ovqrq.html

[10] *Udn.com.* Retrieved from https://udn.com/news/story/7326/2775164

there are still demands to access those political files and uncover historical truth in our society. "There is no forgiveness if there is no truth" is always the most important principle of promoting transitional justice in Taiwan.

Therefore, "uncovering historical truth" and "pursuing the reconciliation of the society" have both listed as the ideal goals of "The Act on Promoting Transitional Justice". But obviously, we can feel that Taiwanese society does not seem toward the direction of reconciliation in the process of pursuing the transitional justice. On the contrary, we can feel the reality and hidden anxiety of this splitting society. This paper aims to indicate this split vividly for all by highlighting this image war of Chiang's statues.

In my opinion, we are not able to completely interpret the inner structure of the image war if we identify the split as the manipulation from some politicians. This misinterpretation sees the "state of exception" as the historical accident beyond the rule of law, it seems suggesting that we will be able to go back to a country under the rule of law if the state of exception is eliminated. In addition, if anyone who attempts to stop the process, he/she is equal to attach to the state of exception and should be disgusted and excluded by the community during the process of transitional justice.

It is the emotion of "disgusting" or "being disgusted" to urge us rethinking the interpretation of state of exception from Giorgio Agamben. If the state of exception has become the regular condition of modern democracy, we, everyone, could be *homo sacer* (sacred man) who "may be killed and yet not sacrificed." (Agamben, p. 8) On one hand, the nation could suspend the fundamental human rights of its people by announcing the nation is being in "the state of exception"; on the other hand, each citizen could be excluded by the community and became the *homo sacer* and lose his/her fundamental human rights anytime. "If today there is no longer any one clear figure of the sacred man, it is perhaps because we are all virtually *homines sacri*." (Agamben, p.115)

I believe that the supporters of removing authoritarian-era symbols could sense certain sympathetic understanding to the opponents if they could juxtapose the image war of Chiang Kai-shek's statues with Giorgio Agamben's interpretation of "state of exception". The state of exception has become regular condition in modern democracy, and won't disappear just because of promoting the transitional justice. For those opponents, although the ideal of transitional justice is worth pursuing, it has created another state of exception that will eliminate those opponents out of this community.

Perhaps this is the inspiration we could receive from this war of images, which continuously challenges whether Taiwan would reach this contradictory and strained ideal goal of "uncovering historical truth and pursuing the reconciliation of the society" in the process of promoting transitional justice.

References

Agamben, Giorgio. *Homo Sacer: Sovereign Power and Bare Life*. Trans. Daniel Heller-Roazen. Standard University Press. 1995

Mitchell, W. J. T. *What Do Pictures Want? -The Lives and Loves of Images*. The University of Chicago Press. 2005

Teitel, Ruti G. *Transitional Justice*. Oxford University Press. 2000

No More Professional Writers in the Future?

Agnieszka Sural

Agnieszka Sural presents how directions, conditions and manners of discussion, evaluation and distribution of art have changed in the last years and how – in the context of converging technological, economic, socio-demographic and environmental forces – the world will look and feel within next decades. We live through a fundamental transformation in the way of working. Digitalisation, robotisation and artificial intelligence replace human role; and change skills and tasks that organizations look for in the people. What are after-effects for a society and institutions right now and in the future? What is the future of professional writers? How can we shape the world we live in and respond to it?

Agnieszka Sural is a writer, curator and producer in the fields of visual and performing arts, and architecture. From 2016 she's a contributing editor for the Flash Art International. Between 2012–2017 she was an editor on the culture.pl. She was a curator (together with Julia Staniszewska) of the Witryna gallery project in a window shopping in Warsaw (2007–2014) and the interdisciplinary platform Temps d'Images Festival at the Centre for Contemporary Art Ujazdowski Castle (2005–2011). She's a co-author and editor of books: "Polish Phrase Book with Art in the Background" (with Maryna Tomaszewska) and "Witryna 2007–2009" (with Julia Staniszewska). She runs the Witryna Foundation and works independently with artists and public and private institutions in Poland and abroad. She lives and works in Warsaw.

Unlimited Uncertainty: A Critical Narrative of Art Self-Powered by the Virtual

Lisa Paul Streitfeld

1. INTRODUCTION

The turn of the millennium came with two parallel events affecting the art world system: the demise of the newspaper critic and the rise of "do it yourself" digital technology. In the United States and elsewhere, newspaper art critics became a dying breed. Yet, the rise of the self-empowered blog and the social network in the 21st century gave more freedom of expression to artists and critics alike, bypassing the gatekeepers to seek one's own niche.

Shunned by the art world, the New Age Movement scanned infinite space for signs of a new cosmology. The Internet provided the global network for an early leap into real time collaboration, a Web 3.0 ideal made possible by quantum computing surpassing the binary code. An early example of this future leap was Jose Arguelles' call for a Harmonic Convergence meditation on August 15, 1987. A decade later, a website devoted to global harmony (www.gaiamind.com) was able to do the same for January 23, 1997.

Speeding forward into 21st century virtuality, boundaries between art and entertainment exploded. *Gangnam Style* (7.5 million views) from the east was superseded by *This is America* (203 million views in three weeks) in the west. These videos expressed the dialectic of the *Kulturindustrie* in the age of the Internet by way of the virtual extension of the body gesture through the new mass medium in which past/future are simultaneous with present motion. In examining this virtual expression, we don't need to ask if it is art; instead, we ask what the implications are for art when creative expression with a self-reflecting gesture is offered for free, and yet infinitely reproducible.

How is a critic riding the wave of new technology to react to such developments in which virtuality supersedes the views of any mechanism the art world can produce? In an age when celebrity is a global currency, how can ubiquity favour a critic tracking the emergence of a new art movement? These are questions I asked myself as I bumped along the quantum wave as it began to collapse on my profession. From the loss of my position as newspaper critic in 2006 through several online applications to the present use of medium.com, I bypassed the art world to interpret cultural events through the lens of *Kultureindistrie* theory acquired as a doctoral candidate.

This paper reveals the strategy underlying my virtual process. While there was no financial compensation and little recognition from my peers, my passage ensured a self-contained *GESAMTKUNSTWERK* (Total Work of Art) untainted by the trendiness of the marketplace that hijacked the art world during the death of postmodernism and the rise of a New Modernism (Streitfeld, 2014). In this quest into the Unknown, virtuality was key as it permitted self-determined actions to be initiated in the proper timing for Kairos.

2.0. Virtuality, Virtuosity & Ubiquity

Virtuality was transforming art dissemination parallel to the rise of the after-postmodern reflecting the globalisation of the celebrity by means of 24/7 media. While the narrative of celebrity is defined by ubiquity, the ability to be in several places at once is only humanly possible in the "virtual" realm of the Internet. The ubiquity of celebrity figuratively reflects the "unlimited uncertainty" of the virtual—from the limitations of gallery space into the eternity of cyberspace.

A conscious progression from mainstream media into cyberspace is a paradigm leap integrating body, *the real*, with virtuality, *the hyperreal*. Yet, this middle passage dangerously blurs the border between critical observer and artist. From a conventional role as critic in the dying daily newspaper, a leap into virtuality with the 2007 New Media launch of the blogel (blog novel) in a midtown Manhattan storefront demanded a new dialectic for boundary crossing. The interpersonal physics of the paradigm shift became the topic of two papers at conferences merging art and science: "The Uncertainty Principle in 21st Century Art" (Streitfeld 2009) and "Overcoming the Heisenberg Principle: Art theory arising out of Wolfgang Pauli's collapsed wave" (Streitfeld, 2011).

While the subject required breaking any rules enforcing "critical distance" to establish a (r)evolutionary new critical narrative, this conscious leap into quantum physics required a surrender to the feminine principle, i.e. intuition, in order to effectively interpret a new medium of expression. This is particularly true of virtuality, distinguished by unlimited cyclical narratives of life/death/rebirth and interactive audiences.

Whether artist or critic, the potential rewards of engaging in virtuality are as unlimited as they are uncertain. Theatrically-staged slick cultural commentary mocking its own self-reflective embodiment of the *Kultureindustrie* conquers virtuality with virtuosity.   Without the common superficial entertainment value, there would be no immediate connection with the audience: the key to the success of the performance is the postmodern wink letting us in on the joke. Such virtual works as the two examples in this paper are critic proof. This is true not only because of the speed of transmission; the self-reflective exaggerated gesture defies any other interpretation than the strictly intentional—the ubiquity of the virtual expression.

Chasing the ubiquity of the virtual as a new challenge for critical interpretation drove me further into the unknown, one online application at a time. I never came close to the aspired goal of "going viral" but the quest kept me playing for higher stakes. My position as critic for the newly established *Huffington Post Arts* in 2010 proved to be a crucial virtual platform for effortlessly crossing borders between artistic mediums. I was covering conferences, film festivals and concerts, as well as art exhibitions. This broader panorama allowed me to keep playing the virtual game of upping the Google score while conquering my own fears as the only blockage standing in the way of ubiquity. Could a critic forfeit a hard-won reputation for Unlimited Uncertainty if notoriety was part of the game?

2.1. Virtual Leap into A New Paradigm

With this understanding that the illusive promise of the virtual is ubiquity, each leap into a new technology reflects a personal evolution blurring the boundaries between critic and artist. These borders were strictly enforced by my newspaper editor in the past and I was quick to learn that the shifting ground for collaboration required a complete devotion to the embrace of uncertainty. My reporting on the exploding Application Service Provider market for internet.com agreed with my knowledge of quantum physics to interpret the early the adapters of this new technology as riding the quantum wave collapse into the future. My creations, therefore, increasingly expressed the character of the *hierosgamos*— the emerging archetype that Wolfgang Pauli and C.G. Jung agreed to be the icon of the 21st century which Pauli interpreted as emerging from under the collapsed wave (Roth 2012).

Pauli's prophecy cut through Unlimited Uncertainty to determine the virtual destination—which meant embodying the characteristics of the *hierosgamos* with every new experiment. Clearly, this held out the danger of the loss of identity; yet with growing evidence of the death of my former profession, there was less at stake in holding onto the rigid parameters of separation, not only with the artists I chose to write about, but with my audiences. In other words, the rules of engagement had broken down for the critic to the point of death. This is precisely how "Gangham Style" mocking of western imperialism—which South Koreans can do like no other nation—could "go viral" as an artistic expression completely free of art world institutional gatekeepers.

But this left a significant question: what is the role of the critic in this abyss? I reverted to the definition of shaman as interpreter given to me by a Native American medicine man. Clearly, to be able to cross borders between the collective consciousness and collective unconscious required some revolutionary new contemporary methods of critical interpretation that were as old as human civilisation.

3.0. Cosmology As Art Theory

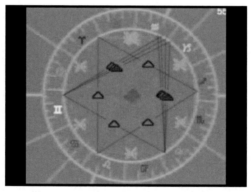

FIG. 1.   AT 2:30 PM EST on January 23, 1997 there was a Seal of Solomon in the Heavens, the gateway to the Age of Aquarius.

The father of modern physics, Wolfgang Pauli, believed the hexagram, known as the Seal of Solomon, to be the configuration for the icon of the 21 century arising from under the collapsed quantum wave (Roth 2012). The interlocking triangles represent the alchemical *coniinctio*, or sacred marriage of opposites (Streitfeld 2006).

On January 23, 1997 a six-pointed hexagram appeared in the sky (FIG. 1) under a rare Jupiter/Uranus/Neptune alignment. Astrologers and metaphysicians declared this configuration as the gateway to the Age of Aquarius (gaiamind.com, 1997).

This configuration was detected from my January 23, 1997 solar return. Three weeks later, I attended a historic San Francisco "Cycles and Symbols" conference that brought astrologers and scientists together for the first time. The organiser was the philosopher Richard Tarnas, who declared the *hierosgamos* as the icon of the 21 century.

On Valentine's Day, I initiated my first interventionist performance with James Hillman, the father of archetypal psychology, to demand why he referred to Venus as the Greek goddess, Aphrodite. In doing so, I revived the archetype of the Sumerian goddess, Inanna, self-declared Queen of Heaven and Earth who personified the ancient icon of the *hierosgamos*.

This powerful holistic energy was channeled into an intense cross-disciplinary investigation resulting in an ongoing series of texts on the subject. As I became driven to uncover and interpret new forms of the icon in art, my career path transformed from journalist into professional art critic. This journey explored an art theory prompting pioneering expression as curator and New Media artist.

With the ambition of bringing the *hierosgamos* archetype into form in accordance with celestial timing and the "sacred space" of the art gallery, I embarked on a series of *acciones reciproques* timed for the January 23 anniversary.

3.1. Trajectory of The Spoken Word, January 23, 2005

The Lab Gallery of the Roger Smith Hotel on Lexington Avenue, a few blocks from Warhol's original factory, proved to be the ideal "middle realm" situated on the clearly-defined geometrical grid of Manhattan to bring heaven down to earth through hermetic acts aimed at bringing the emerging archetype into form.

My first curated event was a dinner with spoken word performance. The guest of honour was the legendary avant-garde critic/artist Richard Kostelanetz. Through spontaneous performance, three outstanding New York poets—Valery Oisteanu, Max Blagg, and Edwin Torres—narrated the trajectory of 20th century Spoken Word to create a new language for the *hierosgamos* reflecting the integration of right/left brain. The event was so successful that it led to "Generational Genus" with the three poets at a salon in the penthouse. This attracted many figures in the New York avant-garde that I subsequently worked with in new collaborations.

3.2. Icons of The 21 Century, January 23, 2006

FIG. 2.   "In the dream I drew an oscillation process beneath the window – actually two oscillations, one beneath the other. By turning to the right from the curves, I try to see the time on the clock. But the clock is too high, so that doesn't work. Then the dream continues. The 'dark unknown woman' appears. She is crying because she wants to write a book but cannot find a publisher for it. In this book there is apparently a great deal of material on time symbolism – e.g., how a period of time is constituted when certain symbols appear in it. And at the end of one page of the book, there are the following words, read aloud by the 'voice.' 'The definite hours have to be paid for with the definite life, the indefinite hours have to be paid for with the indefinite life.'"
—Wolfgang Pauli, Atom & Archetype: The Pauli/Jung Letters, 1952-1958

My first art exhibit curation was the result of research into prophecies of the icon of the 21st century. I discovered a dream that Wolfgang Pauli had on January 23, 1938 in the Appendix of the text, *Atom & Archetype: The Pauli/Jung Letters, 1952-1958* (Pauli/Jung 2004). This was five days after the opening of the International Surrealist Exhibition in Paris, which introduced the public to the unconscious. The synchronicity between this inner and outer event led to my realisation that I had been living the "indefinite life" for 14 years with my literary experiments with the Surrealist invention of automatic writing, and now needed to begin a "definite life" to gain the balance called for in Pauli's dream.

Icons of the 21st Century opened on January 20, 2006 with 23 works in all mediums. The   opening night window performance was Laurel Jay Carpenter's *Red Woman,* which created a spiral train of a hundred red dresses from the window into the gallery. As postulated by Pauli, the center piece demonstrated the resurrection of Eros as fundamental to the emerging archetype arising from under the quantum wave.

On January 23, I hosted a dinner with the gallery director, Matt Semler for artists, curators, dealers and critics. As a performance piece, I wrote Pauli's dream of January 23, 1938 in the window with his dream symbols: a rectangle and round clock face with the hands gesturing at the "indefinite hours" of 9 p.m. above the double wave. The rectangle became the "definite life" of the dinner table whose participants listened to my gallery talk triggered by the unseen cosmological time clock – the astrology chart. The marking of these symbols in the window constituted the passage of the dream images into the collective consciousness. My interpretation was the "indefinite hours" pointing to the timing of the wave collapse, the double wave signifying the Age of Aquarius.

3.3. The Alchemy of Love, January 23, 2007/08

I continued to identify with the "dark unseen woman" in Pauli's dream who cried because she couldn't get published. For my next January 23 project, I launched a vehicle for instantaneous virtual publication. This involved using the blogger.com application to depict the Kundalini passage through the seven chakras. My goal was to create a colour coded visual language for the alchemical experiment known as The Great Work.

As a structure for my next exhibition inspired by fictional experiments, I followed the alchemical process in five chapters of an installation/performance at the Lab Gallery entitled *The Alchemy of Love in Five Elements*. My goal was to have my writing married on earth (the gallery) and heaven (cyberspace) as the figurative manifestation of Pauli's dream of drawing "a double oscillation beneath a window". The double wave of the Aquarian symbol is reflected in the integration of conscious/unconscious in a holistic style of writing utilising both sides of the brain.

FIG. 3.   An innovative literary form enabling instantaneous publishing launches the blogel (coined by critic Jeffrey Wright) with "The Alchemy of Love: Calcinatio/Fire", the first stage of a year-long five chapter alchemical transformation at the lab gallery, NYC: www.thealchemcyofloveinfiveelements.blogspot.com

The alchemical experiment was initiated with a ritual ceremony in the gallery. Under the Moon/Venus conjunction in Aquarius at 12:18 PM on January 20, a priestess established a sacred space to birth the Aquarian Age icon. The second day of the writing performance was January 23. On this anniversary of the *hierosgamos* gateway, my quest of ubiquity was launched with "Flame: Page Six". After spending the night on the bed in the center of the gallery, I published the entry at the moment of my solar return shortly after dawn on January 24 when there was a line-up of Aquarian planets (Sun, Mercury, Venus and Neptune) on the horizon. The quest for ubiquity was manifested by the September 23 performance when my name appeared in a gossip column in *The Daily News* during the September performance of *The Alchemy of Love: Air/Sublimatio*.

FIG. 4.   Lisa Paul Streitfeld performing "Bliss" under the Stepanova "Waterfall" on January 24, 2008.

Under an impending Lunar Eclipse on February 7, a two-night performance was to demonstrate how synchronicities regulate consciousness into revival of the Lost Bride uniting with the Resurrected Groom through a video interweaving recent series by allegorical painters Tatyana Stepanova (Russia) and Michael Manning (U.S.). On the first night anniversary of the cosmology of January 23, 1997, Stepanova created *Waterfall* in the center of a black circle with an astrology chart of the solar return and during the performance painted the upcoming solar eclipse in Aquarius/Leo on the gallery wall. I entered the light projected by the paintings to integrate Pauli's dream symbols with the astrological symbolism of 2012, synchronizing my movements to Lutz Rath playing the violincello. My final act was painting the double oscillation image from Pauli's dream in the window as the the the sign of Aquarius. In keeping with the final stage of alchemy, the experience of the final performance of *The Alchemy of Love in Five Elements* was *Bliss* (FIG. 4).

4.0. Marrying The Virtual/Real (2008-2011)

The virtual publication of symbols uniting Pauli's dream (indefinite hours) with live performance (definite hours) on the January 23 anniversary of the *hierosgamos* cosmology reflects a new era in which mythical content of the collective unconscious is instantaneously made conscious through the World Wide Web.

This inquiry into consciousness in time and space erases the boundary between critic/observer and performer/participant. Immediately prior to the performance, my sister contacted me with a dream in which the symbolic timekeeper was no longer the old man with an hourglass but a crone. This could indicate a return to lunar time as postulated by Jose Arguelles. The dream message also seemed to foretell the resolution of the dilemma of the unpublished woman in Pauli's dream who has written "a great deal of material on time symbolism – e.g. how a period of time is constituted when certain symbols appear in it." She had to wait until she was a crone to be published! This proved prophetic.

To enforce my ability to detect time symbolism, I would have to bring my alchemical process for the resurrected feminine into the art world as a strategy of marring the Virtual with the Real. This mission was ignited by the alchemical embodiment in the final January 23 performance going virtual a day later with the posting of myself naked in *Bliss,* a prophetic view of the entire performance picked up by *The Daily News*. The dialectic of the *hierosgamos* in art was to be established by my curation of three subsequent multimedia exhibitions, both with a virtual component.

4.1. Evolver: Wake Up & Dream (FEB 2, 2008)

FIG. 5.   YouTube still of John Knowles' "Evolver WakeUp & Dream" video FEATURING "Bliss" with the double text signifying the emerging icon.

Evolver: Wake Up & Dream was a multimedia happening conceived by Daniel Pinchbeck, author of *2012: The Return of Quetzalcoatl* (Pinchbeck 2006) as a fundraiser for his Internet project marrying heaven and earth through a website (evolver.com) featuring consciousness thinkers giving live talks at venues provided by "consciousness spores" around the nation. The planning required a lot of brainstorming meetings to develop a language merging Internet with consciousness without reverting to the New Age lingo shunned by New Yorkers. I was named art director with my roommate, Alison Levy, and our input was welcomed with a caveat—no astrology. This proved a lesson about the "consciousness fringe" entering mainstream where mystics were allowed, without their mystical apparatus.   Nevertheless, I succeeded in convincing them of the Aquarian timing for the event: the February 2 Jupiter/Venus conjunction offering a new vision of interactive art. John Knowles, my video collaborator at the Roger Smith Hotel, fought back against patriarchal resistance to my ongoing practice of *hierosgamos* embodiment which he had filmed in the Lab Gallery. His intervention video branded *Evolver Wake Up & Dream* (FIG. 5) by capturing the opening night extravaganza with my *Bliss* (featured at the event as a video installation) as centrepiece. The Evolver project was successful in achieving its mission and my offerings were predictably rejected by the male gatekeepers of the site, yet Knowles' video signified the event with the effect of radically expanding the virtual audience of my personal project.

4.2. Black Madonna (2009)

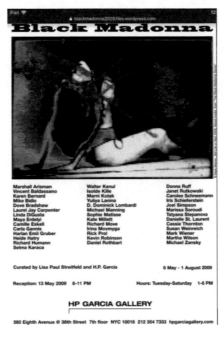

FIG. 6.   Black Madonna E-VITE on www.Blackmadonna2009.wordpress.com

Black Madonna opened on May 13, 2009 at HP Garcia Gallery. I met H.P. Garcia when I was invited to give a talk about the mythology influencing the election of Barack Obama at his gallery the previous fall. He was so impressed by my understanding of the archetypes that he presented his authentic identity as I was departing: the direct descendent of Hughes Payans, the Founder and First Grandmaster of the Knights Templar.

The blog (www.blackmadonna2009.wordpress.com) was launched under the Full Moon as a virtual leap into an ongoing collaboration of events in the gallery intended to bring the Kundalini serpent power into conscious artistic expression. A new virtual experiment consisted of a closing performance in which Mark Weiner and Michael Manning created a performance painting channeling an abstracted figure of the Black Madonna archetype over the astrology chart. This event used the latest technology of streaming media to marry gallery space with cyberspace.

4.3. Woman in The 21ˢᵗ Century (2010)

FIG. 7. The signature sculpture for the multimedia exhibition is by Tania RAJIR.
www.womaninthe21stcentury.wordpress.com

Woman in the 21st Century: Margaret Fuller and the Sacred Marriage was a multimedia exhibition launched to celebrate the 200th anniversary of the American Transcendentalist and editor of Emerson's magazine, *The Dial*. Margaret Fuller was essentially the Mother of American literature and the bicentennial of her birth became a major event in her hometown of Cambridge. The opening performance (FIG. 7) was the curator conjuring her spirit, made virtual through the blog containing writings on Fuller and images of the exhibition and opening.

5.0. Gesturing Towards Web 3.0

My adventures in virtual space confirmed my hypothesis that the new role for the revived critic is interpreter. The artist is traditionally concerned with materials which render immaterial in the virtual, while the critic is devoted to ideas reflecting the forms art takes in a new modernist era. This quest inspires the critic to leap beyond the artists' Web 2.0 quest for amassing the quantitive "LIKE" into a qualitative leap into Web 3.0 in which quantum computing makes real time collaboration possible. This took place in Cyprus when I launched a new blog aimed at uniting the divided island. Umit Inatci, the renowned Cypriot artist, became an immediate collaborator with the offering of a signature artwork for the project expressing the duality of Cyprus personified by the original Cypriot love goddess, which we named together.

5.1. (R)evolution Series Huff Post (2010-2017)

THE BLOG   09/09/2014 05:09 pm ET | Updated Dec 06, 2017

Schirmacher (R)evolution in Saas-Fee: The Badiouan EVENT Takes For(u)m with Michael Hardt, Antonio Negri, Graham Harman and Geert Lovink

 By Lisa Paul Streitfeld

Alain Badiou: AN EVENT IS A SURPRISE; IF IT IS NOT A SURPRISE, IT IS NOT AN EVENT.

Like the proverbial fall of dominos or throwing of the Deleuzian dice, the black and white of the ever-domino(ant) continential philosophy text is blending into a distinct shade of grey...

Badiou's diagram of the EVENT, from its epicenter locality: European Graduate School in Saas-Fee, Switzerland (August 2012).

...illuminating the third path of the Homo Generator...

Dr. Wolfgang Schirmacher, founder and director of the alpine laboratory, the Media and Communications Division of the European Graduate School.

FIG. 8.   The apex of my Huffington Post reporting was the Badiosian Event taking place in the Saas Fee laboratory of continental philosophy in August, 2014.

When Huffington Post initiated an arts section in 2010, I was invited to contribute. It was a privileged position under founding editor Kimberly Brooks, and my reviews were frequently displayed as the daily feature on this prestige site.

My first review was the digital paintings of the American guru, Adi Da. An interpretation of his work as the manifestation of the *hierosgamos* union between heaven and earth inspired the title "(R)evolution in Chelsea". This launched the (R)evolution Series that took me around the world in search of new forms of the emerging archetype.

Writing for *Huffington Post Arts* gave me permission to expand my interpretation of cross-disciplinary art and the opportunity to act on a dream: writing about film. I applied for the 2011 Venice Film Festival with an assignment for a new film magazine launched by HP Garcia. My quantum leap into the virtual now set me on a new course of interpreting the 21st century icon in film, which I was eventually able to do with two of my professors who innovated the archetype in the medium: Wim Wenders and Terrence Malick.

I became a correspondent at the Berlin Berlinale from 2013-2016. This live experience with streaming media led to a new opportunity to create a dialectic directly aimed at the virtual with the real presence of a movie star trapped in the virtual streaming press conference.

5.2. Missing James Franco 3.0 (2015-2017)

FIG. 9. This image from Athens that captured James Franco's attention posted: "http://www.MISSINGJAMESFRANCO.COM"

My four years of experimentation with the marriage of gallery and virtual space culminated with a public leap into the Third with James Franco, the movie star newly defining ubiquity as the conquest of all disciplines through the social network by way of his 7.5 million Instagram followers. This multi-hyphenate crossing the border into the New York art world (2010-12) had the effect of his celebrity shadow cast over the corpse of postmodernism, as I was preparing for global circumnavigation seeking the forms of a new modernism.

My pursuit of James Franco's "aha moment" that birthed what I termed "the James Franco phenomenon" of ubiquity resulted in a book length text promoted prematurely of publication. The *Missing James Franco 3.0* project intended to bridge urban tagging (FIG. 9) with cyberspace tagging essential for the Goggle placement of my MJF 3.0 postings (www.missingjamesfranco.wordpress.com).

5.3. Gofundme/Excavating The Treasure (2016)

"Excavating the Templar Treasure: Re/Searching the Hieros Gamos in Artistic & Critical Practice" was presented at the Contemporary Arts Research Unit (CARU) 2016 conference "What does it mean to research art / to research through

FIG. 10. The marrying of my public HuffPost (R)evolution series with my personal Missing James Franco project inquiring into the fame shadow obscuring the emergence of the Aquarian icon took place through this posting: "Missing James Franco in Oxford" (January 19, 2017). I managed to complete my journey marrying the virtual with the real PRECISELY one year prior to the shutdown of the Huffington Post blogger network, which happened simultaneously with the sudden public fall of James Franco; just as I was submitting my January 19 posting "Time's Up James Franco", I got the email of the end of the Huffington Post virtual experiment with prestige blogging, effective immediately (Streitfeld 2018).

The Missing James Franco 3.0 Project marrying cyberspace with urban space resulted in an invitation by Contemporary Arts Research Unit (CARU) to deliver a paper for their 2016 conference (FIG. 10) demonstrating the use of artistic process as research at Brookings in Oxford. This resulted in a leap into a new app that would fund the conclusion of my journey in Jerusalem.

The thrill of discovery in this new app was the unlimited space for unedited narrative to describe the project. This served as a hidden reservoir for my disclosing about the Templar Treasure, the target of adventure seekers for over 800 years (excavatingthetreasure.

wordpress.com).

I made over $700 inviting friends and family to join the paradigm leap by funding my journey to Jerusalem (in exchange for stickers, art and astrology readings) where I was guided to the mythical figure in Israeli archeology who told me what to do about the secret. I left the holy land with a concrete plan of action that resulted in the closure of the journey when I arrived in Paris. Synchronistically, this was also the closure of my experiment with James Franco. My final email exchange with him was from Tel Aviv, the day before my Paris flight (February 1, 2017).

6.0. Kairos, December 18, 2016

GOFUNDME.COM/p/ccsv

FIG. 11. This acknowledgement by James Franco of the Missing James Franco Project was a Web 3.0 certificate of our virtual collaboration instigated by my interventions the streaming press conferences.

The Heidegerrian disclosing of Being (Heidegger 2008) resulting from my leap into uncertainty was the *hierosgamos* arising from under the collapsed wave that I was riding, from one synchronicity to the next. The *definite hours* "critic/al narrative of art self-powered by the virtual" resulted in two crucial discoveries for the emergence of the *hierosgamos* in the collective consciousness founded in the *indefinite hours* of my solitary experiments with the Great Work. These establish the Möbius strip inner/outer marriage reflecting the balance of a holistic icon merging the opposites in the human heart.

The first was the Templar Treasure that has been sought for over 700 years, the existence of which was confirmed by a three-page email sent by Hughes Payans

(February 14, 2015), just as I was writing the first draft of the text, "Missing James Franco 3.0: Nine Days at Berlinale 65".

The second is the Lady of Lemba dug up from 2500 BC in Cyprus which came to my attention in 2012 and was an object of study during the summer of 2017, resulting in a new text revealing how this major archeological find has been kept a secret.

6.1. Marrying Cyprus (2017)

13:58

MARRYING CYPRUS

MARRYING CYPRUS: THE RETURN OF EROS IN KALO CHORIO (GOOD VILLAGE)

The Homage to St. Paul, who made Cyprus his first missionary site so to rid the island of the Sacred Marriage Rites.

"Pleasure Ritual" Intervention into the continued patriarchal repression of Eros!

FIG. 12. The erotic interventions led to the hidden relics unearthed on the island revealing a worship of transgender idols.   This was an ontological confirmation of my quest to disclose the multitude of forms of the hierosgamos, past and present

This virtual project (www.marryingcyprus.wordpress.com), had a projected gallery component as an attempt to bridge the division between the Republic of Cyprus (south of the Green Line) and the Northern Republic of Cyprus (north of the Green Line) through erotic interventions with ontological objects. This began with a pair of red Playboy Bunny shoes that manifested after appearing in my dream and became linked through my travels with the wild red Cypriot tulip, the red veil and henna used in Turkish Cypriot bridal ceremonies.

A Cypriot artist, Umit Inatchi, provided an image for the launch of the project that summed up the marriage of the Goddess and her Shadow on Aphrodite's troubled Island. This ritual, integrating the virtual with the real, resulted in Kairos: the discovery of collaborative installations between Greeks and Turkish within the divided capitol.

The virtual expression proved essential to the quantum leaps that permitted these connections between objects as a relation within time and space, signifying timing of the ontological disclosure as the intersection of virtual/real, along with definite/indefinite life indicated by Pauli's dream.

The Trumping of the Anti-Kanye "This is America"

CHILDISH GAMBINO DEBUTS AT #1 ON THE BILLBOARD HOT 100 CHART WITH "THIS IS AMERICA"

FIG. 13. This posting awarded payment of $8.00 and 135 claps

6.2. Claiming The Third Space (2018)

The final stage of my decade-long conversion was marked a Kairos leap onto an innovative virtual application strictly for writers, medium.com. In May 2018, I signed on as Dr. Shiva Lisa Paul, with an expressed mission: to apply the use of astrology as hermeneutics to pop culture, which has become increasingly drenched in occult imagery.   After embracing uncertainty in the decade since my dialectic of the *hierosgamos* (Streitfeld 2006) was launched in cyberspace, I found a new identity as media philosopher and cultural critic. The transformation from dying critic was the outcome of the leap into virtual uncertainty, one application at a time.

Transformation is not a conventional view of art practice. Yet this is what happens instantaneously when one engages cosmically timed ritual in the eternal realm of the virtual. You may even become the next Childish Gambino...or his virtual critic!

7.0. Conclusion

FIG. 14. Dr. Lisa Streitfeld launching her global dissemination of the Lady of LEMBA on June 22, 2018 at the 2018 AECA SPAIN Congress: "Critica de Arte: Crisis y renovacion.

Consider the trajectory—from Jose Arguelles' pre-Internet call for a Harmonic Convergence to the 1997 virtual invitation to join a global meditation by way of a website (gaiamind.com 1997) inviting the cosmic thinkers of a new millennium to interpret a rare cosmology; leading to the 2008 "EVOLVER: Wake Up & Dream" launch of a blog inviting new thinkers to be virtually recorded live at urban "spores" of consciousness; and finally the 2015 Missing James Franco 3.0 Project gesturing towards Web 3.0 live collaboration with the ubiquitous celebrity shadow in cyberspace via urban tagging across three continents. In this virtual evolution, there is a narrative of human awakening told through evolving gestures in virtuality, each more refined and reverent of "beginning in darkness to merge with the light" than the last.

The virtual revolution is not only technological, but an artistic discipline of perfecting virtuosity in real time through instantaneous processing of a feedback loop following action. The definition of virtuous is "having or showing virtue, especially moral excellence: led a virtuous life" (freedictionary.com). This paper closes with an interpretation of virtuous as quality, associated with women (chaste), and therefore the feminine, and virtual as (unlimited) quantity, associated with the masculine. These dual characteristics comprise the autonomy of number, as demonstrated with philosophical texts in my Master's thesis (Streitfeld 2014).

Therefore, the evolving mission of this two-decade project culminated through the marriage of the virtuous with the virtual as a reflection of Pauli's prophetic dream regarding the timing of the Age of Aquarius. When "definite/indefinite hours" are balanced in an innovative form of image/text reflecting the Pauli dream, the Aquarian archetype of the *hierosgamos* is made real through the demonstration of human embodiment: the *corpus* of the art reflecting the *corpus* of the artist.

The cosmic leap into the uncertainty is clearly the determining force of ubiquity—the value of being everywhere at once. The bigger the risk at the precipitous moment, the greater potential for universality. In continental philosophy, this is known as the Badiosian Event: "An arrow projected into the world" (Streitfeld 2014).

Stepping out of one's comfort zone requires an act of faith. The pioneering artist makes this giant leap for humanity by gesturing beyond the limited realm of the mind, that self-critical gesture known as conceptual art, and transforms into something not quite determined—the Third entity between creator/doer and scientist/observer. In this ambiguous realm all possibilities can be achieved at once. What artists with this consciousness would refrain from making the leap? They may not have the global reach of a Childish Gambino, but the possibilities will always be unlimited once the gallery walls are broken down.

The bold new multi-direction that art takes in the 21st century returns us to our ancient roots in shamanism revived in the Italian Renaissance by Marsellio Ficino, the influential humanist philosopher, whose hermetic practice reprised creative acts in time and space as mediations between heaven and earth. My real-time creative manifestation of Pauli's dream established a literal middle ground by drawing my natal astrological chart on the gallery floor as the "definite hours" of embodiment (my natural astrological chart with Uranus rising squaring Pluto on the Midheaven) of the "indefinite hours" in the dream (the hands at 9 pm on the dream clock). By forging the path of the "in between" through the tension of the opposites, known in the art world as Harman's third table (Harman 2014), the artist guides a new cosmology into the culture, as was done in ancient times when the priests determined the timing of sacred ceremonies through their knowledge of planetary relationships. Thus, we have a return to the model of the Italian Renaissance, when Ficino inspired artists to revision humanism with his hermetic infusion of astrology into everyday life by way of practices such as the revival of orphic hymns playing homage to the planetary gods.

To bring the knowledge of the paradigm shift symbolised by the mythology of 2012 (the end of the Mayan calendar representing a new beginning) into the body through everyday rituals of *Unlimited Uncertainty in Virtuality* establishes a process of an evolutionary consciousness of the cyclical in our bodies. This is where the Web 2.0 impossible quest for the quantifiable "Like" is refuted by the quality of virtuosity; co-creating with the cosmos the synchronistic-laden passage to the icon of the Self through daily acts of consciousness in time and space is how we can travel the middle path into the *hierosgamos* icon. Surrendering the obsession with material consumption destroying the ecological balance of the planet to a virtual practice of evolving consciousness with the spirit of holism may seem like a minor accomplishment in the face of such grave challenges, yet multiply one raised consciousness to the potential of millions hooked into the Internet and you have a collective leap into a New Paradigm of an interconnected universe honouring the planetary ecosystem across all human borders.

References

gaiamind.com, "The Hieros Gamos: Gateway to the Age of Aquarius", January 23, 1997.

Graham Harman, "The Third Table", *100 Notes - 100 Thoughts*: Documenta Series 85, (Kassel: Documenta, 2014).

Heidegger, *Being and Time,* trans. John Macquarrie and Edward Robinson (Harper:NewYork, 2008 [orig. 1927]).

C.G. Jung and Wolfgang Pauli, The Pauli/Jung Letters, 1932-1958, ed. C.A. Meier, trans., David Roscoe (Princeton University Press:Princeton, 2004).

Daniel Pinchbeck, *2012: The Return of Quetzalcoatl"* (Jeremy Tarcher/Penguin:New York, 2006).

Remo Roth, "The Return of the World Soul, I & II (Pari Press: Pari, 2012).

Lisa Paul Streitfeld, "Applying the Uncertainty Principle to 21st Century Art," (paper delivered to "Art and Science", 2009 AICA Congress, Dublin).

   The Hermeneutics of New Modernism, (Atropos Press:New York/Dresden, 2014).

   Huffington Post Archive: *http://www.huffingtonpost.com/author/lisa-paul-streitfeld.*2010-2018.

"Magic & Media: Conclusion", *Media-N Journal of the New Media Caucus*, Spring 2012. Vol. 8, No. 1, CAA Conference Edition, http://median.newmediacaucus.org/spring-2012-v-08-n-01-caa-conference-edition-2012-magic-and-media/.

"Missing James Franco in Oxford", *Huffington Post Arts*, January 19, 2017,   https://www.huffingtonpost. com/lisa-paul-streitfeld/missing-james-franco-in-o_b_14204100.html.

"Overcoming the Heisenberg Principle: Art theory arising out of Wolfgang Pauli's collapsed wave" (paper delivered to "Art and Science", Sixth International Conference on the Arts in Society, Berlin-Brandenburgische   Akademie   der   Wissenschaften,   May   9-11,   2011), https://cgscholar.com/bookstore/works/overcoming-the-heisenberg-principle.

   "The Rise of the Unifying Symbol in 21st Century Art", *Critical Trilogy: A Critic's Millennial Journey* (author blog), August 15, 2006,   https://kundalinisdaughter.wordpress.com/hierosgamos-art-theory-and-practice.

"Times Up James Franco", *Hermeneutics of New Modernism* (author blog), January 19, 2018, https://hermeneuticsofnewmodernism.com/2018/01/19/times-up-james-franco/.

"Schirmacher (R)evolution in Saas-Fee: The Badiouan EVENT Takes For(u)m with Michael Hardt, Antonio Negri, Graham Harman and Geert Lovink", *Huffington Post Arts*, September 10, 2014, https://www.huffingtonpost.com/lisa-paul-streitfeld/the-event-in-saas-fee-bad_b_5737080.html.

"The Trumping of the Anti-Kayne 'This is America'", medium.com, May 17, 2018, https://medium.com/@shivalisapaul/the-trumping-of-the-anti-kanye 'this is america'.

"Umit Inatci: Full Circle to the Hieros Gamos", Retro catalogue, Istanbul, 2017.

Lisa Paul Streitfeld, blogs (listed by inauguration date):

thehierosgamosproject.com, 2005

thealchemyoflove.blogspot.com, 2007

blackmadonna2009.wordpress.com, 2009

criticaltrilogy.com, 2009

(R)evolution: hierosgamosdotnet.wordpress.com, 2010

womaninthe21stcentury.wordpress.com, 2010

hermeneuticsofnewmodernsim.com, 2014

missingjamesfranco.com, 2015

excavatingthetreasure.wordpress.com, 2016

marryingcyprus.wordpress.com, 2017

Politics of Performance Art Before and After 1989

Małgorzata Kaźmierczak

The history of performance art in Poland reaches back to the year 1978 when the word was used for the first time on the occasion of the I AM (International Artists Meeting)—a performance art festival at the Remont Gallery in Warsaw. As Łukasz Guzek pointed out, when thinking of this kind of art, art critics use either a diachronic (historical) or synchronic (ahistorical) approach. The first one leads towards depicting performance art as a practice always present in art and immanent in artistic activity. It blurs the specificity of performance art as a genre and its connection to the modernist avant-garde. It also neglects the local circumstances of its birth.[1] This kind of approach is represented e.g. by Rose Lee Goldberg.[2] The synchronic approach presents performance art as a separate discipline. Its advantage is the recognition of local characteristics, which is important in this case, as it is tightly connected with political and social environment. In this approach the key point is the emergence of the word "performance art" as a moment when the discussion about this genre of art begins. For the purpose of this paper I will take a synchronic approach and will take 1978 as a date when performance art emerged in Polish art history, although many performance artists call their earlier actions "performances" *post factum*. Among artists who participated in the first performance art festival in 1978 only Krzysztof Zarębski continued to practice performance art.[3] He started his career as a painter and his performances were very erotic and sensual. He used erotic gadgets such as phalluses, artificial nails and lingerie. The artist went to New York in 1981 before Martial Law and therefore decided to stay abroad when it was imposed. In his performances he fetishizes mass culture products and media, which distinguishes him from the Western trend of criticism towards mass culture.

---

[1] See: Łukasz Guzek, "Above Art and Politics - Performance art and Poland," in *Art Action 1958 - 1998*, ed. Richard Martel (Quebec: Intervention, 2001), 254.

[2] Por. RoseLee Goldberg, *Performance Art. From Futurism to the Present* (London-New York: Thames & Hudson, 2010).

[3] There was also Janusz Bałdyga, but he participated as the Academia Ruchu Theatre group.

Another performance artist from the oldest generation was Zbigniew Warpechowski whose background was in poetry. He did his first performances together with Tomasz Stańko—a jazz musician. Jazz was obviously connected with freedom and improvisation in art and for Warpechowski it was a way of presenting poetry in a non-traditional way. He called his first performances "poetic realities".

As we can see just based on those two meaningful examples, despite the conditions of the regime—of isolation and state control over most aspects of life—or maybe actually because of that, art was supposed to be pure and free from politics. Artists had in mind the way art was instrumentally used by the communist regime at the time of social realism so they did not want to engage directly in politics. Engagement in politics has been doubtful since Walter Benjamin wrote: "Such is the aestheticizing of politics, as practiced by fascism. Communism replies by politicizing art."[4] The other option at that time was to associate oneself with the Church but for most artists this represented a similar form of a mental oppression.   However, practicing an anti-institutional art which was functioning outside the official circuit, the academy and official Artists' Union were under these conditions—became paradoxically—a political gesture as Jacques Ranciere would like to see it. The politics of art here means an interference into the sphere of senses and it shows something that was unimaginable before. Above all – in the case of performance art—it changes and questions the language that was used to describe the life of the community—making it possible for new subjects and new postulates to exist in the political field. Since performance art has no definition, from now on, art is not what fulfills the imposed criteria, but what revolutionizes and creates its own rules. At the same time, art loses all norms that decide what can be or what cannot be art which goes in accordance with a permanent crossing of its own borders by art, which is a certain paradox. Among the pioneers of Polish performance art only Jerzy Bereś—who called his actions "manifestations" or "holy masses" (e.g. *Political Mass, Romantic Mass, Philosophical Mass, Polish Mass* etc.) thought that art is a moral sphere, hence the political engagement of the artist is his/her moral duty.[5] But the strong moral stance was characteristic for performers of that time in general. Zbigniew Warpechowski before one of his performances wrote a *Decalogue for Performance Art.*[6] Also, Władysław Kaźmierczak says that: "To be a performer is an attitude towards the world and oneself, not towards art. Performance's struggle is a silent, heroic fight for the freedom of

---

[4]   Walter Benjamin, *The Work of Art in the Age of Its Technological Reproducibility, and Other Writings on Media*, trans. Rodney Livingstone Edmund Jephcott, Howard Eiland (Cambridge, MA-London: The Belknap Press of Harvard University Press, 2008), 42.

[5]   Guzek, "Above Art and Politics - Performance art and Poland," 258.

[6]   Ibid.

expressing momentous and significant ideas."[7]

In the USA the birth of performance art is tightly related to the art of protest. Lucy Lippard indicated that art activism and organizations such as AWC, Black Emergency Cultural Coalition, Women Artists in Revolution did not come "from the raised fists and red stars of the 'revolutionary' left as from the less consciously subversive reactions against the status quo that took place in the mainstream—primarily in minimalism and conceptual art."[8] The critic then pointed out that they were blunt and blatantly noncommunicative. This statement comes in accordance with what Polish performance artists active in the 70s and 80s say. Kwiekulik (a duo: Zofia Kulik and Przemysław Kwiek) wrote, that in the reality of the regime it was impossible to create conceptual art, hence the success of contextualism formulated by Jan Świdziński. Zofia Kulik said "We, however, could not be pure conceptualists, because we would have cheated ourselves into believing that we are fine, there are no institutional nor existential problems, there are no potboilers etc. How could one then practice conceptual art in Poland? Till now I can't comprehend that."[9] The example of the group is interesting as one could say that their methods such as the project: *Art of the Ministry of Culture and Art* which was a mail art action—sending letters to the Ministry of Culture and Art—was a proto-activist action. As Klara Kemp-Welch noted: "the sense of the correspondence with officials steps outside of the problems raised by it that refer to art, and becomes a fight for human rights, pointing at the pure human aspect of being an artist."[10] An interesting exception in Polish performance art was the Orange Alternative—a group which organized absurd demonstrations since 1986. Today we could also call them pioneers of Polish art activism.

Martial Law in Poland in 1981 meant the beginning of the so called Dark Ages of performance art and any art in Poland. Artists announced a boycott of official / public galleries. Some events were organized in artist-run-galleries or private studios. The majority of performances were about the state of emergency, oppression and uneasiness. Even though the context of Martial Law evoked a political interpretation of all actions—artists did not declare openly their engagement in politics. Peter Grzybowski—a member of Awacs group (with Maciej Toporowicz) once said that: 'our performances

---

[7]   http://www.kazmierczak.artist.pl/

[8]   Lucy Lippard, "Trojan Horses: Activist Art and Power," in *Feminism Art Theory: An Anthology 1968 - 2014*, ed. Hilary Robinson (Malden, MA-Oxford: Wiley Blackwell, 2015), 76.

[9]   Tomasz Załuski, "KwieKulik i konceptualizm w uwarunkowaniach PRL-u. Przyczynek do analizy problemu.," *Sztuka i Dokumentacja*, no. 6 (2012): 79,

[10] Klara Kemp-Welch, "Sztuka dokumentacji i biurokratyczne życie; Sprawa Pracowni Działaniom Dokumentacji i Upowszechniania," in *KwieKulik. Zofia Kulik & przemysław Kwiek*, ed. Łukasz Ronduda and Georg Schöllhammer (Warszawa: MSN, 2012), 517.

may be interpreted as political, but we didn't want to make them this way. We wanted to be as far from politics as possible'.[11] One of their actions was the performance *Awacs*[12] (Klub Pod Ręką, Kraków 23.05.1981) in which a blindfolded Toporowicz led by signals from Grzybowski was supposed to jump on light bulbs lit on the floor. The performance was potentially life-threatening as the action scene was surrounded by an electric wire and Toporowicz had a heart condition. As Łukasz Guzek noticed, artists at that time were not apolitical but non-political. This non-politics had a political reason—it resulted from the lack of faith in that an individual may change anything. Escapism was more and more understandable under the conditions of Martial Law but it was even more difficult to isolate oneself from politics because of it. Focusing on existential problems was therefore a form of political stance.[13] It is interesting, as the same structure of the performance was later used by Grzybowski when he did his solo performance *Remote Control* between 2003-2006—supplementing it by images from capitalist and post 9/11 world reality. Here he was himself jumping on the bulbs and the remote control was operated by another person. So the political and economic system changed but the artist remained oppressed by it.

Even though Poland was isolated, the politics of gender was slowly getting through. Some female artists (Ewa Partum, Teresa Murak, Maria Pinińska-Bereś, Zofia Kulik and Natalia LL) moved proto-feminist topics. The only known proto-queer artist from the 80s was Krzysztof Jung. The postmodernisation of art shifted its interest from the form to the context. The democracy that was brought back in 1989 meant that Polish performance artists started to be able to travel freely around the world which is extremely important in the case of art which requires the physical presence of the artist. The date also marks the beginnings of institutional critique and becoming a part of the international circuit. The 90s, were a time of transition and so called critical art which meant criticism towards capitalism, Church, globalism, ecological issues etc. The artists became more and more aware of the global social, economic and political problems. The content became more and more socially engaged, commenting on the surrounding changes in reality, however the language of expression was still the same as the one developed in the 70s and 80s. The new generation of artists who started their careers in the conditions of a newborn democracy were more likely to be involved in social activism. In the year 2000 the C.U.K.T group traveled around Polish clubs and alternative spaces with a presidential

---

[11] The interview recorded on the CD enclosed to the catalogue: Ruchome-nieruchome. Performensy Marii Pinińskiej-Bereś, (Kraków: Bunkier Sztuki, 2007).

[12] Maciej Toporowicz, "AWACS Performance Kraków," *High Performance* 17/18 (Spring / Summer 1982): 57,

[13] Łukasz Guzek, *Rekonstrukcja sztuki akcji w Polsce* (Warszawa-Toruń: Polski Instytut Studiów nad Sztuką Świata; Wydawnictwo Tako, 2017), 453-54.

campaign for a virtual candidate, Victoria Cukt, whose main slogan was "politicians are redundant". The public were asked to enroll into the political party Victoria CUKT, to sign a petition to the Parliament to make her become an official candidate (in Poland one needs to collect 100 000 signatures in order to register) and to write down their postulates, which automatically became a part of her political program. Nowadays, 18 years later, the scandal of Cambridge Analytica proved that real politicians do use Victoria's method.

Even more so, the crisis of 2008 caused a new wave of art activism in the world. Boris Groys wrote: "A certain intellectual tradition rooted in the writings of Walter Benjamin and Guy Debord states that the aestheticization and spectacularization of politics, including political protest, are bad things because they divert attention away from the practical goals of political protest and towards its aesthetic form. And this means that art cannot be used as a medium of a genuine political protest—because the use of art for political action necessarily aestheticizes this action, turns this action into a spectacle and, thus, neutralizes the practical effect of this action."[14] But the question is: is this always a spectacle? Stephen Wright in his famous *Toward a Lexicon for Usership* suggests that participation and usership are a remedy for spectacularizing.[15] As Andrzej Turowski wrote: "If democracy is a means of improving collective life (rather than a political utopia), and politics a means of achieving a socially desired order (rather than political power), then the art of the *particular* sparks that unrest without which democracy as a form of critical participation in the collective project would be unthinkable."[16]

Jn 2011 Cecylia Malik and Modraszek Kolektyw mobilized hundreds of young people who, dressed in blue butterfly wings, protested against developers who intended to build another estate in the last green enclave of Kraków, where a rare butterfly (a blue) resides. The artist is a well known activist, her recent actions also include the action against tree cutting *Polish Mothers at a forest cleaning* and the *Mother River* action against the artificial regulating of rivers and building of dams, during which women entered the Vistula river holding signs with other rivers' names. Paweł Hajncel joined a Corpus Christi procession as a "Butterfly Man" for the first time in 2011, for which he was prosecuted later. He has repeated the action every year in various costumes since 2011 and was arrested for a last time on May 31st, 2018 as offending religious feelings in

---

[14] Boris Groys, "On Art Activism," *e-flux*, no. 56 (2014), http://www.e-flux.com/journal/on-art-activism/.

[15] See: Stephen Wright, *Toward a Lexicon of Usership* (Eindhoven: Van Abbemuseum, 2013).

[16] Andrzej Turowski, Sztuka, która wznieca niepokój. Manifest artystyczno-polityczny sztuki szczególnej [Art That Sparks Unrest. The Artistic-Political Manifesto of Particular Art (Warszawa: Książka i Prasa, 2012), 88.

Poland is prosecuted. Monika Drożyńska is an artist who uses embroidery as a means of expression—however, she turns it into an "embroidery activism" by organizing a collective called Golden Hands which embroiders slogans weekly and also before manifestations. Anyone can join. The form of embroidery is of course a feminist way of expression and, as traditionally associated with beautiful and "feminine" objects, when contrasted with explicit content it became a subversive form of expression in which delicate form meets a radical message.

Political engagement of the new generation of artists who now often become art activists is relatively new in Poland, even though performance art has been always connected with social activism since its birth in the 70s. This shift causes conflict between artists in the discussion about the role of art and artists in society, especially in the context of art education which, in its nature, aims at preserving and strengthening the old forms rather than provoking a new way of thinking. Therefore, most interesting cases of perfo-activism in Poland come from artists from different backgrounds than performance art. And this is exactly as it was in the 70s when performance art was a marginal genre for the most radical.

References

Benjamin, Walter. The Work of Art in the Age of Its Technological Reproducibility, and Other Writings on Media. Translated by Rodney Livingstone Edmund Jephcott, Howard Eiland. Cambridge, MA-London: The Belknap Press of Harvard University Press, 2008.

Goldberg, RoseLee. Performance Art. From Futurism to the Present. London-New York: Thames & Hudson, 2010.

Groys, Boris. "On Art Activism." e-flux, no. 56 (2014). http://www.e-flux.com/journal/on-art-activism/.

Guzek, Łukasz. "Above Art and Politics - Performance art and Poland." In Art Action 1958 - 1998, edited by Richard Martel, 254-77. Quebec: Intervention, 2001.

Rekonstrukcja sztuki akcji w Polsce. Warszawa-Toruń: Polski Instytut Studiów nad Sztuką Świata; Wydawnictwo Tako, 2017.

Kemp-Welch, Klara. "Sztuka dokumentacji i biurokratyczne życie; Sprawa Pracowni Działańm Dokumentacji i Upowszechniania." In KwieKulik. Zofia Kulik & przemysław Kwiek, edited by Łukasz Ronduda and Georg Schöllhammer, 515-17. Warszawa: MSN, 2012.

Lippard, Lucy. "Trojan Horses: Activist Art and Power." In Feminism Art Theory: An Anthology 1968 - 2014, edited by Hilary Robinson, 69-78. Malden, MA-Oxford: Wiley Blackwell, 2015.

Ruchome-nieruchome. Performensy Marii Pinińskiej-Bereś. Kraków: Bunkier Sztuki, 2007.

Toporowicz, Maciej. "AWACS Performance Kraków." High Performance 17/18 (Spring / Summer 1982): 57.

Turowski, Andrzej. Sztuka, która wznieca niepokój. Manifest artystyczno-polityczny sztuki szczególnej

[Art That Sparks Unrest. The Artistic-Political Manifesto of Particular Art. Warszawa: Książka i Prasa, 2012.

Wright, Stephen. Toward a Lexicon of Usership. Eindhoven: Van Abbemuseum, 2013.Załuski, Tomasz. "KwieKulik i konceptualizm w uwarunkowaniach PRL-u. Przyczynek do analizy problemu.". Sztuka i Dokumentacja, no. 6 (2012): 79-88.

Art as Events with the Virtual: Rethinking about the Democracy and Bureaucracy

Raylin Tsai

For art criticism, the definition of contemporary art is no doubt a complex thing. Defining art as an actual object of work is too narrow, and that as a social context is too broad, therefore we have to properly describe it as 'event' (événement) along with the virtual, although ironically there are many incident things so-called 'eventual art' everywhere we saw.

There are two aspects of the events, that as 'pure art' for its such sake and that as 'public affairs of art' for the public. One aspect, art itself is purely an object-event, it relates to the integration of technology and the media, whereby to the result of its digital manipulation is 'the virtual' (virtuality). Surely we must have digital literacy in order to integrate our life into a virtual sphere. The task of contemporary art criticism is to bring the virtual reality back to the actual reality, similar way to Prometheus mission. Nowadays it is crucial tasks of artists, curators and critics to consider how to actualize art events with the virtual. Unquestionably, many examples are given around.

Another aspect, the art events are always carried out in the public affair and explored themselves to human rights in political effecting, to benefits from commercial marketing, so we saw their involving with fairness and justice (in pursuit of greater individual freedom) as well as open sharing experience (collective asking for more 'for free') . For economical and democratic operation by the public, those two demands are interconnected more and more assimilated in virtuality. Moreover, whether we conceal ourselves in consumerism or populism, our art activities segregate less and less actual interest out of bureaucratic procedures. Does contemporary democracy fit to be a gorgeous clothing of the global bureaucracy trend? How can we ask art events, the incident art, to endorse any democratic transition in art discourse? In this article those questions will be analyzed in some cases, even we finally will find that art is nothing but surplus plots for matters of democracy.

All that imitating 'Yang',
are saying good to engage a start;
all that imitating 'Yin' are saying
evil as a strategy for ending it.

— *Guiguzi. Chapter I. Poking and Closing*

I. What Art could do?

I should avoid praising too much avant-garde art so that I can share nostalgia and retrospect to art criticism. We do not ask the obsolete question of 'what is art,' which has been placed on the bookshelf of art historians. To ask about 'What is not art' seems too harsh, to question 'What else is not art' is too shallow. In critics' responsibility here, we are obliged to concern what contemporary art might be or could do to the world.

For improving our perspective on art criticism, in this article, I list nine motifs by analyzing the trends of contemporary art and its definitions which were commonly based on the relevance of *texts, works, events,* and *context.* I also put forward some ideas to rethink what an adequate relationship between critics, artists, and curators should be. In particular, the concept of the *event* (*événement*) is used to describe what happens or occurrence of the arts and to trace their various relevant contingency, of these phenomena it can be called *eventualities* of the original event, which will be explained later. Thus, *the distinction between events and eventuality* is not a priori, nor is it compulsive. This distinction is mainly concerning critic's detached stand position in an appropriate distance from characters, objects, interests, and media that concerned with. If we can follow the normative *principle of arm's length*, it may be called a descriptive asking for *a step away* from others, that means we are not often stand in the same situation as artist and curator do in public affairs. When the event was over there were only the eventualities can be saved as if it will be diverging and reoccurring continually. Focusing on artistic generation is the first motif.

Motif 1:   The *autopoiesis* (self-generation) of art cannot be explained clearly by word at all.

Art creation is usually unbelievable but can be indirectly clarified in a metaphor. Let us first think about there an affiliation with ponds, stones, and ripples. Metaphysically, if we depict the art field as a pond within the universe, the artist's good creation is like a stone thrown to a splash of water, causing ripples on the surface. A sensitive arts critic will pay attention to all of this.

Without a doubt, artists should have a mystery in their inner life, a source to creation, some from the power of the universe, some from the memories of the past, and some from the reality encountered with others. Using the term *autopoiesis* to describe the significance and possibility of art creation is convenient to that art is in itself the purest power of generating. It is like *Ereignis* as Heidegger said:

> The word *Ereignis* (concern) has been lifted from organically developing language. *Er-eignen* (to concern) means, originally, to distinguish or discern which one's eyes see, and in seeing calling to oneself, *ap-propriate*. The word *con-cern* we shall now harness as a theme word in the service of thought.[1]

It means it is not merely something coming into view like an event, but also arising into its own becoming. When the light shines into the open space in the forest giving us the most unrestrained silence, it is authentically an art exists. A little bit of a pre-modern plot here. Nevertheless, the contemporary art is involved with the action, conflict, social reform, and revolution. How do we get to know their passion in such movements?

II. Text and Events Strategy

In order to analyze the nature of art, we examine the concept of text. The so-called 'text' is produced in art activities, so much that the result of art creation is the production of various texts. Of course, such producing process of art was involved with the public affairs, which can be considered as the simplest element to constituting an event. We do not object that there are artistic elements like basic atoms, raindrops, foam, spray, dust, and starlight are closer to our imagination, those are aggregated and naturally shaped into any different state of assemblage. They are natural text with organizing texture. But mainly through artificial and artistic doing a thematic, it becomes an actual text break away from the natural state, although it may also have a simple naïve style.

Motif 2: Art produced the text.

Where there is an art text in producing, there is accompany with events in emerging. It is like the phenomenon of things with adumbration given in our aesthetic activities, means that art text is usually accompanied by shadows for public's imaginary. After

---

[1]   Martin Heidegger, *Identity and Difference*, trans. Joan Stambaugh. New York: Harper & Row, 1969.

busywork, no matter the art text will meet the public's taste or not, it completes its first task. Then it recorded in any way to turn into a variety of documents as historical things if they are really excellent in the result. This secular course is an ordinary phenomenon of contemporary art. Not merely in literature art, the text of a work may be indicated a sacred task and the artist has to complete it step by step. After identifying the fictional nature of literature, Eagleton sees the events that make up the literary text is as an *action* more than a work. Especially when it comes to drama, *"that is, literary works are regarded as strategies."*[2] Therefore, "the strategy has established a vital bridge between the work and the readers. As an intermediary coordinator, it is the driving force behind the birth of the work."[3] We can divide the way we process text into two categories, that is, treating the work as an object or as an event.[4] He stated in *The Event of Literature*:

> Once the object/event distinction is taken into consideration, what about structuralism and semiotics? ... Umberto Eco called "symbol-production" activities from the reader's point of view, using inference (hypothesis), induction, reasoning, overcoding, undercoding and other strategies to break the translation The "information", the latter is an "empty form that can be given any meaning." The text is no longer a solid structure, but a "great labyrinth garden" full of interpretations and possibilities. ...inviting readers to participate... Text information is not just an object to be read from a symbol, they are a set of events or symbolic behaviors that cannot be reduced to the code that produced them.[5]

When we look at the art text, we all focus on the work, concentrating on the aesthetic qualities it expresses and wondering what material it is made of or what form it has. No doubt that the composition of artwork is mainly medium and subject matter, and it is eclectic; in addition, it has style and meaning, and its performance is diverse. These are too important, but now to no avail. What matters is the writing strategy, and writing is sometimes done to produce events that can be read fresh.

As Barthes described, especially in literary texts, both writing and reading are enjoyable, that "I am interested in language because it wounds or seduces me."[6] Even

---

[2]   Terry Eagleton, *The Event of Literature*. p.169; c:191.

[3]   Ibid., p.186; c:210

[4]   Literature concerning the concept event, see Derek Attridge, *The Singularity of Literature* (London and New York, 2004), pp.58-62.

[5]   Ibid., Eagleton, pp.190-91; :215-16.

[6]   Roland Barthes, The Pleasure of the Text

painter or dancer has the same expression in their language that is also the case with other art categories. More aesthetic experiences we will have through the text. In fact, the aesthetic principles of the text are practical and meticulous and are generally used in various art types. I had summed up before at least three aesthetic principles that of *pleasure, trepidation*, and *disgust*. Enjoy it, or vomiting it! It's easy to understand, but the meaning of trepidation is not obvious. While exceeding the aesthetic intensity that our sensory ability can withstand, in a state of trepidation of death or face the God, we feel almost collapsed that Kierkegaard will depict it as *tremble*. Nowadays in the challenge of contemporary art, there is a new one, an aesthetic *rupture* of our virtual sensibility in the digital world. Later we will explain how it is produced, as well as its content.

The aesthetic principles above are descriptive on subjective feelings that could be applied to the audience. In contrast, what is the normative for analyzing the objective presentation of a work? In terms of external presentation, the text of the work can be confirmed in three ways: works, events, and contexts. The text in the narrow sense is the work itself, sometimes called '*object-text.*' As for the text in a broad sense, it refers to all the items related to the creative work so-called '*contextual-text.*' Here, narrow and broad senses are relative and static as we find that these two forms are not applicable in the task of defining what contemporary art is. One is too narrow and the other is too wide, so it is difficult to properly describe the true process of the producing of art text at all. Consequently, we must put forward a precise view that can be floated to actual situations: when the work takes place and changes in the corresponding context, this is the dynamic text, which is completely in line with the description of the artistic event. Conscientiously, what we care about is an artistic event described by dynamics.

Why do we want to emphasize that art is a text event? This can be combined with Aristotle poetics and Barthes literary theory. Aristotle discusses the elements of tragedy or comedy, which should include a series of plots, arranged in an orderly manner that towards an unexpected event occurs. If this is an incredible turn and disrupts the original plot sequence, it will eventually lead to tragedy. Events and plots can achieve the function of purifying society. "Tragedy is not just an imitation of a complete action, but an event that causes compassion and fear." And it is "that the sequence of events, according to the law of probability or necessity, will admit of a change from bad fortune to good, or from good fortune to bad."[7] Barthes mentioned in *the Pleasure of Text* that a kind of *jouissanc*e (enjoyment) becomes real, which has been actually obtained through reading is much more than the *plaisir* of the text, and finally, both reach their extreme in an indescribable beauty of life.

---

[7] Aristotle, *Poetics*

Motif 3:   If the text forms an event and breeds problem, whether good or bad, then there is a *strategy*.

There must be a reason for the strategy to be proposed. Without the event as a motive, it is difficult to come up with a strategy. The artistic event is not empty, but a process of finding the pure position where the phenomenon can occur. When thinking about the subject matter, the event is already brewing. It posits itself to let everything posited inadequate position. We borrowed the contribution of Badiou to better illustrate where the event occurred, and of course, it is the view of set theory. In order to facilitate us to describe the follow-up concept of 'art event and its divergence', there are at least *four 'postures'* in need. The first is *the eventual site* (*evental site*), which means the edge of the void that is about to happen.

Posture 1. The events as *Being* satisfied within *evental site*.

First, an event has its own look and it will wrap the content. This is the pure existence of all things as 'one.' It has a posture, a self-sufficient state of aground, faintly presenting a void space, waiting for position and matter. The existence is close to the edge of nothingness, just like the art activity jumps from the nihilist.

> It is therefore essential to retain that the definition of evental sites is local, whilst the definition of natural situations is global. One can maintain that there are only site-points, inside a situation, in which certain multiples (but not others) are on the edge of the void. In contrast, there are situations which are globally natural. …Every radical transformational action originates in a point, which, inside a situation, is an evental site.[8]

And,

> I will term evental site an entirely abnormal multiple; that is, a multiple such that none of its elements are presented in the situation. The site, itself, is presented, but 'beneath' it nothing from which it is composed is presented. As such, the site is not a part of the situation. I will also say of such a multiple that it is on the edge of the void, or foundational (these

---

[8]   Badiou, *Being and Event*, transl. by Oliver Feltham; (New York: Continuum, 2005), f:196-7; c:219; e:176

designations will be explained).[9]

Moreover,

> I will call this organised control of time fidelity. To intervene is to enact,
> on the border of the void, being-faithful to its previous border.[10]

We can say that the follow-up phenomenon will happen as *fidelity* on the edge, let it be exclusive to the thematic art events. The art text is an event, which means that the work takes place in the corresponding context, as well as the text is formed in the *Event* of this happening—they are belonging together. We are used to seeing works in isolation, which is the smallest state of the event itself. On the contrary, as long as we do not look at the work in isolation, the event may expand to the whole world. In short, the text is centered on artwork (object-event), while the text-event emphasizes the work as the starting point. It is a burst of self-generated creation, and then with the development of the plots: there has been an unexpected turn.

In the eyes of artists and curators, there should be strategies for the occurrence of events. In our day, the global vision of art distribution strategies is an attractive topic, especially in the digital and online world. We find a reference option for the strategy and tactics of making events to distribute art. It is the tradition of philosophy of Guiguzi provides a rhetorical theory and key persuasive strategies to deliver the events. In his text, this passage is very useful.

> To deal with internal and external events, we must define theories and
> methods. To predict future events, we must be good at making decisions
> in the face of various difficulties. We must not lose our calculations
> when applying strategies, and constantly establish our work to
> accumulate moral policies. Being good at managing people and
> engaging them in production is called 'consolidating intrinsic unity.'[11]

Indeed, this concept *intrinsic unity (internality)* is one of the keys to decipher Guiguzi to let us pay attention also to the externality of the occurrence of artistic events. When we

---

[9]   Ibid., f:195; c:217; e:175.

[10] Ibid., f:233; c:263; e:211

[11] *Guiguzi*, a group of writings between the late Warring States period and the end of the Han Dynasty. I-3, sets
      17-19.

regard art text as the process of occurrence and change of events, artists have to use strategic imagination to create works, and curators must use strategic thinking to market artists' texts. This strategy is entirely a text-event creation, just like organizing a mobile script, or even magnifying it into a historical script. Again, we take literary events as an example, Eagleton said: "Strategy projects out of innards the very historical and ideological subtext of literary work of art."[12] And Deleuze alleged a further image "Writing has nothing to do with meaning. It has to do with land surveying and cartography, including the mapping of countries yet to come."[13] Of course, this is to "Bring something incomprehensible into the world!"[14] In contemporary art, strategic thinking will become the core mission of artists or curators, including their characters, motivations, abilities, and efforts. I think Spinoza's concept of *conatus*[15] will be more crucial to the strategy of art and it requires to persist endowment on the events. In art marketing, '*event-text*' must have the power to make the script full of plots and transitions and overflow into reality. Perhaps this phenomenon is somewhat isolated, but the works of art are always the best witnesses of the social encounters of the artist's personal life.

If we do appreciate certain scenes of bicycle graveyards all over the world, to which contrast an odd-looking of Ai Weiwei's 2011 exhibition entitled *Absent*. One of the works, the 'permanent bicycles' stacked 1,200 bicycles, occupying (2630 x 353 x 957 cm of) interior space. It is said that his strategy is merely to express his respect to Taiwan, and he himself said that "absence itself is the status of my art."[16] In fact, the exhibition is not hot and not deserted, and the official propaganda and had a hardly positive response from the public and the media. It can be used as a negative teaching material for public art affairs. Why does it not happen as an actual event? In the beginning, the artworks included a crafty plot for predicting his absence as well as curators planning, which had seldom stimulant elements to cause useful eventualities so that the events had to exhaust itself. Baudrillard would agree on us, this *Absent* did never happen as an event.

III. Events Divergence itself in the Deployment

We do not regard the divergence function of artistic events as the apparatus of the entire general social mechanism, but only by using the implicit meaning of Foucault's

---

[12] Eagleton, Terry. *The Event of Literature*. New Haven: Yale UP, 2012. pp.171-2.

[13] Gilles Deleuze, A Thousand Plateaus: Capitalism and Schizophrenia.

[14] Ibid., Deleuze,

[15] Spinoza, *Ethics*.

[16] Ai Weiwei, Taipei Museum

dispositif to refer to the existing condition of the divergence of individual events as the *deployment*. Of course, it involves more specific time and space and mental factors.

Motif 4:   The occurrence of the event-text always produces its eventualities.

There must be a turning point after the event occurs. It may be hidden for a while, but it will affect the whole situation once it appears. Whether this turning point produces a tragedy or disaster, whether it is a reversal, or turns into joy and climax, its emotional content is surprising. When the 'event-text' itself turns into a tipping point, it must be the primary one with a substantial position, then it will become a real tipping point for more things. The subsequent effects it causes are a series of derived events, in the second order and after, so that we can treat them as *eventuality* i.e., 'eventual nature' of the text.

Following the primary event in a tipping point, these eventualities are more likely to spread everywhere, as they are not first-order but derived, reversed, or retrospective. That is to say, event nature is constantly copied and transmitted by coincidence, which in turn causes the original event (in the tipping point) to absorb more and more energy. Applying the term '*meme*' to the analysis above phenomenon, we will easy to explain the relevance of eventuality of the text appropriately. Richard Dawkins defines meme as a term for a unit of cultural transmission or imitation units, meaning that our brains replicate themselves in the dissemination of information, similar to cultural replication. [17] However, people are not happy with the imitation or reproduction of art. It should be self-requested to be a unique event. The artists will not disagree. This is a major thing that 'self-overcoming,' a long journey, as Nietzsche swears, "When I overcome myself in this respect; I have to overcome myself in a greater event; Victory will be the seal of my completion!" Moreover, it continues to return *eternally*.

> Truly, I say to you, good and evil, that would be immortal - that does not exist! It has to overcome itself over and over again. [Wahrlich, ich sage euch: Gutes und Böses, das unvergänglich wäre - das giebt es nicht! Aus sich selber muss es sich immer wieder überwinden.][18]

Therefore, this process is full of turning points. And the turning point of the incident is accidental, and may not meet the conditions immediately. But in any case, in the aftermath, its ending is realistic, so the previous contingency is for all accompanying

---

[17]   Dawkins, Richard (1989), *The Selfish Gene*. Oxford University Press. P.192; p.352.

[18]   thus spake zarathustra

eventualities. It becomes inevitable in advance, that is, events and possibilities have certain structures that are predictable. Our description methods include logical thinking and scene thinking. Logical and mathematical methods, as pointed out by Badiou:

> I name 'event', a rupture in the normal disposition of bodies and normal ways of a particular situation. Or if you want, I name 'event' a rupture of the laws of the situation. So, in its very important, an event is not the realization/variation of a possibility that resides inside the situation. An event is the creation of a new possibility. An event changes not only the real but also the possible. An event is at the level not of simple possibility, but at the level of possibility of possibility.[19]

We regard these possibilities of the events as a contingent effect in the public sphere, i.e., *Eventuality*. And Badiou recognizes that it is unaccountable,

> An 'event' is something that happens that does not quite fit into our established system of knowledge, and so it will appear to us as something unaccountable, something that we cannot quite get our minds around even as we recognize the great importance of the encounter.[20]

In addition, in the dialogue with Zizek, Badiou proposed 8 theses to explain the event is related to the universality. Of which is "Thesis 3: *Every universal originates in an event, and the event is intransitive to the particularity of the situation.*"[21] Because of the event occurs on the 'edge of the void' (evental site) and the universality separated from the situation. In principle, art critics observe the eventualities of events without participating in the observed events, and can only extract the meaning of the events as '*pure events*' to track and analyze. Especially in the study of eventualities, their purpose is trying to find out what the derivatives could be, which includes paths, vacancies, and gaps to all eventualities, as well as nodes and dispersal. Again, what is eventuality and how they spread to the public, these questions are raised by critics for fully understanding why they are artists as such. Their motives are obvious, but the desire is not easy to dig out. It is precisely Lacan who depicts that anyone should be a life in the process of becoming.

---

[19] Alain Badiou, 'Is the Word "Communism" Foorever Doomed?' http://www.lacan.com/badioulinks.htm.
[20] Mark T. Conard, The Philosophy of the Coen Brothers.
[21] Badiou, Philosophy in the Present, (with Slavoj Žižek); (New York: Polity Press, 2010)

> What is realized in my history is not the past definitive of what it was,
> since it is no more, or even the present perfect of what has been in what
> I am, but the future anterior of what I shall have been for what I am in
> the process of becoming.[22]

The artist's life history has influenced the ecology of his artistic events so that the attitude of divergence is different. This requires a method of plot thinking. This requires a method of plot thinking, so our imagination is not necessarily logical. In the tracking of the event turning path, what kind of state of art eventualities must be understood by us? What kind of magic weapon should art critics have to be used to outline the art text and open the blueprint for the events deployed by curators and artists? What must appropriate philosophical work be done by art critics to cleverly observe events? Non-direct interventional observations will weaken the power of criticism, or in turn, affect the public and interfere with artist creation? In short, if the art critic wants to track events and eventualities, they must ask: What is the attitude of the event? In short, if art critics want to track events and its eventuality, they must ask: What is the attitude to the event? Why do curators need to seize the opportunity to spread the influence of this event through media communication tools? Because it is divergent. Here gives this proposition, Motif 5.

Motif 5:   Any eventuality spreads itself to wherever, namely contingency of event, it diverges.

The eventuality of art event, its contingent effect, constantly repeats the differences by itself and spreads the problem towards the public. This method is also directly considered as an event divergence. Just like the stone provokes the behavior of the water (the original *event*, the central hypothesis point that occurred for the first time) and the subsequent phenomenon (that is, all *eventualities*, they diverge toward the public and reversibly push back to the original center point). The stone sinks down and the water ripples spread out. The divergence of the two is somewhat different, but they are attached to each other. The event occurred but it was not transmitted by itself. Throwing stones into the water, we know that it splashes and then ripples on the water, but the ripples that spread out on the water are not the stones. Strictly speaking, what can be spread is not the event itself, but the text beyond the event, more correctly: it radiates the eventuality of the text.

Since it will be diffused everywhere, we notice at least four typical manifestations:

---

[22] Jacques Lacan, Écrits: A Selection

being, becoming, beyond, and in-between, which is the essential linkages to the world as the event divergence in the text. In short, due to the social role of the mass, there will be corresponding gestures and postures of this divergence in begin and end. As we may repeat the heavy words of Milan Kundera "God laughs when a man thinks," as well as in the beginning, we (pretend we do yet think nothing) should know that no matter whether the audience is laughing or not laughing it is a problem. At this divergence point, as long as the scene is gone, the event itself will not disappear. We should talk about the second posture of the events divergence.

Posture 2. It is the events as *Becoming* to what known or somewhat unrecognizable.

This posture means that the divergent event also generates various paths, some of which are known and some of which are unrecognizable. Deleuze uses the concept of the *rhizome* to describe its appearance that the path and the maze are intertwined and spreading out. However, this posture *Becoming* occasionally ends up at any time. The end event seems to be a world of strange humanoids such as ghosts and aliens that appear after death. But death is not the final plot and life after death is not the death. It requires us to stay as a living person to witness the real power of '*event divergence.*' Spirit or ghost is precisely one of the human generation process, or the Becoming of ghosts, animals, aliens and so on. Are all these desire-machines? That should be the product of desire that stimulates the event of sensation. Therefore, to become an event will not just to fill the evental site. Does it mean that logic also has its own emotions? How can there be various changes in the existence of self-presentation? This is the posture of Becoming. Generate to becoming is crucial to artistic events, as described by Deleuze's 'transcendental empiricism,' in which art events are about becoming the minority, becoming-woman, becoming-animal, and these existences are of marginal, weak and minority in the actual world. For the artist's way of life, Deleuze says this:

> Signs imply ways of living, possibilities of existence, they are the symptoms of an overflowing (jaillissante) or exhausted (épuisée) life. But an artist cannot be content with an exhausted life, nor with a personal life. One does not write with one's ego, one's memory, and one's illnesses. In the act of writing, there's an attempt to make life something more personal, to liberate life from what imprisons it...There is a profound link between signs, the event, life, and vitalism. It is the power of nonorganic life, that which can be found in a line of a drawing, a line of writing, a line of music. It is organisms that die, not life. There

is no work of art that does not indicate an opening for life, a path between the cracks. Everything I have written has been vitalistic, at least I hope so, and constitutes a theory of signs and the event.[23]

Since artworks in the opening are to appear in the path between cracks, Deleuze emphasizes *the path* so far he explored that constitutes a theory of signs and events, which is very important. In the process of Becoming, the artist's life is like this color,

To become imperceptible oneself, to have dismantled love in order to become capable of loving. To have dismantled one's self in order finally to be alone and meet the true double at the other end of the line. A clandestine passenger on a motionless voyage. To become like everybody else; but this, precisely, is a becoming only for one who knows how to be nobody, to no longer be anybody. To paint oneself gray on gray.[24]

To this end, he said, "The self is only a threshold, a door, a becoming between two multiplicities".[25] It is becoming of the self through the threshold to be the double of this-and-that sides of the same door. We know that it is a ritual, returning whence it leaving. It completes the closest intimacy of its own simulative differences. Deleuze defined 'a dead time' to be infinite waiting, which is between two moments, the event as a point of '*entre-temps*', which is Becoming. He said:

It is no longer time that exists between two instants; it is the event that is a meanwhile [un entre-temps]: the meanwhile is not part of the eternal, but neither is it part of the time — it belongs to becoming. The meanwhile, the event, is always a dead time; it is there where nothing takes place, an infinite awaiting that is already infinitely past, awaiting and reserve.[26]

Above, we have described the first two postures of divergence: there are events-being (void), and events-becoming (finalized). As a whole, we already know at

[23] Gilles Deleuze, A Thousand Plateaus: Capitalism and Schizophrenia.

[24] Ibid., Gilles Deleuze,

[25] Ibid., Deleuze,

[26] Gilles Deleuze, *What is Philosophy?* c:158; c:425.

least four postures, later we will mention it again. From the various forms of being, becoming, beyond, and in-between, I found that the artists produced various divergence (in postures of eventuality), and the curators gave more clear and active gestures, which is equivalent to the resonance of the events (and eventualities) to reach the maximum expectation. What is the reflection of the natural and social environment? How far can the original incident spread under the political economy of global governance and media hegemony? This concerns the deployment and disposal to the text-event by the art team. Therefore, we have to talk about the real strategy and the structure that it has to. As follows Motif 6.

Motif 6:   Events divergence has a dual structure: deployment and disposal.

The dual structure is due to the internal and external positions of the core actors (mainly artists and curators) and the relevant structures of the events divergence system. It is not as ambitious as the social operation of *Dispositif* in Foucault's description. However, the overall strategy of the divergence of artistic events is well carried out by taking advantage of the internal and external realities. The art text as an event reflects the social reality. This dynamic process is seen as a complete collective influence with internal and external correspondence. But this state is not constant and there are no fixed boundaries. The duality of internal and external correspondence refers to the 'endo-position' of the inwardness of the group (individual) itself, and the exo-position that is wrapped by the outer circumference. The text-event of art must have an 'endo-/exo-correspondence' of this loop power. Is there really no fixed boundary between inside and outside? It depends on the eventual divergence. But statically, we treat the artist and his work as all the relevant participants as a basic group (involved in the event). In contrast, the context that is affected by events is 'exo-position' provided externally, which could be called an *external deployment*. However, how does the core art group, that is, the gathering of artists, curators, brokers, dearer and even collectors, view the original events and their resulting eventualities? This is the basic problem for them. The overall deployment of the original art activity was to express the art text of self-generation, but after the divergence of the event turning point, its *distance* from the critic was farther away.

The artist's own inclinations are required to be equated with the qualities of human virtues and to be consistent with the quality of the work being created. Arts events occur in the group are both internal and external incoherence, and its eventuality causes in the direction of the exo-position. This requires another divergence posture to look at the overall situation, that is, the self-overcoming. In short, the third posture of the event is

Beyond. The meaning of beyond is vague, it can be advanced and backward, rising and falling, transcending and indulging, or sacred and secular. In any case, the posture Being of arts event is of value and could be contrasted radically. We describe this posture as follows,

Posture 3. It goes *Beyond* its own chain of events to evaluate itself constantly.

This is just like Nietzsche's *'chain of events'* in life. The most indispensable power of art is the attitude of self-overcoming. He revealed, "Life is a dark chain of events."[27] It has a sequence and a necessity for value assessment. Nietzsche said,

> The greatest events- they are not noisiest but our stillest hours. The
> world revolves, not around the inventors of new noises, but around the
> inventors of new values; it revolves inaudibly.[28]"

He hoped that the 'greatest event' will cross all of this, and in history, there has been a relative phenomenon of advanced or backward, superb or ignorant. The greatness of the event lies in the importance of self-overcoming also it is a life prescription to prevent democracy from becoming a bureaucrat. Although, "this tremendous event is still on its way, still wandering; it has not yet reached the ears of men….and yet they have done it themselves."[29] Nietzsche asked for himself,"And life confided the secret to me: behold, it said, I am that which must always overcome itself."[30] He said,

> …Behold, I teach you the overman. Man is something that shall be
> overcome. What have you done to overcome him? All beings so far have
> created something beyond themselves; and do you want to be the ebb of
> this great flood and even go back to the beasts rather than overcome
> man? What is the ape to man? A laughingstock or a painful embarrassment.
> And man shall be just that for the overman: a laughingstock or a painful
> embarrassment…[31]

Is the event always mastered by the overman? Why can it not be? or why should Nietzsche "overcome and why it on this ladder to his hope increases" [Überwindungen

---

[27] Friedrich Nietzsche, Thus Spoke Zarathustra.

[28] Ibid., Nietzsche.

[29] Ibid., Nietzsche.

[30] Ibid., Nietzsche.

[31] Ibid., Nietzsche.

und Warum es auf dieser Leiter zu seiner Hoffnung steigt]? The artist's hopes are pointed out in the divergent posture of his/her own life and his works.

IV. Virtuality and Aesthetic Rupture

The divergence of artistic events involves a set of public aesthetics. In addition to the digital representation, the symbol theory in this also has a new situation of virtuality. We say that gesture of sign is an enhancement of posture because it's signifier function is more obvious. Sometimes, the gesture of the body, face, and fingers is a particularized posture in universal. The symbols in political activities reinforce the signifying power of the event divergence, and the artistic events based on social reform or transitional justice are involved in the public life world. This forms the theme 7.

Motif 7:   Art event diverges in various postures to intervene the public.

In order to make the art text a reality, artists and curators must intervene in public life for information dissemination, that is, they must use different gestures to make the event more diffuse. The divergent posture is a direct claim of existence, and the gesture to be imitated is the indication function. We will see the announcements and numerous instructions on the art exhibition, that is, the posture and gesture are fully utilized. Of course, the functional intervention of such art does not conflict with the purposelessness of traditional aesthetics. Now there is also the purpose of virtual reality, although this virtual is not a direct reality. Among all of these functions, we know one of the most important indicators of globalization is *transitional justice*, the most typical intervention force for contemporary art activities. Therefore, the events in the public events are not other creative ideas, but 'Events' that go deep into the political arena and carry out art expression of democratic needs for us.

Posture 4. It seems *in-Between* the events as the vanishing mediator, but it is actually *a meanwhile*.

The final posture is an imaginary plot that constantly reverberates in all events of 'within,' 'among,' 'between,' or 'mediate.' This fourth gesture is not easy to compare with the first three. Strictly speaking, it is a mixed event, a hybrid eventual collection of all divergent paths to becoming a bundle of events. Moreover, they are not connected and are not affiliated with each other. This gesture is closest to political events and is one of the most expressive expressions of contemporary art text: *in-Between*. From the perspective of the left, the grand [art] event will become a major project of political calculation. However, the art action strategy can be a deconstructing of the event itself, for instance, "flaunting the red flag to oppose the red flag" in the event (the Cultural Revolution). Now as one of the weapons of the Left Alliance, isn't it the first story to shoot an arrow and then draw a target? "In political practice, we must be both 'the arrow and the bull's eye', because the old worldview is also still present within us."[32] Zizek interprets Lacan's other language as a *pure negation* to intervene in reality, and is often the role of political intermediary.

> And of course, Lacan's point is that if one fully exploits the potentials opened up by our existence as parlêtres ('beings of language'), one sooner or later finds oneself in this horrifying in-between state – the threatening possibility of this occurrence looms over each of us.[33]

So Zizek said frankly:

> The subject is thus split even if it possesses only one "unified" Self since this split is the very split between $ and Self... In more topological terms: the subject's division is not the division between one and another Self, between two contents, but the division between something and nothing, between the feature of identification and the void.[34]

Zizek's solution is special. The event assumes a mediator between "something and nothing," but it is not the becoming as '*a meanwhile*' that Deleuze said. Strictly speaking, in terms of an *in-Between*, one must choose one of the edges, was different from that of *a meanwhile*, one is letting the event continues to occur between the both. Badiou would rather call it an 'intervalle' of events but not fall into it. Even so, can we simply describe Deleuze as a rightist relative to the above lefts?

This 'in-Between' state does not have to be laborious to explain, because as long as the public is asked, "Is the murderer in the middle of us?" then the event divergence will begin to collapse. It means that I am among the perpetrators? Do not! On the contrary, I am one of the victims and did not indicate that it was because I did not want to be remembered. In the conspiracy of politics and history and the pseudo-called great events,

[32] Alain Badiou, The Communist Hypothesis.
[33] Slavoj Žižek, 1999, *The Ticklish Subject*, London: Verso., e:p.156
[34] Slavoj Žižek, 'Cyberspace, Or the Virtuality of the Rea.'

we are forgotten and have already become self-abandoned existence.

> Lacan's notion of the act as real is thus opposed to both Laclau and
> Badiou. In Lacan, the act is a purely negative category: to put it in
> Badiou's terms, it stands for the gesture of breaking out of the constraints
> of Being, for the reference to the Void at its core, prior to filling this Void.
> In this precise sense, the act involves the dimension of death drive that
> grounds a decision (to accomplish a hegemonic identification; to engage
> in a fidelity to a Truth), but cannot be reduced to it. The Lacanian death
> drive (a category Badiou adamantly opposes) is thus again a kind of
> 'vanishing mediator' between Being and Event: there is a 'negative'
> gesture constitutive of the subject which is then obfuscated in 'Being' (the
> established ontological order) and infidelity to the Event.[35]

We should pay attention: this *'vanishing mediator'* is not the *'entre-temps'* described by Deleuze. He sees the event as Becoming as a wait or reserve that occurs 'between two moments,' but not just a purely negative usage of reality. Inevitably too fast maybe it is, Zizek's left 'parallax' does not see the philosophical creativity (this *meanwhile*), he fell into the reality of manipulation. However, the text is the eye of the event. It is the temptation to seduce, and Barthes's text politics is depicted like this:

> Is not the most erotic portion of a body where the garment gapes? In
> perversion (which is the realm of textual pleasure) there are no
> "erogenous zones" (a foolish expression, besides); it is intermittence, as
> psychoanalysis has so rightly stated, which is erotic: the intermittence of
> skin flashing between two articles of clothing (trousers and sweater),
> between two edges (the open-necked shirt, the glove, and the sleeve); it is
> this flash itself which seduces, or rather: the staging of an
> appearance-as-disappearance.[36]

The depiction here about two edges, can it not be a narcissistic complex of the text? The event diverges itself to return to its own temptation at all. When the artist continually diverges on the text-event produced by himself, his passionate attachment is as old as the lover's endless love. But we have to ask: Can the enjoyment caused by such divergence

---

[35] Ibid., *TTS*, e:p.160
[36] Roland Barthes. The Pleasure of the Text.

be directly abandoned by the audience? If the world as a whole is a great event that has not yet been concluded, then we are a temporary thing in the world that contains extremely complex eventualities residues in its overall divergence.

Thus, this strategy has political implications and has practiced critical literature. This intervening posture is a powerful divergence, but full of risks. Putting it on political issues is easy to fall into an unbalanced, disproportionate, unequal position, or even pretending to be a peaceful blender, but it is actually unjust. Eagleton sees this risk of Zizek, he commented:

> Would one also seek to reconcile slaves and slave masters, or persuade native peoples to complain only moderately about those who are plotting their extermination? What is the middle ground between racism and anti-racism?[37]

Additionally,

> Anyway, let's see how Zizek plays between the left and the right, a middle that is useful but disappears after completion. Not a glance, but a parallax! In the art event, the available and disappeared in the middle becomes 'art of events.' It's just that Zizek often plays too much.

Although there are criticisms as we read, also know these mixing, among, parallax, between, in-between, and fall into the secular world are inevitable. On the video of *Cyberspace, Or the Virtuality of the Real*, he informed us that the event-related in the event of involvement! This is the fright of the art review. Although we hear those criticisms, we also know that these blends, parallaxes, between, during, between, between, and into the secular world are inevitable. He seems to tell us that as long as one is involved in the eventuality, you cannot avoid this event! This must be the scare of art criticism. Indeed, it is a political risk of artistic events. So, Eagleton had to ridicule Zizek:

> Like the rest of his work, these two latest volumes are postmodern in form but anti-postmodern in content. Žižek has the eclecticism of the postmodern, along with its mixing of high and low genres. His books are broken-backed affairs which leap erratically from topic to topic.

---

[37] Terry Eagleton, Why Marx Was Right.

What is more,

> The parallax point of view happens when an object is viewed from two different places (almost at once) realizing the object itself moves when the point of view changes. In the parallax, there is the apparent displacement of an object, caused by a change in observational position. Zizek is interested in the 'parallax gap' which happens when you are caught between the two points where no synthesis or mediation is possible.

In other words, eventuality is always the ghost of the event! 'Am I a ghost? But it will have been my shadow.' In other words, eventuality is always the ghost of the event! If we remember the posture—beyond of the event, we should listen to Nietzsche's muttering, "I am a ghost? But this will be my shadow." (Bin ich denn ein Gespenst? Aber es wird mein Schatten gewesen sein).[38] The time of the East and West Ghost Festival is different, it is said that the ghosts were wandering around among us during that time.[39] A Taiwanese commercial propaganda film in 2018 was considered to reflect the appearance of victims of past political persecution and caused discussion.[40] This is a political murder in the depths of Taiwan's collective memory, but it reflects the real examples that must be faced in the global transitional justice trend. The art expression technique is understandable, so social disputes have emerged. As long as it is the subject of artistic creation related to political reform and social resistance, especially the reflection on criminal justice, compensation or generational justice, media effects are quickly generated in the process of its artistic event divergence, and it is often praised or rejected by the public.

Undoubtedly, historical events are long-term social movements from potential events to collective coexistence. Many artists know the purpose of this reality and can use various aesthetic principles to intervene in social movements, motivate the public, and face the righteousness. Curators know that deliberative as well as prudent democracy is the most concrete art practice and can raise the motive and power of the public to reform society. However, it is not a lot of successful of them who could advance the eventuality of the artistic event-text to the farthest place. Under the premise of art autonomy, artists and curators often lose their autonomy and become passive roles because they must

---

[38] Nietzsche, Also sprach Zarathustra.

[39] Liqiū, one of the 24 solar terms, it is the beginning of the fall.

[40] This film can be found at https://www.youtube.com/watch?v=TEU-mk4r_oU ; The relevant report on this political event is at http://www.taiwandc.org/twcom/tc05-int.pdf

interact and communicate with the bureaucratic systems of various government departments. They can only consider reciprocal behaviors and dare not express too many protest opinions. This falls into the bureaucratic game. This is weaker than Kafka's Gregor's breathing and is dying. As for the pure or practical art text, it is more difficult to act autonomously in commercial marketing, and it is even more difficult to speak loudly.

Basically, art activities do not conflict with commercial interests. Usually, they are also desirable, but the event-text is self-recording. There is hardly any art that can be separated from capitalism and can resist the temptation of capital. Then, to think about the public appearance of these artistic events in essence, will it be precisely 'in the Name of art, by the Desire of capital?' If we fully know that the Lacanian nightmare 'in the Name of the father, by the Desire of the mother' will not wake up, we will be accustomed to the signs and imaginations of the bureaucracy and the market, or simply turn a blind eye. For the digitalization applied to the text and event and involved in the public life, the power and substantial benefits of this virtuality cannot be ignored by us. But we find that, in general, the ultimate value of contemporary art is pretending and fake. Is this a shock we have to ask about the real insight of the end of art is coming? Is this the real insight of the end of art? This is a shock, so we have to ask if the end of art is coming soon?

Especially under the impact of new media, online and digital technology, our aesthetic experience has been drastically changed, and the transition mechanism between virtual and reality has become a game of art expression. Therefore, we must put forward a corresponding aesthetic principle for the analysis of the new media art's control over the audience's sensory ability.

Motif 8: The virtualization of the event often leads to *aesthetic rupture* in perception.

The result of this shock is to blame the contemporary aesthetics for describing the sensory function and trusting the artist too much. There are many traps for our aesthetic integration. There has never been a map that has met the ecstasy of the artist's ingenuity, and the curator has deliberately designed more complicated mezes to mislead the public. People's confusion does not require art critics to solve them, because they are able to discard the lost path or labyrinth faster than our footsteps and comments. However, we still have to analyze what the aesthetic crisis of the contemporary art event hides in the future when it will be more complicated and digitalized.

We can intervene in text-events and eventualities through digital manipulation or new media, but in fact, this is usually done by inducing the senses of digital devices to indulge and immerse our senses into the virtual domain. In terms of divergence, this is the process of parody of events and replication of differences. Similar to a perceptual jumper, this sensible mechanism that can be re-introduced but interrupted at any time is almost unprecedented in the development of human experience and is brand new because it utilizes high-tech devices and equipment. This corresponds to the traditional aesthetics, but since there is a jump between virtual and reality, which can be noticed as a 'rupture' by devices user as one of the aesthetic principles.

How does our aesthetic integration in sensory function to be the event with virtuality? Similar to a perceived hop, this interrupt can be called an 'aesthetic rupture' on perception, close to an anesthetic state in an instant. If the event has a rupture, it may recur to the bounce of the retrospective sensory recovery, as a momentary daze (dizziness) resulting from the offshore of the sensory senses of 'off-shore and ashore' between reality and virtuality.

Barthes said with emotion that "boring is not far from bliss: it is bliss seen from the shores of pleasure." But how much is boring and stagnation? We don't know, but the aesthetic break that occurs after the virtual interference is similar to the case of *gaze-daze*. This is an example of pop music of digital art, and it satiates the true sluggishness, as the lyrics of Lady Gaga's album sing. Our vision and hearing are automatically dissolved from words to electronic sounds, and then the body is separated out of reality in the beat, become dazing and looping thing:

Pre-chorus: I am having a dream(s) as I lay me down to sleep
Chorus: Gaze electronica daze / Beautiful charades / Colors and rage

Can people stop the meme of rhythm? Yes! But it breaks in the floating sense of the digital sea, on the shore back to reality. Scholar Chloe Watson has done research and art criticism from visual psychology, she said. "What is Gaze-daze? Gaze-daze can be understood as an environmentally specific iteration of vertigo, best described as the illusion of movement at a moment of stasis."[41] We were digitally sent to the stagnation in the exhibition and repeated the same gaze in the digital virtual. Why is the aesthetic break in the gaze jumping out of sluggishness? Because it consumes all of the fascinations, it compresses into an audiovisual stimulus and a bundled body. The internal position is so that the exterior is more compressed and distorted, becoming a special dictatorship of artistic events. Being accustomed to it, bureaucratic democracy has its own symptoms of the corresponding illness, which is precisely the common language of schizophrenia.

---

[41] Chloe Watson Victoria Maxwell, 'Gaze-Daze: An Open Letter of Concern'

V. To Paralyze the Autocratic, an Eventual Art!

It is difficult to convince people to treat *autocratic activities* directly as an *autopoiesis* of art. But art is often hidden in an autocracy, which events itself with authoritarianism. Therefore, any deliberate creation of an event becomes an art, and the occurrence of an event is the end of art. No doubt, *autopoiesis* supports the desire for art autonomy, but its eventual divergence must be heteronomous. This brings the risk of autocratic because when the deployment of art is confused with bureaucrats or businessperson, their boundaries are so floating that the power of the key poiesis has disappeared. The art-text event can easily fall into the mud of formalism in its divergence operation. Becoming a formalist zombie, and then it adds a piece of 'eventual art' in the public sphere. The word may have been beautiful, but it is corrupt here. It ended and was buried. The pathological signs are also the study of how to navigate the path and channel of artistic events. It became 'one thing of multiplicity' and was placed in bracketing (*epoché*), suspended, and usually did not become a property of art history. But if it does not fall into the formalist autocracy, it is not the case. This is the risk of the event, so there is a reminder of Motif 9.

Motif 9:   The contingency of events could be involved in more *autocratic affairs*.

This Motif 9 has a conditional clause: Autocracy is derived from the fact that if the *democracy* we thought is actually claimed by the *bureaucrats*.

The event itself may end, but the eventuality it breeds is hard to end. Specifically, in the endless repetition of eventuality, in the loop, the event is constantly repeated with the illusion that it is ended. The illusion that the event has ended is exactly what we need to be commemorative after the event. Therefore, the commemoration is only for the sake of forgetting. In order to package the emotional attachment of life, we can only choose the incomplete form of life after death. Because we don't want to remember the sad things that were not recognized as self-identity in the past, our collective memory automatically loses memory, that is, we suddenly suffer from amnesia.

What is going to happen is just the way to forthcoming but never going. If it is not implemented in front of us, it can only become a contingency that later belongs to other events. On the wedding day, the marriage contract was announced, and the bride's makeup turned into a pure symbol to bury the virginity. The inevitability of the event was diluted, and the so-called *Gegenwärtigen* (living now)[42] became its own void. Although

---

[42] See Husserl, 1928. Vorlesungen zur Phänomenologie des inneren Zeitbewusstseins (Lectures on the

it is empty, it is eternal waiting for the event to happen. The artist wants to market his own artistic events that have occurred, and eventually, no events have occurred. This still has to return to the old tone of the contemporary textual view. When the art event occurs, the author's death is declared, and the reader's birth process of the generation's memory of the work is inevitable, just like the inscription, just writing a political reconciliation. It's helpful to revisit the old words of Barthes:

> The reader is space on which all the quotations that make up a writing are inscribed without any of them being lost; a text's unity lies not in its origin but in its destination. Yet this destination cannot any longer be personal: the reader is without history, biography, psychology; he is simply that someone who holds together in a single field all the traces by which the written text is constituted ... Classic criticism has never paid any attention to the reader; for it, the writer is the only person in literature ... we know that to give writing its future, it is necessary to overthrow the myth: the birth of the reader must be at the cost of the death of the Author.[43]

In a field similar to the symptom[44], what Lacan pointed out, we left a deep philosophical question: Why does the event itself end, but its eventuality may not end? To be clear, in the event-forming circle, the events that have become empty shells are constantly repeated to end the story. In terms of appearance, for artists and curators and brokers, it is necessary to produce events and make use of sporadicity, and try to spread the incident in the event. As for art critics to conduct reconnaissance missions on incidents, but must stay away from incidents and maintain appropriate distances, it is more important to be cautious to avoid the output of events.

But the participants in the artistic event are different from the observers. Although the art critics are not directly involved in the incident, they participate in the eventual divergence. With the globalization of Bureaucrats and capitalism, contemporary global governance has reached a new high point. The birth of artistic events by the name of cultural democracy and the abolition of events due to the divergence of events are more common.

If the event must give a conclusion, it will no longer diverge in the loop, and the event is terminated as if it did not happen. After the event diverges, the imaginary

---

Phenomenology of the Consciousness of Internal Time)

[43] See Roland Barthes, 'The Death of the Author,' in Image-Music-Text, by Trans. Stephen Heath (1977)

[44] Cf., Jacques Lacan, Fetishism: the Symbolic, the Imaginary and the Real,

eventualities will not disappear. It means the surplus plot may fall off the motifs to be another event begin. Compared with the formalist art event, it is packed and buried in the grave. The remnants here are attractive diversity, and the ghostly residual plot tends to infinity, leading to the universe life without boundaries. The events that took place in the ponds were dissipated as events, becoming burial events in the forest, and the remaining plots were treated arbitrarily. But this is the *aporia*, a real diffusion of all events, the response of the endlessly divergent in all directions. As a Taiwanese philosopher, Jiang Nianfeng, who has committed suicide, said:

> *Wild grass climbing vines~, full of rich years!*

Even, we can only let the more trivial plots deconstruct the concept of events. Because the remaining, which may not be described with respect to the 9 Motifs listed above. Because it is the remainder, this description cannot be listed in the above topic. As people are often reminded, events will always end, events will be resolved, and the natural state will be restored. But we recalled by chance and did not have the opportunity or willingness to confirm with others. Therefore, these episodes of events are still there, they remain in the collective imagination of the public. Imagine a picture: if art is the ice, the public is seawater, and philosophy is fervor, with that a residual poem we draw a line for this article as the end:

> An ice, after its melting on an iceberg,
> still attached to the iceberg to becoming ice;
> In the memory of the seawater.

Summary

Motif 1: The *autopoiesis* (self-generation) of art cannot be explained clearly by word at all.

Motif 2: Art produced the *text*.

Motif 3: If the text forms an event and breeds problem, whether good or bad, then there is a *strategy*.
Posture 1. The events as *Being* satisfied within *evental site*.

Motif 4: The occurrence of the event-text always produces its *eventualities*.

Motif 5: Any eventuality spreads itself to wherever, namely it is the *contingency* of event.
Posture 2. It is the events as Becoming to what known or somewhat unrecognizable.

Motif 6: *Events divergence* has a dual structure: deployment and disposal.

Posture 3. It goes *Beyond* its own chain of events to evaluate itself constantly.

Motif 7:   Art event diverges in various *postures* to intervene the public.

Posture 4. It seems *in-Between* the events as the vanish mediator, but it is actually a *meanwhile*.

Motif 8:   The virtualization of event often leads to *aesthetic rupture* in perception.

Motif 9:   The contingency of events could be involved in more *autocratic affairs*.

A conditional clause: Autocracy is derived from the fact that if *the democracy* we thought is actually claimed by the *bureaucrats*.

The Post-Enlightenment Fallacy:
Political Art and the Fate of Aesthetics

Joe Nolan

Art never has been, nor will ever be, totally divorced from politics [Justinian mosaic, San Vitale].[1] To ignore an artwork's political influences or agendas on the grounds of aesthetic purity can only find as much success as a doctor who lops off a patient's arm to get a better look at his head. But today's art critic is in no danger of espousing such a rigid position. As artists' works increasingly reference culture [Rauschenberg's Collection, EXPORT's Touch and Tap Cinema], art discourse has necessarily become more political. Indeed, today's artist is tempted to believe that her art is meaningful only insofar as it translates into political change, or social awareness. This is a weak idea, but it is perpetuated by the way we speak about art. As we reflect on the relationship between art discourse and challenged democracies, awareness of art's enduring relationship to the Enlightenment will caution against art discourse getting too cozy with politics, as well as with other areas of human thought.

Our present has a history. This is glaringly apparent in an age that can only describe itself with that pesky prefix, "post-". We are post-truth, post-structuralist, After Virtue, After the End of Art—but all of this is ponderously wrapped up in post-modernity. We cannot understand the dangers facing art and art discourse today without understanding that thing to which today's thinkers, writers and artists are responding. And they are responding to a specific failure of modernity. Levine's 1981 *After Willem De Kooning* succinctly articulates the crisis of modernity.

[*Woman I*] De Kooning's Abstract Expressionist paintings were heralded in the 1950s as modernity's new direction (Rosenberg). As we look at his abstraction of a woman's figure, we are invited into the artist's subjectivity. The harsh strokes, the emphasized yet flattened breasts initiate the viewer into the afflicted allure the female figure holds over the artist. Even though it is a little dark and unabashedly subjective, de

---

[1]   Brackets refer to cues in the powerpoint slideshow that will accompany this presentation

Kooning's painting exhibits the optimism found in many strains of modernist art, including Kandinsky, the Cubists, the Constructivists, De Stijl, and especially the art critic who explained them all to the English-speaking world, Clement Greenberg. All of these, with De Kooning's work, posited art's objectivity. Whether it's Greenberg's "flatness" or Kandinsky's "pure artistry," modernist art can be understood as the quest for the objective expression of art. It is the search for the ideal art form native to art's "inner logic" (Greenberg). But it was exactly this modernist optimism that, by the 1960s, had launched a whole galaxy of quasi-reactionary cultural expressions [*After Willem de Kooning*]— called postmodernity—which, while resisting neat definition, is clearly a departure from De Kooning and modernist optimism. But this is where it gets complicated. Modernist art was the norm-defying quest for freedom. It rejected the bourgeois commodification and academic reification of art, and it thrived on opposition and revolt. The difficulty of postmodernity, as Hal Foster puts it, is how to "break with a program that makes a value of crisis."[2]

The complex nature of postmodernity and its testy relationship with the past is distilled in Levine's appropriation of de Kooning. A charcoal retracing of AbEx gold makes for a somber reflection on a past that can no longer be. But Levine is also subversive. The bareness of the media with the clout of de Kooning gives the drawing the feel of a novice's half-finished study of an Old Master, as if Levine were learning how to properly render the female figure by studying de Kooning's method. On the other hand, Levine's academic formalism clearly fails AbEx standards of authenticity. So Levine's drawing claims on one level to be a study of de Kooning's emotional experience, but on another level contravenes the logic of de Kooning's style. By foregrounding an inherent contradiction in copying a de Kooning, Levine brilliantly frames a critical evaluation of the AbEx thesis of authentic artistic expression.

The subject of Levine's work is not just Abstract Expressionism but the crisis of modern art in general. After decades of different manifestoes and opposing schools, modernity did not converge on a single theory of art. Instead, its several schools eventually lost energy, and their divergences cast doubt on the common doctrine among them, faith in an objective language of art. Levine, and postmodern art in general, are deceiving themselves if they try to adopt their predecessors' faith in art. Unsure of what to do next, postmodernist art can only strive, with Levine, to apply more and better critical analysis. But is criticism in art really the way forward? Inquiring into the root cause of the crisis of modern art uncovers not a lack of critical reflection but a philosophically groomed ignorance of art's language.

---

2   Hal Foster, *The Anti-Aesthetic: Essays on Postmodern Culture* (Port Townsend: Bay Press, 1983), ix.

Much as Levine's postmodernity preserves elements of modernism (reason-based criticism) while leaving other elements to history, German philosopher Jurgen Habermas explains how postmodernity cannot, and should not, reject all of modernity. He distinguishes between "cultural modernity" and the "project of Enlightenment"[3]—modernism's revolutionary naiveté from the serious philosophical project that drives it. Though the enlightenment project certainly helped form cultural modernity, the end of cultural modernity, which was inevitable and has already taken place, does not necessarily imply the end of the enlightenment project. The oppositional aesthetic that saw itself as the fulfillment of history, the materialistic solipsism of atomized individuals, the consequences of bureaucratic capitalism—these are cultural effects that can be distinguished from the enlightenment project that was (in part) their cause. In other words, the essential "modernist project" has not run its course; it has only been pruned. But what exactly is this noble heart of modernity that must be pruned and saved? For Habermas, it is not some utopian, historically-extricated ideal but has its roots in the Western philosophical tradition.

The "project of Enlightenment" aims to reorganize everyday life according to reason. It is the effort to open all tradition, all norms to the light of rational discourse. The central method is to found each of the various fields of knowledge onto their proper plane, their own "inner logic."[4] The fruits of the resultant accelerated specialization is then expropriated to the roots of society. We see the virtues of this separateness when we remember early modern Europe before the Enlightenment. Culture was beholden to the Church. Copernicus and Galileo's findings were suppressed because they challenged Church authority, and religious wars made politics a matter of theological doctrine. In part, the enlightenment project is an attempt to free the sciences and the state from the whims of outside agendas, ecclesiastical or otherwise. Hence, the political question evolved from "Who has God put in authority?" to "What is the fairest way to govern humans?" And the sciences developed their own academies to protect and encourage free inquiry.

As Habermas emphasizes, the ultimate purpose is for this specialization to be expropriated to all of society and not locked away in reified, esoteric academic vocabularies.[5] Such is the method of the enlightenment project; its overall thrust is to beat back the shadows of tradition and authoritarianism with the words of Monet: "I can only draw what I see."[6] The anatomy of modernism thus displayed, Habermas shows

---

[3]   [2] Jürgen Habermas, "Modernity- An Incomplete Project," in *The Anti-Aesthetic: Essays on Postmodern Culture*, ed. Hal Foster (Port Townsend: Bay Press, 1983), 8.

[4]   Habermas, 9.

[5]   Habermas, 9.

[6]   Eric Protter, *Painters on Painting* (Mineola: Dover Publications, 1997), 140.

how certain reactions to modernism fail because they misdiagnose modernism. The way forward is to learn from the excesses of modernist culture, but to preserve and carry on the project of free inquiry on the basis of reason alone. Postmodernity does not need to return to tradition or authoritarianism just because it better understands the difficulty of determining "what I see."

Habermas' historical framework helpfully complicates a simplistic modernist-postmodernist duality. Understanding modernity and postmodernity as diverse responses to an unfolding Enlightenment question allows a method of analyzing productive and counterproductive art attitudes in postmodernity.

As a serious player in the enlightenment project, Western art had to determine itself just as physics did. It had to discover its own inner logic. This tripped the wire for much philosophical reflection on what art is and corresponding narratives to show art's progress toward this self-realization. Thus, Greenberg drew new attention to Renaissance Mannerism and El Greco, Cezanne, and Pollock as pioneers toward art's "ineluctable flatness",[7] the inner logic of pictorial art that no other art shared. For Hegel, art was no more than embodied content, and artists are free to employ art to whatever ends they see fit. He narrates the strange formalist wars that color its history as the plot development in a *bildungsroman*, or story of self-discovery.[8] Across the art scene, illusionism lost favor, increasingly seen as disingenuous, a sort of lie. Enormous pressure was felt to discover an art form faithful to itself, not just because illusionism became linked to the bourgeois, but because it was not the essential, stripped-bare logic found in a tube of paint and a stretched canvas. It did not answer the question of the enlightenment project.

In contrast to all of these approaches to the enlightenment project's challenge to art, Kandinsky offers, in my opinion, the most sensible distillation of art's essence. In his treatise *On the Spiritual in Art*, the Russian Abstract Expressionist painter refocuses the discussion of art's essence from its material expressions to the human "inner need" that causes them.[9] Abandoning attempts to explain art solely in terms of a succession of isolated artworks, he enriches art by re-rooting it in the human creator that brought it about. Kandinsky is certainly a formalist. The treatise features his thoughts on what he believes to be the objective quality of certain colors, besides an overall defense of

---

[7]   Clement Greenberg, "Modernist Painting," in John O'Brian, ed., *Clement Greenberg: The Collected Essays and Criticism, Volume 4: Modernism with a Vengeance* (Chicago: University of Chicago Press, 1993), 87.

[8]   Arthur Danto, After the End of Art: Contemporary Art and the Pale of History (Princeton: Princeton U.P., 1997)

[9]   Wassily Kandinsky, *Concerning the Spiritual in Art*, trans. M.T.H. Sadler (New York: Dover Publications, 1977) 26.

abandoning illusion to unlock the as yet unexplored "pure artistic composition."[10] In this sense, it would seem possible to group him with Greenberg and Hegel's attempt to discover art's inner logic in terms of material form. But Kandinsky resists this easy categorization. His theories of pure artistry aside, whose modernist ring sounds only too clearly, Kandinsky repeatedly affirms the primacy of the inner need to the artistic act. The artist is not a slave working toward a definable, material, or psychological goal, like flatness or self-consciousness. The artist is rather a prophet that hears a truth of humanity or the world, which is irreducible to words. He uses the art form to express this inner need, which is his duty to communicate to humanity. Good art is faithful to the message; bad art merely responds to the formalist standards of the day. The first modern artist to paint pure abstraction, Kandinsky is responding to those critics who thought art had to represent something. But clearly, he would find that form of avant-gardism that rejected illusionism for the sake of rejection, equally superficial and arbitrary. For Kandinsky, a good artist uses form to respond to his spiritual sense; a shallow artist responds to form, deaf to the spiritual.

Retooling Kandinsky for today feels like surrendering reason to the comforts of tradition. Is there such a thing as a spiritual realm? Isn't he overdramatizing the artist's role? And yet, his voice is only one of many who highlight artists' prophetic duty to society.[11] The religious vocabulary, though integral to Kandinsky's spirituality, is not necessary to articulate his concept of the mysterious nature of the art act. Karsten Harries, the atheist philosopher, explains the same thing in non-spiritual terms:

> If modern art is not to be supplanted by Kitsch, artists must know how to listen and must try to reveal what it is that calls man. This is not to say that we must return to the tradition;… But to say that God does not call man is not to say that man is not called at all. We may no longer know our place in the world, yet the world still speaks to us. A geometric figure, a crack in a concrete wall, neon reflections on wet pavement, melting snow, a wrinkled skirt, the motion of a hand—we have to listen carefully to hear this language at all.[12]

What can be said about a crack in a concrete wall that cannot be said by the material

---

[10] Kandinsky, 30.

[11] See Jeff Koons, "Full Fathom 5," in *Theories and Documents of Contemporary Art: A Sourcebook of Artists' Writings*, 2nd ed. Kristine Stiles and Peter Selz (Berkeley: University of California Press, 2012), 438-439.

[12] Karsten Harries, The Meaning of Modern Art: A Philosophical Interpretation (Evanston: Northwestern U. P., 1968), 159.

sciences? We can learn the cause of the crack, how fast it happened; we can measure its dimensions or even analyze our emotional response to the crack as a function of wounds of a psychological past. Clearly, Harries is not speaking of these. There is something else in that crack that the physical and social sciences cannot explain. It is the particular way it speaks not just to one person, but to mankind. For Kandinsky, this is the spiritual dimension. Harries does not go so far as to name it. But both agree that, unlike the sciences, the thing that calls man to produce art cannot be grasped and analyzed—it must be received.

These two philosophers of art suggest that art's proper logic cannot be reduced to form (as Greenberg would have it) or psychology (as Hegel) because form and psychology are graspable, analytical regions of human knowledge. Since great art responds to and engages with the nonmaterial call of man, art's inner logic must be categorically different from the sciences. We will combine Kandinsky's "inner need" and Harries' "call" in the term, "art impulse." The art impulse is an aesthetic response to an objective reality the sciences cannot explain.

The enlightenment project's protection of autonomous disciplines spurred unprecedented progress for the hard sciences, psychology and others that continues today. Art seemed to be riding the same wave. The period from 1880 to 1950 houses perhaps the most extraordinary explosion of artistic creativity in history. But, by the dawn of postmodernity, it was clear that this energy could not be centralized and codified into a common language and method. Where the enlightenment project successfully re-organized the material sciences, it placed art in a dilemma. Because the enlightenment project failed to develop a dignified category for nonmaterial objectivity, art was required to account for the art impulse in terms of material objectivity. If everything can eventually be resolved into "clear and distinct," objects cleanly laid before an all-discerning subject, then the inner need of the artist cannot be coordinated to some truth beyond reason's grasp. That thing that calls man cannot be anything more than the irrational echoes of an unhealthy psyche. The artist cannot be a priest, mediating spiritual nourishment to the starving masses. The artistic impulse instead gets tied down to earth in one of two possible ways: it is reduced either to media-research or to criticism or to political activity. Notably, physical research belongs properly to science, criticism to sociology, and political activism is an application of political science. But remember that the enlightenment project calls for a rational re-organization of the several fields of knowledge according to their own inner logic. If suppressing the nonmaterial logic of the art impulse forces art to employ research-logic or social critic-logic, art as a field of knowledge will collapse. Denied an autonomous language, the forces of the project of Enlightenment will break up the institution and divvy its several contributions and experts into their proper fields of knowledge based on the sort of logic they employ.

The first desublimation of the artist's inner necessity explains art in terms of media research. This desublimation owes much of its energy to Greenberg, who interpreted the enlightenment project's implications for art, not (as we have here) as re-establishing art on the inner logic of the art impulse, but as re-establishing each specific art on the inner logic of its medium. He explained the frenzied creativity of modernist painting in materialist terms: the great geniuses were approaching the Enlightenment desiderata, truth to medium. Greenberg caused a great deal of excitement because he offered formal criteria that could make sense of impossibly heterogeneous paintings: Cezanne was a genius; the Fauves a distraction. The goal of painting is to engineer flatness.

Greenberg retains an awe for artistic creation even as he reduces it to media research, but the artists who picked up his theory found a scientific posture more transparent to the scientific aims of art. In a 1960 lecture, AbEx painter Frank Stella explains his art in an engineer's idiom thusly:

> There were two problems which had to be faced. One was spatial and the other methodological. In the first case… the obvious answer was symmetry—make it the same all over. The question still remained, though, of how to do this in depth. A symmetrical image or configuration symmetrically placed on an open ground is not balanced out in the illusionistic space. The solution I arrived at… forces illusionistic space out of the painting at constant intervals by using a regulated pattern. The remaining problem was simply to find a method of paint application which followed and complemented the design solution. This was done by using the house painter's technique and tools."[13]

You do not need to understand Stella's compositional dilemma to pick up on his cool, distant researcher's attitude. He doesn't want us to imagine his psychological state expressed in concentric boxes, nor find in it a social critique. He is merely a researcher looking for solutions to his occupational challenges. We will not endeavor here to make an argument about the nature of Stella's work as flatly scientific based on his writing about his art. The point is not about the actual art, but about the language in which art is understood. Here, an artist explains his art impulse in terms of a researcher's perseverance and an engineer's wit. He sounds like a creative architect working out his

---

[13] Frank Stella, "The Pratt Lecture," in *Theories and Documents of Contemporary Art: A Sourcebook of Artists' Writings*, 2nd ed. Kristine Stiles and Peter Selz (Berkeley: University of California Press, 2012), 136-137.

concept with industrial materials, or an engineer tinkering with a machine.

The ramifications of Greenberg's exaltation of media research extended beyond Abstract Expressionism. Minimalism's great expositor, Donald Judd, exploits this understanding of art to endorse otherwise legitimate aesthetic goals. In his seminal essay "Specific Objects," Judd's aesthetic attraction to Minimalism ("power," "oneness," "lack of duplicity") are an after-thought.[14] His larger thesis uses Greenberg's truth-to-medium to claim painting and sculpture are exhausted. Painters have felt out all their limits, since "the rectangular plane is given a life span. The simplicity required to emphasize the rectangle limits the arrangements possible within it." But with Minimalism, "the several limits of painting are no longer present. A work can be as powerful as it can be thought to be."[15] Judd speaks of the limits of media as inhibitors of artistic creativity and characterizes creativity as frontier-exploration. Painting has been figured out, so artists will move to three-dimensional work because the limits have not yet been discovered. Whereas it is conceivable that painters can fruitfully respond to their art impulse even after Malevich's black squares, Judd characterizes art as media research to claim that it is impossible. Judd speaks of painting like it is Euclidean geometry. Artists may paint if they like, but it has all been done before; there is no more room for creativity. The real artists, the real explorers will find freedom in Minimalism, whose undiscovered limits and manifold possibilities can be explored like the undetermined frontier of general relativity.

Explaining the art impulse in terms of media research has benefits. It places art on a plane of unquestionable objectivity, which generates schools of thought and rigorous research. However, art within these boundaries cannot explain why such research is worth pursuing. It hides its mystery in the objective lab coat, but, since the sciences exhaust the domain of physical research, the media research desublimation can only be seen as obfuscating the clarity demanded by the enlightenment project.

The second desublimation of the inner necessity is criticism. Rather than following some vague creative-intuitive sense, the artist's role is to drag an unwilling humanity out of the cave, exposing and calling out hypocrisies or contradictions. This has two main expressions: art criticism and social criticism. Art criticism is best illustrated in Duchamp in the 1920s. [*Fountain*] Duchamp's work is not transcendent; it is not trying to be beautiful. Rather, it plays on this very expectation for art (which Duchamp saw as bourgeois fantasy), making a show out of a public who will nevertheless stare at a toilet

---

[14] Donald Judd, "Specific Objects," in *Theories and Documents of Contemporary Art: A Sourcebook of Artists' Writings*, 2nd ed. Kristine Stiles and Peter Selz (Berkeley: University of California Press, 2012), 138-140.

[15] Judd, 138-139.

to find some glint of artistic personality or ethereal beauty. The fountain is not just viewed. It is viewing. It stares the public right back in the face, like a mirror, to show them who they are and what they are doing. This sort of art functions like an examination of conscience, like an American reading de Tocqueville's *Democracy in America*. Only, it is delivered via art, so it has a "meta" quality about it. The enlightenment project lent art as art criticism particular urgency, since the experts are responsible for discovering the inner logic of their field. It became an occupational necessity to reflect seriously on the process of art, the difference between a work of art and an object. But it seems this duty was better handled by art critics and art philosophers, who can be trained in these dilemmas and concepts without any artistic ability at all. In fact, embodied art criticism like Duchamp's may bring art criticism to the masses, who would otherwise not read an essay on "what makes art art," but it does seem to rely on an expository essay in order for the lesson to be unlocked.

Perhaps the most highly regarded function of art today is socio-cultural criticism. Art has found a safe niche here, perhaps because the accelerating forces of globalization and technology shape and reshape the human experience with such speed that we are in need of more self-reflection than sociology can produce. Artists become sociological sages whose art is expropriated to the culture by trained art critics intelligent enough to catch the social commentary packed into the work of art. Lorna Simpson's *Five Day Forecast* is a fantastic critique of representations of the black experience in the US. Darting back and forth over the five figures, to the words below that seem to be describing the experience of the photographed woman, to the weekdays above each picture where her head should be, our eyes try to interpret what the black female artist must be saying about the difficulties of the black female experience. Does she feel locked into a monotone work week? Does she feel misunderstood? Does it mean anything that Monday and Thursday's arms are folded differently than the rest? Is the white smock contrasted with the black body meant to reflect the text style, white text on a black background? We scour her body for signs of her perspective, but the folded arms and slightly differentiated posture reveal no clear diagnosis. But this is exactly the point. We are the viewers misdiagnosing, misinterpreting. As we struggle to find the key to the artist's message, the 'mis-' words seem to describe our frustration with the work. With an evocation of art gallery space, achieved by the text panels that accompany the neatly spaced prints, Simpson frames our experience trying to understand the experience of her body through art. With this interpretive key, she can lodge her critique. As a black female artist in the 1990s, her art experiences new, more subtle forms of marginalization. Her art may be shown at the same gallery as other artists, but where other artists are free to express anything, her art can only be seen in the light of her marginalized social category.

By virtue of being a black female artist, she is restricted to making art that represents the black female experience. And the proof of this is in our own reading of her artwork: we turned a neutral, regular portrayal of a black body into some critique of racial marginalization. Our eagerness to avoid past marginalization ironically censures Simpson's artistic vocabulary. The culture's history of domination determines Simpson's future subordination to a fixed role in the same way that she organizes a photographical history of a body, a "forecast." The mode is new, but the marginalization is the same. Black women's intellects, their humanity are conscripted to the service of representation by virtue of their black and female bodies.

Simpson's work is brilliant, but its aesthetic quality is, like Duchamp's, critical. Remember that, for Kandinsky and Harries, the art impulse is open. It requires receptivity to something we cannot grasp, or the articulation of something we cannot put in words. But Simpson's work is a closed-loop, like a dictionary definition. Yes, her work refers to things outside itself: the viewer, the artist, and cultural habits are all implicated by the artwork. But all of these cohere into a self-sufficient whole. The work refers only to definite, materialist terms. The exploration of mystery, essential to art, is replaced with the riddling obscurity of an—ultimately—definite message.

So we have uncovered two desublimations of the art impulse in modern and contemporary art: research and criticism. Without a serious intellectual framework to hang it on, artists' art impulse had to be expressed in a culturally-approved vernacular. And this vernacular is the language of material science (again, I include the social sciences in this category). However, the cultural atmosphere, still devoted to the enlightenment project, requires art to isolate its own inner logic and specialize within these boundaries. Now, the gravity of modern art's dilemma shines clearly. After committing to material logic, it finds that there are no more tickets to the party. We can look down the road and see that any form of material knowledge art tries to speak can be more clearly articulated by an existing field. Sociology is better equipped to research and communicate the cultural biases of a patriarchal society or the poverties of a Western lens. The philosophy of art seems the best institution through which to reflect on the nature of art. Even art criticism has grown into something of a field, as written essays about art trends become ever more indispensable for appreciating art. If all these fields are advancing their research with increasing rigor, it isn't clear what exactly the artist can legitimately 'research' that isn't his own subjectivity (which would probably be better worked out in a session with a trained psychiatrist). And all that is left for art to do is politics—educating the people on true justice.

The work of Rirkrit Tiravanija [Untitled (Free)] and Thomas Hirschhorn [Bataille Monument] are among the more successful examples of political art. The success of these artworks depends on their ability to spark political or social awareness. Art, according to this tendency, is a sort of educator in civic virtue. Tiravanija's art, rather than foregrounding his own authorship, creates a space for human encounter by preparing food in his gallery space and making the public's free consumption of food his artistic exhibit. Theoretically, the exhibit helps reintegrate separate social spheres in the same way that it integrates the old dividing line between art producer and consumer, which underwrites the logic of modern museums. Tiravanija is as much a producer as are the people who wander into his exhibit—without these participants, there is no exhibit. At the very least, his art calls to attention the present reality of social distinctions. The problem with Tiravanija's work is not that it tries to reintegrate society's several threads, but that it abdicates artistic privilege for this end. His work achieves the titillating sensation of revealing what is veiled, and for this reason it strikes us as "enlightening" or "honest." Tiravanija has boldly exposed art's Wizard of Oz hoax. Participants can physically inhabit the old hiding place from which artists used to spin their myths to exercise authority over the people. He claims to disabuse the people of artistic privilege and to divide the spoils among the people, like a Robin Hood stealing heroically from some aesthetic despot. He achieves his democratic purpose, but sells out art to do so. Who is the artist? Everyone, Tiravanija seems to say. What is the art? All of life can be art. Art, diffused everywhere like this, lacks the rational substance requisite for a legitimate form of human knowledge.

At first blush, Levine's piece appears to be an artistic reflection of Habermas' enlightened postmodernity. She neither opposes modernity nor pretends that it didn't happen, but urges its critical evaluation. Could there be a more reasonable response? But as we have seen, her critical approach, while remaining valuable as a critical reflection on art history, is a dead end for art. Rather than answering the enlightenment question, Levine rehearses the same critical reflex that motivated Duchamp in the 1920s. So her "After All" series, appropriations of past artists of which "After De Kooning" is a part, only place her after modernity with a touch of irony. By trying to critically undress past artists, she makes tired, modernist claims about the function of art, and sidesteps the enlightenment question altogether.

It is, in part, a failure of art discourse that leads art to other domains of knowledge to brand its legitimacy. It is impossible, when unpacking a piece of art, not to touch every other aspect of human life. However, this does not prevent art writers from exploring the essential nature of art. And given the paralyzing effect of art's present self-ignorance, executed by a cultural blindness to the nonmaterial, the need for art writers willing to deal in the mysterious is increasingly felt. Art has tried to avoid this uncertainty, which seems so improper for a field that wants to establish itself as a form of knowledge. It has done so through mimicking research and criticism. But it has quickly exhausted these and found that they are not art's essence. We cannot be tempted any longer from art's proper realm of knowledge—art discourse must fully immerse itself in this mystery, sharpen its senses to its quiet voice.

Within Digital Culture:
The Hyperimage Perspective on Art and Criticism

Alfredo Cramerotti

In this paper I debate for institutions of culture – including art criticism – to become more 'expanded' in their strategy to affect society. I argue for the "age of virtuality" and the Internet not merely as distribution channel or market place manifestations. Rather, I see these as the rationale for, and configuration of cultural work.

There is a need to coordinate, if not align, visual art values with an expanded public sphere that embraces image making as the default choice for relation-building, professional-orienting and personal development. Those deputized to the production, presentation and critical evaluation of visual culture need to figure out how to reconsider artistic and analytical models.

Our concern should be how to make art criticism relevant for a generation for which image-value now resides not in content type and quality of the presentation but rather in velocity (of generating), intensity (of impact), and speed (of circulation), creating a condition of contemporary living where reality is produced, and not only reflected, by images and interaction with screens.

We need to position art criticism within this new context where the contemporary attitude towards the image—a performance, or rather, set of behaviors that I call 'the hyperimage'—shows that visual practice precedes theory; demonstrates that we increasingly learn by doing. This, I argue, can be equally disorientating and liberating.

I begin this paper by stating a belief. I firmly believe that the institutions of culture—including art criticism—need to become more 'expanded' in their definitions and perceptions of what constitutes art. This would involve their following a process undertaken by art practitioners over the past two centuries where painting and sculpting has expanded to include photography and film, and then television and mass media visualization, moving on to scanning processes and automated (also autonomous) visual renderings. My contention is that institutions and art critics as well as visual authors must embrace the "age of virtuality" in their strategy as well as their expression.

I agree with Hanno Rauterberg[1] that criticism is, at its core, a catalyst. It must identify points of conflict or tension, name differences, isolate themes and formulate theses in order to foster a broader understanding of art and the world. The art critic has to open domains of meaning, rather than decree meaning. This would mean that the institutions and people deputized to the production, presentation and critical evaluation of visual culture have to figure out how to reconsider artistic and operational models. There is a need to at least coordinate, if not align, the values purposed by visual art. The expanded public sphere now embraces image making as the default choice for identity shaping and determination, personal development, and governance strategy. We need to acknowledge that cultural expression is just one function amongst many.

The art critic cannot afford to disregard within her or his practice this expanded public sphere, spawned of the digital lives we all lead. Audiences of 'prosumers' no longer need to be physically present in a gallery, museum, auditorium or biennale to experience image-based cultural outputs. They no longer limit themselves to the act of reading a magazine or newspaper to access those domains of meaning I was mentioning earlier. Thus prosumers—simultaneously producers, distributors and consumers—are no longer bound to the personal interaction of paying for admission to see a show, accessing art content in various formats or attending a festival or event.

So the questions are, paraphrasing the words of Omar Kholeif:[2]

- How does the commodification of our most shared space, the Internet, affect not only works of art and curatorial practices – i.e. the making, organization and experience of them – but also art criticism itself, i.e. the critical reflection, revelation of criteria, and assessment of those works and practices?
- How is the democratization of art writing through the web and virtual platforms transforming the traditional art-historical approach to art criticism?
- Is this a true democratization, a dilution of a serious discipline, or both?

It has been proposed that the alignment can start from reaching a better balance between audience experience and critical assessment combining these with initiatives like crowd-sourcing evaluation such as the Tripadvisor / Amazon click mentality, based on "the more, the better" principle.   I have taken a personal decision not to rate or review hotels, restaurants, stationery suppliers, clothes stores or car rentals, but that is my choice. The times I've done some research in advance based on other people's views, invariably I

[1]   Rauterberg, Hanno, 2004. Critic's Turn. *BE Magazin*. No.11: 'Critique', Spring Issue.
[2]   Kholeif, Omar, 2013. The Curator's New Medium. *Art Monthly*. No. 363, pp. 9-12.

set myself expectations that exceeded the reality of the experience. I have therefore stopped using the service or providing customer feedback. It's not that it doesn't work; it's more that for every visit I make to a coffee shop, or every printer cartridge I buy, I get asked to fill in a 'quick survey' and provide feedback to improve the service. Perhaps controversially, I have decided that life's too short for writing reviews about everything.

Back to the matter. If we eliminate crowd-sourcing opinions, how do we coordinate the value of criticism with an expanded public realm—offline and online? How do we make sense, for instance, of our contemporary free-flow attitude towards the image i.e. how do the relations, behaviors, performances, beliefs, and mediations we associate with images and art affect us? And how—in turn—do our actions affect these?

Let us take image making as a metaphor for visual arts in general. Today's environment is made up of the interaction of creative practices, technological developments, and social bonds.[3] Artistic production, in particular, is increasingly dispersed across various formats—exhibition, discussion, publishing, performance, and publicity. I contend that there is even a certain tendency to 'reverse' the creative process. Let me explain this in concrete terms. Pre-Internet, an artist, curator or writer started with an idea for an essay, artwork or exhibition, and then proceeded with extensive research. The gathered material—knowledge, people, thoughts around and about it—were ultimately used by the artist to sharpen the artwork through a narrative presented to the public.   Today, almost the opposite is frequently happening. There is a clear sense of privileging cultural contextualization and dispersal over artistic making, writing or fabrication.

Artists, specifically, use the available online distribution and diffusion channels creatively as sketchpad and as feedback system, rather than simply as circulation tools.[4] A visual author starts from an observation of the works, data, visual clues, references and information available. These are mediated by reflections that occur to her or him often while doing other things or engaging in other activities. From this 'magma' the artist compiles physical, digital or mental lists, indexes, classifications, clusters of data – until slowly some patterns emerge. I find myself frequently in this mode. That arrangement becomes the core of the work, its nucleus. This is then shaped in one or more formats, channeled through a text, artwork, exhibition or cultural program.   In contemporary

[3] Cornell, Lauren and Halter, Ed, eds., 2015. *Mass Effect: Art and the Internet in the Twenty-First Century*. Cambridge, MA and London: MIT Press.

[4] Bell-Smith, Michael, 2006. *Net Aesthetics 2.0 Conversation* [transcript]. New York City. Discussants: Cory Arcangel, Michael Bell-Smith, Michael Connor, Caitlin Jones, Marisa Olson, and Wolfgang Staehle. Moderator: Lauren Cornell. In: Cornell, Lauren and Halter, Ed, eds. 2015. *Mass Effect: Art and the Internet in the Twenty-First Century*. Cambridge, MA and London: MIT Press, pp.99-106.

cultural production, practice definitely precedes theory.

It follows that every work is permanently in a beta state, never resembles a finished output, and affects equally the previous and the next manifestation. It is an approach intrinsically related to the web structure, but the results are not necessarily digital. In fact, the impact of image making can be grasped more in the underlying structure and organization of the work of art than in the use of digital means. Digitalization has transformed visual arts into performing arts, where the performance itself is not a finished product but more of a score that is interpreted differently every time. This, incidentally, is not an entirely new thing. It was common before the age of professionalization of the arts. The history of human culture in music, dance, or cooking for that matter, can tell us something in this regard.

Certainly, learning by doing is the typical approach of the digital native, those 'native speakers' of the language of the Internet.[5] It is an attitude that embodies the concept of pragmatism implicit in the idea of the prosumer described earlier—producing content by adapting, modifying, circulating and re-contextualizing what is receive. Every kind of cultural practice has been touched by the Internet, first as a tool and then as something that affects us in a broader sense. The fact that every web browser allows to select, save or send an image on its pages, and that practically every communication device sold today has built-in tools to edit and change images, enables the image, and in turn visual art, to perform as a cultural (and critical) staple of life. The web becomes an environment through which we relate in many ways (personal, professional, social, economical, political), and it is the image that makes this happen, regardless of how we actually generate the image in the first place.

Progressively then, artists and art writers are finding new ways of expressing their creativity outside of prescribed behaviors, whether by critically appraising the system in which the Internet works, or by re-contextualizing their 'being' into their work. I will unravel this by discussing a term that helped me to realize this fact, and to make more sense of what I am doing as an art critic. This term is the hyperimage.[6] It describes the contemporary attitude towards the image, or rather, the set of behaviors through which an image circulates, and through which we—metaphorically speaking—circulate with it.

This attitude is equally disorientating and liberating. To cope with the disorientation, and reap the rewards of the liberation, we have to shift perspective, take a lateral step,

---

[5] Prensky, Marc, 2001. Digital Natives, Digital Immigrants Part 1. In: *On the Horizon*. MCB University Press, Vol.9, No.5, pp.1-6. Available at: https://www.marcprensky.com/writing/Prensky%20-%20Digital%20Natives,%20Digital%20Immigrants%20-%20Part1.pdf. [Accessed 2 March 2018].

[6] Cramerotti, Alfredo, 2018. *Forewords: Hyperimages and Hyperimaging*. Imola: Manfredi Edizioni.

and consider not the visual output, the product, the object (or version of it), but the very 'performance' of it. The hyperimage is therefore a proposition of a type of behavior towards the image, and its critique, that privileges fragmentation, indeterminacy, and heterogeneity and that emphasizes process or performance rather than the finished object. And this means that how to assess that movement, that flux, the very in-betweenness of it, must then become the focus of the art critic.

I focus therefore on the ways in which our visual relations affect the concepts of art and culture, more than on the actual production or organization. According to Hito Steyerl, image-value resides not in content type and quality (as in size or pixel resolution of an image) but rather in velocity (of generating), intensity (of impact), and speed (of circulation), creating a condition of contemporary living where reality is produced, and not only reflected, by images and screens.[7] It's a fascinating argument, albeit highly speculative. It can be easily dismissed as a theoretical plaything, but I actually agree with the notion. I'm keen to stress though, that it's not only about image-value, but evaluation–, assessment–, and criticism-value too. I argue that what we ask art criticism to be—a catalyst, an instrument (not itself the content) for drawing limits, naming differences, isolating themes, formulating theses, and ultimately opening domains of meaning, is to be found in recognizing and assessing the performance of the image (and visual art), more than in its content. Drawing upon the possibilities of the journey, not of the destination.

This focus on the "performance of the image" reveals a tension between the ubiquitous and 'formless' visual attitude that we adopt in our lives, and the struggle to contextualize, control, author and purposefully use the resulting images. We are in a situation where we cannot determine, nor even suggesting, how an image is, or will be, used, for what purpose and under what conditions. We cannot even demand such clarity, especially as art critics.   Equally, we no longer have an idea of the circumstances that generated an image (human or machine-made), let alone the original intentions behind it. That's why my argument focuses not on the final output, but on the version, the iteration, and the excursion.

Basically every image that we receive acts on us and affects our behavior. Our reaction changes the world around us, and that, in turn, re-mediates the image's meaning. The collapse of digital and physical space and the infinite reproducibility of digital materials are the set of conditions through which we, as critics, confront a new reality and

---

[7] Steyerl, Hito, 2013. Too Much World: Is the Internet Dead? *e-flux journal* #49. [online] November 2013. Available at: http://www.e-flux.com/journal/49/60004/too-much-world-is-the-internet-dead/. [Accessed 15 January 2017].

ontology of the image and its behavior, and this then channels and affects our decisions. To reiterate, it is this 'performance' that I term hyperimage. It is this performance that I contend we should tackle as critics.

Given the incomprehensible number of images we are subjected to and interact with on a daily basis, we can say that we are facing a sort of 'aesthetics of uncertainty' regarding the impact, politics and philosophy of the image. This uncertainty is fostered by the digital, and it is probably its most significant feature and achievement. It renders our attitude towards an image functional, rather than cognitive or critical. Visual agency and 'numerical' mediation do something to us as viewers, authors, and users.

When I say that the image is 'performative,' I am referring to what images do to us as much as what we do to them. The performance therefore is enacted in two ways. Firstly, by the very act of generating images throughout a networked environment, the nature of anything displayed on a monitor is performative as it implies a complicated structure and a process, which is both immediate and ephemeral. Secondly, it is performative as it continuously changes its reference points and cultural hinges. Not only is the idea of what constitutes 'the world' tied to processes of image production and circulation that may or may not induce us to take action, but it changes the formats used for such action-generating systems (a case in point is the Instagram square format, upon which many artists and other art professionals now base their visual output).

It's not just about the formats either. Technical mundanities such as availability of power grid, navigation options, screen resolution, size formats, backlit screens, and filtering opportunities are built-in conditions that affect our behavior towards and through the image. We are witnessing the change from images presented as visualization (result of intention), to images as interaction (result of agency and mediation), affecting our awareness as 'bodied' and visual entities, embedded in our physical and virtual environment. Such a transition also changes our perception of the 'finished' and its definitive meaning. It is as if the performative aspect of image making in the media age (which I take as being the modern day manifestation of the visual arts) is only capable of producing process-based, not outcome-based work and results. It is not what a picture is 'of' but rather what it 'does' in the timeframe and spatial situation within which we engage with it. And where it is going. Smoothly, instantaneously, unapologetically; knowing that our outcomes will be subject to the same treatment instantly.

In closing, I want to underline the role I envisage for art criticism within this triangulation between the appearance (the manifestation, the environment in which it takes place), the code (the instruction, its translation), and the experience (the impact, the multiplicity of meaning). In this context I see the status of art criticism as being less about producing a certain outcome and having a certain position on culture, and more about setting the scene and embodying the development.

We can roughly equate the agency of art criticism with being prepared for something, a "conditional readiness,"[8] which implies that one's understanding of a message is not limited to what to do in response to it, but is expanded to include what one is ready to do if certain circumstances arise. It is more an unconscious preparation for an exploration rather than a conscious setting off for a journey. This is about art criticism at its core. Meaning is produced neither by the 'sender' nor by the 'receiver' of the message; it is formed by a readiness to relate to external factors, in terms of 'performability.' What the hyperimage attitude fosters is a context where we interpret and 'make sense' of art by what it does, the functional aspect. The agency of art criticism therefore arises less from the act of contextualizing and interpreting what we see, and more from the internalized suggestions for possible actions to take.

---

[8]   MacKay, Donald M., 1969. *Information, Mechanism and Meaning.* Cambridge, MA and London: MIT Press.

Total Control and Censorship:
Towards a New Humanity?

Bernhard Serexhe

Whereas not so long ago digital forms of communication were seen as the hope for new forms of democratic participation, they have recently been converted and perverted into ideal door openers for the perfect control of billions of people. Being at the mercy of overwhelmingly powerful authorities of control and censorship has become the conditio humana, the basic condition of our culture and society. We have become accustomed to this situation, just as we are not deterred by the myriads of video cameras we encounter on the way to work or on our way back home. And this resignation paired with our love of ease and selfishness has the potential to invite new forms of totalitarianisms to install a new society with a pre-programmed divide between an elite of hyper-agile information users and a broad mass of interactive consumers restlessly zapping futile audio-visual products and services offered at dumping prices in order to control all of their practices and preferences. This re-coding of humanity could result in the worst of all totalitarianisms, that of a brave new world, in which everyone will be content, well-informed of everything he or she should know in order to play a useful role in society, but remain ignorant of everything that does not need to be known, and consequently be permanently amused to the point of complete satiety.

> *"There is a real risk, that technological innovation slips out of civilian control."* Izumi Nakamitsu, UN Under-Secretary-General and High Representative for Disarmament Affairs

We have in fact crossed the threshold to a new age, although we have still to outgrow a previous, unfulfilled vision of the future. This vision, a legacy of the 19th century, promised happiness and prosperity as the fruit of the increased production of goods and free world markets that would regulate themselves for the good of one and all.

The age of hardware industrialization included among its chief characteristics two world wars and countless other armed conflicts that were no less bloody. In the course of these wars the industrialized nations consolidated their position of economic dominance in a period also distinctive for wreaking an environmental destruction that threatens the basis conditions for life on earth. While the industrial era was powered by the unshakeable belief in the wondrous powers of the machine, a different promise is being held out to the world at the dawn of this new age: happiness, prosperity and peace on earth thanks to networked information and global on-line communications.

Since three decades, we are drowned in a flood of promotion on the benefits of digitization. But today, it is high time to reflect on the risks of digitization as intensely as its benefits have been appraised and promoted. In the midst of this ceaselessly accelerating re-coding of all things, of the society, and of humanity itself, we urgently have to understand where this is leading us.

It has always been said that knowledge is power. Not a power among others, but just power in itself. But today, power is above all possessed by whoever controls the coding and analysis of data and the flow of information. One of the fundamental principles of digitization is that all accessible information processed by machines can be tapped, combined, analyzed, surveilled and manipulated, unhindered. The inherent substantial characteristic of digitization, its fundamental aim, so to say, is the algorithmic reduction of the analogue world into computable information and processes. The total control of information is thus inherent to digital technology. Making the world substantially computable has been understood as the basis of numerous benefits fur humankind. But at the same time, the logical consequence and potential of this is the inherent threat of the implementation of a perfectly controlled society.

The technical basis for this is given with the fact of the recent wide-ranging digitization of communications. On the background of the enthusiastic embracement of specially mobile communication, these days, billions of people all over the world are connected to each other. Billions of all kinds of content and data are generated every day and transmitted across the globe within seconds. Even while it is generated and even before it reaches its recipients, massive amounts of this data are intercepted in real-time by private companies and government agencies, checked, analyzed, categorized and then used for their purposes. As consumers we have accepted that it has become standard practice that we can not take advantage of special offers while online shopping or even while booking a plane or train ticket or hotel room without granting to access to our personal data. Very few people are aware that there are actually no cheap or free offers at all. We always pay with our data and with our most precious belonging, our privacy, as well as with our attention to the advertising that bombards us on every website.

Whereas not so long ago digital forms of communication were seen as the hope for new forms of democratic participation, they have recently been converted and perverted into ideal door openers for the perfect surveillance and control of billions of people. Those who use such devices are being used. This is the proviso to which we have all submitted in order to profit from these convenient forms of communication. Smartphones, and wearable computers, which accompany their users with every step they take, are invariably infected with spyware without their owners' consent or knowledge, and can be used as surveillance cameras and listening devices even when they are turned off. Our locations and movement profiles can be accessed at any time. Our browsing and consumer behavior, our contacts, our preferences, our pleasures, and our weaknesses can be analyzed and passed on at any time without us knowing or being asked. In our so-called democratic society, it has been imposed as a general rule that agreement to data mining is automatically granted by using these devices and their applications.

And yes, it is also correct that during the last years we have become aware of constant violations of privacy in the domain of electronic communications. But at the same time, it seems that we have realized and badly accepted our inability to chance this. Looking backwards, it seems that since the revelations by Edward Snowden, the world has changed in 2013. As a former NSA subcontractor Snowden had indeed collected and disclosed top secret NSA documents leading to the exposure of massive US surveillance practices. But this was by no means the beginning of a new era, and these far-reaching disclosures have been but the tip of an iceberg. Who ever wanted to know, could have known about these practices long time before. But awareness of disturbing things does not make live more comfortable. And comfort turns out to be the relevant driving force in our society. The special thing nudged by Snowdens revelations was that the factual deep data mining by state agencies became undisputedly public. And going public with what state authorities want to hide from publicity is denounced as a crime; publication of existing power structures is a scandal not only in totalitarian regimes.

The world has definitely not changed in 2013. But as citizens and as critical observers of the accelerating trend towards a controlled society, we have dared to understand that this trend is not only operated by state and public agencies, but that it has become the essential business model of a new economy which strikingly stimulated global stock markets. As consumers and observers we have been strictly adverted that data shall be the new raw material of the 21st century. And we have surrendered to this lucky tale without opposition. We have gradually accepted, that tapping, mining and smartly processing our own data was becoming the general key to controlling society.

This is compounded by the fact that in these days the world is gazing spellbound at the spectre of a new, populist conservatism that comes with a just as populist promise of salvation of an also new, but distinct kind of revolution. Two hundred years after the birth of Karl Marx, this new revolution is not rooted in the working class but summoned by the prophets and evangelists of the global economy. The assumption that this impending revolution of the world will lead to more wealth, more jobs and more freedom, as well as to more democracy and peace, has become the favourite credo of politicians of all parties who offer the prospect that the digital world order will come true for the benefit of all mankind: A highly desirable, technological revolution and incidentally, already a process in full swing, the irreversibility of which must even not be questioned.

That is how the dawn of a Fourth Industrial Revolution as a lucky consequence of the ongoing digitization was proclaimed in a January 2016 speech at the World Economic Forum in Davos, before the cheering representatives of the global economy: This much expected Revolution "*will fundamentally alter the way we live, work, and relate to one another. In its scale, scope and complexity, the transformation will be unlike anything humankind has experienced before.*" From the blurring of the boundaries between the physical, digital and biological spheres by means of artificial intelligence, robotics and the Internet of Things, by self-driving cars and new findings of biotechnology, it is expected to "*redefine human being*" and "*improve the wages and the entire world's standard of living*".[1]

Redefine human being! This is once again a strong word. But it does not tell in which direction human being will be redefined. In order to make this promised brave new world more attractive to the crowd, we, all of us as the general actors and subjects of this commencing new age, are being briefed under the headings of simplified buzzwords like "*Robotics*" and "*Artificial Intelligence*", which will make life so much more safe and comfortable. However, the intrusive all-party push for a comprehensive digitization and automation of all aspects of life, including the private sphere, leisure time, culture and the arts, is rarely beforehand scrutinized for its potential risks. What is expected to unfold into the most important chance and challenge of human future is until today not subject of a broader public discussion. Up to now, the general public is treated as if a political opinion formation was not fully desirable. And politicians of all camps and countries are incapable of doing anything except claiming that we must not miss the boat, in order to secure our future prosperity.

In this situation it is still fortunate that at least parts of the art world and some NGOs have initiated and taken over the necessarily critical reflection on what digitization, robotics and artificial intelligence actually could mean. Among the few

---

[1]   Klaus Schwab, *Die Vierte Industrielle Revolution*, translated from English by Petra Pyka and Thorsten Schmidt, Pantheon Verlag, München 2016.

excellent exhibitions on the subject, two are mentioned representatively: the exhibition *OPEN CODES. LIVING IN DIGITAL WORLDS* from 20.10.2017-05.08.2018 at the ZKM | Center for Art and Media Karlsruhe, and its second phase *OPEN CODES.THE WORLD AS A FIELD OF DATA* (01.09.2018-06.01.2019), and the festival ARS ELECTRONICA 2017 under the heading *"AI. Artificial Intelligence. The other I"*, and 2018 entitled "ERROR the art of Imperfection".

Discussing these items is also one of the good reasons why we are gathered here today, thanks to the initiative and invitation of AICA. But at the same time we should be aware that like many other people exhibition curators, biennial chiefs, festival and marketing directors are still today naively fascinated by the velocity and virtuosity of new digital virtual realities. Venerating the new gods of the digital era, with their applauding shows they keep disseminating the new message of salvation to the visitors of their big events.

At this point, it would be opportune to enumerate the never ending list of examples of violations of privacy by state agencies and private companies. Besides knowing that state agencies are conducting far reaching, politically motivated spying activities, we have also known for a long time about the massive influence of commercial companies on the public and the private sphere, on political and economic decisions, and on our real everyday behavior. Already during the big takeovers and mergers in the capital markets of the 1990s, it had become obvious that media power was more and more concentrating in the hands of only a few global players. Today, in 2018, more than 20 years later we are still wordlessly stupefied by the cold arrogance of a young unlettered Mr. Zuckerbergs meaningless apologies in front of the US Congress.

The newly triggered human need for communication and entertainment that never stops has all the hallmarks of an addiction. While even very small children are being introduced to constant digital amusement to enhance their little lives, at the same time their future profiles as consumers are being scrutinized and developed further. One of the latest project of this branch of the industry is "Hello Barbie," a talking version of the eponymous doll that kids are supposed to talk to and tell about their secrets and dream. The doll is connected to a central server of the manufacturer which then analyses and evaluates the data collected by eavesdropping Barbie.

Another one of the recent examples for this trend towards a new humanity is to find in China. The upcoming superpower, proudly referring to its five millennia of high culture as well as to its overwhelming progress in digital technology, is today testing and partly already experiencing a social credit system, which in the future will not allow one single civilian to escape from being scanned and rated on his or her good (or evil) conduct in society. And if we are horrified of this vision which is being actively translated into reality, we need not at all look far: In the aftermath of the Cambridge Analytic controversy Facebook in an interview with Washington Post has recently admitted that since more than one year it is developing a system which secretly classifies the trustworthiness of each and every one of its users.[2] The so-called "score" is intended to be used for eliminating fake news, but in the future it can as well be instrumentalised for easily controlling its users opinions. Big Brother of Orwells 1984 was a lame duck measured against this kind of potentialities. Modern history demonstrates: Whatever is technically possible, will also be done.

All of this is well known to those who want to know. And whoever reads relevant newspapers, whoever seriously searches the internet for information about current methods of data mining and data analytics, about upcoming social scoring systems in the People Republic of China as well as in the so-called free world, about control and censorship as an immanent epidemic of the information society - will find any number of relevant facts and perspectives of this alarming item. In this sense, the promising term "information society" reveals a new dimension: it is the society where all information, be it banal or important, be it of public concern, or of purely private nature can be intercepted by government agencies as well as by the private sector. The first-mentioned strive to control the society, the last-mentioned has long since build its business model on the interception, analyze, exploitation and manipulation of digital data. It has become a matter of fact, that the most successful companies, such as Apple, Amazon, Alphabet, Facebook and many more, have based their profits on their users intercepted private data. All of you know these companies, because all of you are unknowingly working for exactly these companies. It is a matter of fact that public agencies of all states practice deep analysis and data mining on their citizens. And it has long since become an undeniable practice that private companies - like Cambridge Analytica - which know more about their consumers than the state knows about its citizens, on behalf of government services and political camps selectively influence the voting behaviour of citizens. All these invaders bluntly deny their profitable activities.

Being at the mercy of overwhelmingly powerful authorities of control and censorship has become the *conditio humana*, the basic condition of our culture. To some extent we realize this and reflect upon it, but we cannot reverse or undo it. We are well on the way to accepting surveillance and censorship as a given, just as we have learned to accept other conditions as facts of modern life – traffic noise, ubiquitous advertising, environmental pollution, and our insignificance in the political arena.

---

[2]   see: Washington Post of 21.08.2018: https://www.washingtonpost.com/gdpr-consent/?destination=%2f...%2fpost...%2fwhat-facebooks-trustw...%3f of

Already today, notable success has been achieved through the replacement of human intelligence by algorithmic systems. The long since set in train electronic connection of all human beings and devices in the Internet of Things (IoT) as main instrument of the coming economy bases principally on the use of intelligent control algorithms. In having access at any moment to our behaviour patterns, which are provided by us in the form of our digital data as consumers in a relentless production process, they control us as prosumers by a direct feedback with behavior-guiding impulses we are receiving in sync. In this field, the promised "*merging of the boundaries between the physical, digital and biological sphere by Artificial Intelligence*" has long taken root. It is precisely at this interface where presently will be redefined our understanding of being human. The great allurement of the popular new revolution may consist in giving up the humanistic ideal of a self-determined life.

However, this is not merely a covert conspiracy of the new economy against the civilian society, but the consequent enforcement of a data based capitalism, which has never been restrained by politics. Right in contrast to necessary regulations, politics of all countries have welcomed, encouraged and facilitated the new economic model which is actually based on the flagrant violation of one of the most fundamental human rights, the right of privacy. As long as we are willing to recognize these rights, we have to assume, that the invasion of privacy through unauthorized data mining is a crime against humanity, a crime that will not be sentenced, nor prosecuted.

In spite of the alarming things we now know, a large section of the public has already resigned in the face of the ubiquitous presence of state and commercial surveillance. Our grandchildren will hopefully still be able to ask us what we did about it; in the forthcoming digital-totalitarian society such questions will not even be posed. We have become accustomed to this situation, just as we are not deterred by the myriads of video cameras on the way to work or on our way back home. And this resignation paired with our love of ease and selfishness has the potential to invite a new totalitarianism to install a new society with a pre-programmed divide between an elite of hyper-agile information users and a broad mass of interactive consumers restlessly zapping futile audio-visual products and services offered at dumping prices in order to control all of their practices and preferences. This re-coding of humanity could result in the worst of all totalitarianisms, that of a *brave new world*, in which everyone will be content, well-informed of everything he or she should know in order to play a useful role in society, but remaining ignorant of everything, which does not need to be known and consequently permanently amused to the point of complete satiety.

Eco-Democracy and the Romanian Contemporary Public Art

Marilena Preda Sanc

The development of the cities, the changes in the human life and in the structure of the urban communities, the evolution of architecture forms, the new means of artistic expression generated by new techniques, technologies, and materials have influenced and transformed, in the last century, the typology of Public Art.

Starting with the second half of the XX century, along the permanent interventions, such as bronze or stone sculptures, commemorative/celebratory monuments and traditional murals, the public space became also a stage for new, temporary and ephemeral art forms and events: installations, projections, street art, graffiti, performances, electronic murals, light art, locative art, media events and live art, among many others. We now witness a spectacular evolution of the Public Art: a merging, re-mixing and hybridization of traditional and new media, a creative process which is contextualized and grounded in the thorough research of the relations between artwork, location and audience, and which generates an entirely new urban visual dynamic.

We speak about a re-articulation of the city, a street urban psycho-geography and the hope for a meeting and communication Agora. The artists and specialists practicing Public Art dream of the city museification but also of the city as an open scene, or a work-in-progress: the city as a place for experiments and esthetic games, the city as a field for social and political investigation, education and cultural activism.

Today the visual cityscape is increasingly dynamic and unpredictable, and so is the Public Art – I refer to site-specific-artworks, site-specific-art-places and performing arts, interacting with the urban space which are strongly related to the life of the communities.

These works reshape the urban space in a complex approach of the art – urbanism – living spaces dynamic relationship. The esthetic dimension develops towards the social and political. People of the cities are no longer mere spectators, contemplating the artistic work. Their part is increasingly participatory, as in many cases they directly interact with the artworks and become co-authors of the visual arts performances.

Contemporary artists empathize with their peers and the world we all live in today. The many forms of the contemporary democracies seem to foster an unstable N.W.O. (New World Order), under threats of all kinds and concerned with concepts such as 'political correctness', 'collateral victims' or the more theoretical 'ethical universalism'. We live in a world destabilized by violence – ethnical, religious, gender related, by hybrid wars for territories, markets, oil, natural resources, wars which generate realities and geo-political or personal histories filled with pain: local, global, human and ecological.

Responsibility lies indeed with the political leaders, but we all share a moral responsibility. From this perspective, artists often stand for the values of Eco-Democracy.

Eco-Democracy consists in a new set of political theories and decisions based on democratic practices regarding universalism (ethics) and human complexity,

multiculturalism, with a positive influence on the environment and the quality of life.

Visual artists are concerned with the creation of a moral, spiritual living space through their artworks, and for contemporary Public Art artists, this concern is a major concept in their discourse. Their beliefs and hopes for a better society are often expressed through attitudes which can be ironical, reflexive, militant and critical. They are often involved in a cultural activism articulated in relation with local or global crisis, society, cultural politics, contexts generated by the political powers, contexts which they interact with and attempt to change. Art can mirror people's conscience and can indeed challenge people to think, to think actively, and with stand the pressure of authority. An intervention of art in public space can be a way of expressing the citizen / human being rights in a world dominated by the happy few and their interests.

Romania went through several shifts in ideology and political administration in the last century – from monarchy, military dictatorship, communism to democracy (still a transition democracy) and the adherence to the European Union. Romania is now in the European Union and still striving to become a nation able to decide for its own future.

The most important memorial monument in Romania is signed by the renowned sculptor Constantin Brancusi and is well known as The Sculptural Ensemble of Târgu Jiu, or the Walk of Heroes. The monument, completed in 1938 is an homage to the heroes fallen in 1916 during World War 1, and comprises of The Table of Silence, The Walkway of Chairs, The Gate of the Kiss and The Endless Column (The Column of Infinite Gratitude). The stone sculptural elements and the column, cast in iron, follow the same axis oriented west towards east (aligned with St Peter and Paul church, inaugurated in 1937), with a total length of 1275 meters.

Between 1947 and 1989, during communism, Public Art has meant chiefly mural pieces or sculptures in stone, metal or ceramic, decorative pieces or memorial or celebratory monumental art, and everything was strictly censored by the specific criteria of the communist ideology, in short they had to express the values of and victory of communism and its heroes. Nicolae Ceauşescu, the communist dictator, is subject of many public artworks. Communist propaganda named The Golden Age the period 1980 – 1989, cultural period dominated by the Nicolae Ceauşescu's cult of personality.

After 1989, with the opening of both material and virtual borders, the Romanian society has experienced a chaotic growth with positive sides but also alarming ones in terms of behavior, social and political ethics, human consciousness, spiritual values, which all provoked visual artists to become active witnesses in documenting and often exposing this contexts.

In this presentation I have collected Romanian Public Art works and practices focused on topics related to Eco-Democracy concepts – from the site-specific-art- place in Tăuşeni (De-signs towards the Sky for Rain and Rainbow), by Alexandru Chira, to the social / political sculptures by Aurel Vlad (The Convoy of Martyrs), Mihai Balko (Romania's Treasure).

I have included the eco-poetic installations by Virgil Scripcariu (Noah's Ark), Leonard Ursachi, b. Romania, lives and works N.Y., (Hiding Place; What a Wonderful World), and Mihaiu Ţopescu's militant, site-specific-installations (MANIFEST).

The complex Project 1990, from 2010, concept and curator Ioana Ciocan, has comprised of the temporary placement of 20 contemporary artworks site-specific on the empty pedestal of the Lenin monument – which had been removed immediately after the revolution of 1989. The empty pedestal, still standing in front of a building iconic for the Stalinist architecture and period was turned into a space for protest,

in which the artists presented artwork critical of both the former totalitarian regime and the current post-communist society. Among the artists in the project we mention Mihai Zgondoiu (Lenin's Sleep), Alexandru Potecă (Country Lovers), Bogdan Raţă (Handgun), Judith Balko (Melting), Mihai Balko (Red Sharks), Ileana Oancea (Roşia Montană).

Further on I would like to mention a few artists whose creative discourse develops in the urban representational space, and who in my opinion stand as frontier movers, chroniclers, mediators, activists and educators of an audience / public for whom awareness and solidarity for an idea becomes vital. I refer to Dan Perjovschi, Alexandra Pirici, Matei Bejenaru and Cosmin Paulescu.

Dan Perjovschi sees himself as a political activist. His site-specific-artworks consist of large scale drawings on walls, windows, ceilings, doors, floors — drawings of his specific characters and slogans in which he criticizes local, geo-political, social, and cultural crises. He is one of the artists always 'on the watch', constantly commenting on and accusing all local or global deviations from democracy and all behaviors straying from the principles of humanity and civilization. (Horizontal Newspaper; Drawing Book with and for the children from Pata Rât; artWall)

Alexandra Pirici, choreographer and dancer, directs and stages performances that can be seen as 'visual thinking' movements. The minimalist expression of the human body is multiplied and articulated in symbolical structures which are placed in a consubstantiality relationship with iconic sculptures – emblematic for history and power. The whole performance becomes a site-specific tableau vivant which calls for questions and meditation. (If you don't want us, we want you)

Matei Bejenaru is a refined observer who documents and archives reality and searches for a truth which he represents at the same time directly and nuanced, in photography, installations and mixed-media environments. His positive energy makes him see and depict beauty and hope in even some of the most common of the human actions. (Science Gazette; Songs for a Better Future; Performing poetry; Prut)

Cosmin Paulescu comments sarcastically in his apparently funny performances and installations on the need for clichés – nationalistic, religious, and so on, certain signs of a society and world losing their direction. (Maps; EU.ro)

Video projections are a high impact Public Art form, especially when the images bring forward uncomfortable, unsolved issues – avoided by authorities and ignored by most people, due to egocentrism and lack of solidarity. (FemSlogan projections, Marilena Preda Sanc)

Currently, street protests in Romania (and everywhere in the world) have a very powerful visual quality: slogans, sky art, locative art, cartoons, laser projections, light and sound installations, and so on. Protests become thusly true human environments (#Rezist, #DEMISIA, etc.)

Sometimes the artists and mass-media compromise and they self-censor the visual-scape within the parameters of the acceptable and the comfortable half-truth. However, major social, political, geo-political issues, regarding religious and gender freedom, armed conflicts, abuses generated by the fight for natural resources, pollution or climate change are increasingly often, central in exhibitions exploring the complex interactions between people and their communities.

The current Romanian visual arts, curatorial practices and art theory are increasingly developing towards topics focused on Eco-Democracy and the human existence nowadays. Several curators who have a profound knowledge of the local / global visual art scene have curated complex and courageous exhibitions centered on the conceptual investigation of social and political contexts, of gender issues, ecology and local / global histories, analyzing the effects of globalization in the digital age and presenting, in anthropological and geo-political perspectives, the histories of a mankind re-shaping its identity towards a more responsible attitude. I wish to refer to the theoretical studies and the remarkable curatorial practice of professor, writer and art critic Alexandra Titu (Il miraggio politico, Venice, 2011; am I my brother's keeper?, Timişoara, 2012; Man against Life, Bucharest, 2015, and In Memory of the Hero, Focşani, 2017).

From the younger generation of curators I would like to mention Olivia Niţiş, curator and co-director of the Experimental project (Perspective / a contemporary feminist art project, Bucharest, 2008; The Poetics of Politics, Varşovia, 2012; Good Girls, Memory Desire Power, Bucharest, 2013 [co-curator]; Monu-Mentals Historie, Bucharest, 2016) and Răzvan Ion, curator, co-founder and co-director of the Bucharest Biennale (Bucharest International Biennial for Contemporary Art).

In a world in which ethics is an illusion, and a utopic desire rather than a certainty is uneasy for an artist, curator or theoretician to stand for its values.

In historical perspective, monumental art have been an expression of the political authorities, as opposed to the current Public Art forms which comment on the recent history and the present realities. The artist militating in the public space has the vocation of the community. He / She becomes a refined observer, who perceives intuitively and differentially analyzes the superior complexity of our world. She / He subsequently articulates, in a nuanced visual meta-language, the artistic message which reflects and stands for the ideals of the civic society and its members. In this sense social philosophy is an essential dimension of the artistic social practices specific to the contemporary art scene. Social art becomes a complex mechanism generating human awareness and knowledge. Public Art as social practice and expression of Eco- Democracy produces effects on habitats and contributes to the shaping and education of a society aware and able to formulate opinions in order to change politics in the benefit of the citizens.

I believe that the human being and the quality of life will be enriched once the self / geo / political consciousness is fully integrated into an ecological mind of a new identity of a Man reborn. (MPS – Split Reality, symposium on New Media – MUMOK, Vienna 2001)

To the Moon

Laurie Anderson and Hsin-Chien Huang

Whereas not so long ago digital forms of communication were seen as the hope for new forms of de The Moon is projected by Laurie Anderson and Hsin-Chien Huang are doing for the Louisiana Museum and Denmark. This is a very beautiful place in that the color combinations of art and science. So, they asked us to make our versions of the moon. And they are doing a big exhibition - a scientific exhibition about the moon. This is going to be the only art project in their series.

It is of course a kind of imaginary moon where it is anti-gravitational but it's all kind of things happening. As it turns out, it's a kind of a dark version of it because while we are working on it, the announcements of space force that's going to patrolling space; there is a lot of concern with what we are going to do with the earth debris. So, we imagine it circling the earth and travelling to the moon. So, it's a kind of dystopic picture of the moon.

It's a fifteen minutes piece because we learnt in making other works. We have collaborated on Chalk Room and Aloft; we realized fifteen minutes is a pretty good amount of time for people to be in VR. The head sets, for some people are a little bit challenging.

This is a slightly more controlled work because we realized that we need to guide people a little bit more. But of course, it is flying so it's a free form work. And there is another thing that we learnt from working on Chalk Room and Aloft which they are both very much airborne, very much about the air and the flight. So The Moon was a kind of a natural work for us to take on because it involved in bringing that very much. It will be installed very soon and so we are working very hard on the music. For me, it's a huge challenge to do the music because it's nothing like I know how to do. It's not narrative music with a beginning, middle and end. It's spatial so you walk into music. And I believe it's the future of imagery and music too. That you walk into these works of art. They will no longer to be pasted on the wall.

We were talking about a Chinese story that I like very much. I don't know where this comes from. It sounds like a Borges' story. It's a story of a Chinese painter who makes a beautiful landscape piece; he spent a long time working on these beautiful, vertiginous mountains with pine trees and huts and roads that are going up the mountains; he's painting this landscape and then when he is finished, he walks into it. And this is kind of what VR feels like to me that you are actually able to walk into a work of art. That is really very exciting!

It's been wonderful to work on this project. Hsin-Chien Huang is one of my favorite artists in the world so it's a great privilege for me to work with him and see him visualizing these things. When you said, "Well, maybe it could look like this..." And he comes with an idea that is like wow, so much more beautiful than anything I had imagined! So it's very exciting. And it's a kind of work of discovery for us. We discovered The Moon.

This is the second time that I have worked on VR. I am learning a lot. You know. We don't know really how to make music for this art form, how to make a story, so each work is an experiment. It's a very exciting thing to be at the beginning of a medium like VR. Of course it's been going on for quite a while but it's just beginning to be an actual art form. So the people kind of go 'Oh I know what it is…', 'I have seen a couple…' so people are becoming more literate in VR. That's a big challenge to artists who are beginning to work in it because then the novelty and the shock of it are not the most important thing. It's what you begin to do with it; how you shape it. So it's, for me, very, very exciting because I don't know what it is! So we just try to invent things. You kinda go, "Does that work?", "I don't know.", "Does that work?" It's no rules so it's a real adventure!

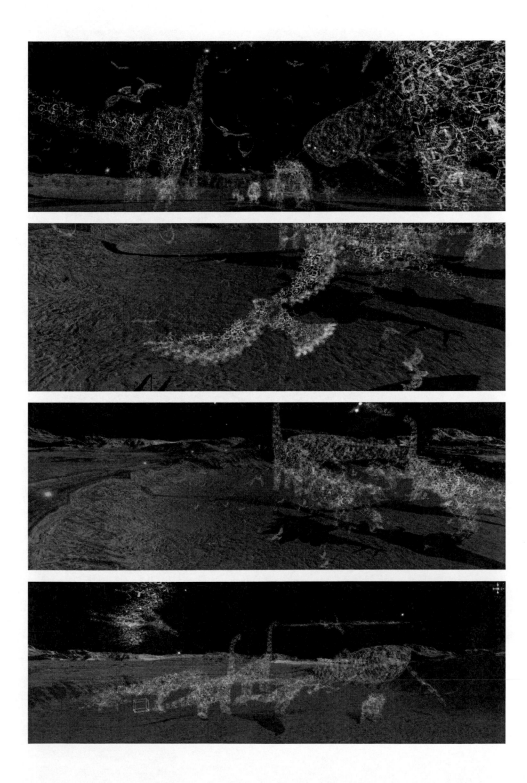

Fireworks

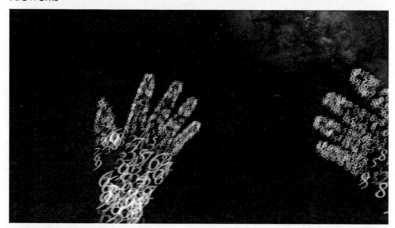

largestPrimeNumber

snowMountain

stoneRose

trashMountain

On "Art Discourse Facing Challenged Democracy"

Bélgica Rodríguez

Latin America is in a dead end and in need of establishing differences before a homogenizing globalization. This disjunctive enters the political ground, and of course the aesthetic one, questioning democracies but also "democratic dictatorships" plaguing the South American continent and permeating art production and, more often than not, the work of critics. Critical activity generated by Latin America's "surviving" art has no "anonymous" existence. It acts in the turbulent present towards a future, if not uncertain, at least quite controversial; this critique and artistic production, however, go on as a lesson of "history," a possible history full of disturbing questions which can be answered through a stimulating, optimistic dynamism.

Exploring Robots

robotlab

The German artist group robotlab works with industrial robots in public spaces. It explores the relationship between man and machine by means of installations and performances. Robots will play a significant role in future societies and will invade more and more human domains. robotlab focusses on the most prevalent robots today, industrial robots. Their number is rapidly increasing worldwide. Their mechanical and electronical capabilities grow with the continual development. The direct coupling of precise mechanics and information processing electronics results in a powerful technology which is discussed in the sciences under subjects like »artificial intelligence« and »artificial life«. robotlab creates experimental situations in exhibition spaces, in which the public has the opportunity to encounter the robots. The massive appearance of the robots, their movements and sounds effect the visitor, are interpreted individually and evoke ideas which may lay in the field of practical purposes as well as formulate a utopian image of a future culture with man and machine.

Introduction about robotlab's work exhibited in Taipei:

The central element of the installation »the big picture« is a creative process that goes beyond the limits of human possibilities: In a months-long, uninterrupted process the robot draws a Martian landscape with one single uninterrupted line. By this inimitable technique it creates a unique artwork with a high level of detail and precision. Hundreds of kilometers of an abstract line converge towards a photorealistic image.

The machine artist takes photographic imagery data from NASA 's Curiosity Mars Rover on the Martian surface and transforms it through algorithmic operations into one path, thus defining 900 million movements. Travelling over the canvas, the thin line constitutes a complex structure on the large format screen, which can be moved back and forth by the machine to reach all areas of the drawing. The generated image gives a partly abstract partly depictive representation of the original imagery information interpreted by the robot itself.

AICA-USA Online: Being Effective, Virtual, and Real in the Twenty-First Century

Judith E. Stein and Jamie Keesling

Increasingly, we live in two worlds, the actual and the virtual. More and more often, people are in contact remotely rather than face-to-face, and experience society as a collection of self-interested and largely self-sufficient individuals who act like separate atoms. When the International Association of Art Critics was founded in the years following WWII, our optimistic colleagues understood the essential contribution of art critics to the health of free ideas and created an organization to counter separation and to rebuild connections. Now, seven decades later, while our goal remains that of the founders, to facilitate and enhance communication as professionals, the way we achieve this mission is new, namely digital technology.

In 2017 the board of AICA-USA found itself with a huge problem after we discovered that we had four different membership lists compiled by different officers at different times. *Zut alors*. Not good. We have approximately 500 members which makes us one of the largest AICA sections, a dubious distinction! Like many AICA's sections, our membership is spread out geographically, from Hawaii to Alaska, San Francisco to Miami. Our greatest concentration is in the New York City area, and our board is centered there.

AICA-USA first went online at the end of the last century. Someone once joked that that a computer-year is roughly equivalent to a dog-year, and over time, our website became a beloved, geriatric pooch. Cyberspace had moved on—the very word is now old-fashioned—and so did stewardship of the website. Remember the children's game "Telephone," where a message passes from one to another and changes along the way? Some of our AICA-USA website passwords, and the very reasons we made certain decisions, did not fully transfer to the next generation of volunteer leaders. Our web presence was spotty, and we were unable to efficiently contact our membership, and in turn, some members found the online renewal process an ordeal. We were nearing dysfunctionality. I can't say what the "last straw" was, but it became clear to the board that we needed to do more than the equivalent of tidying up our closets.

Our digital disfunction—outdated and competing membership lists coupled with lack of consistent web management and social media presence—limited our ability to address the more relevant elements of our organization, namely, to support the working lives of art writers and to protect free expression in an increasingly insecure profession. We began by clarifying for ourselves our large-scale goals and identifying the practical improvements we'd need to make to both our internal and our public-facing digital platforms to realize our goal of refreshing AICA-USA.

In the fall of 2017, we contracted with the redoubtable Bridget Goodbody, who was both an art historian and software designer (and now AICA member), who conducted a thorough assessment of the state of our organization. Bridget began by familiarizing herself with the history of both AICA International and the US section, its mission, bylaws, and branding, and then created a plan to move forward. She interviewed the board members who constituted our "institutional memory;" this proved essential, as not all our history was written down. Then, she proposed some basic upgrades. Our new website would have to be friendly to use for some of us born before 1960, yet lively enough to attract a new, diverse and younger audience.

Clearly, we needed a single membership database that would keep itself up-to-date and be accessible to whoever was in charge of membership records. After some research, we chose Kindful, an online membership management system designed for non-profit organizations. Through Kindful, members can update their contact information, pay annual dues, and request replacement cards and stickers. Too, we accept new member applications through this site. This software change—made before we upgraded our website—meant that all our applicants' information is in one place, easy for the board to review.

Next we considered how we contact our members. Looking around, we found a better digital platform than the one we'd been using. No one remembered when or why we chose the old one, which had fees to pay. The company we chose is Mailchimp, which is free for mailing lists with fewer than 2000 names and allows us to design and send mass emails to our full membership free of charge.

When it came to the website redesign, we weighed the benefits of template-based web management systems—WordPress, for example—which were all low cost and user friendly. Ultimately, we decided to build a custom site which would allow us to best represent AICA-USA and meet the needs of both our members and a public audience. We were fortunate to be able to dip into our restricted reserve treasury for the website designer's fee. We chose the seasoned Perry Garvin, who has worked with multiple arts and non-profit organizations including Performa, founded by long-time AICA-USA board member RoseLee Goldberg. He first acquainted himself with the goals and mission of our organization, and with the changes we wanted to see in the new website.

Judith was part of the board's web committee, and we began the process with several back and forths with Perry, who mapped out the "wireframes" or the skeleton of the site and all the information it must contain. He provided our team with four designs to choose from and adapt. These ranged from classic and conservative—something no one would have trouble interacting with—to bold and daring: a text-heavy design with a homepage devoid of pictures. The choice was challenging. AICA is an organization that supports writing, so why not use a design that avowedly embraces language? Perry advised that the lack of images is highly unusual in contemporary web design, so we'd be at the vanguard of a new style. It was a big step for us to accept a homepage that featured no pictures. As critics, we are highly visual people, but we had to recognize that our activities have not produced high quality, original images that would encourage people to engage with a website. But the aspect of newness, and the sleek, minimalist look of no images were compelling enough to try it. Perry took design inspiration from AICA-USA's logo with its multiple square shapes and their symmetrically stacked relationship. A restrained palette of red, black, and white defines the site's major elements.

We never lost sight of the site's need to be easily navigated as well as engaging in its look and feel. We wanted it to convey newness and originality, yet not seem unfamiliar or alien. Our designer took into account AICA-USA's demographics and the reality of our loyal but graying constituents. He understood that different populations use websites differently. Scrolling, for example, is not as instinctive to older web users as it is for younger people who have had access to digital platforms for most of their lives. Our knowledgeable web design expert also knew that there is a maximum width at which people can comfortably read a column of text on a screen. We learned that this is far less than the width of your typical laptop or desktop monitor. He helped guide us through these design and functionality choices with our user base in mind.

Our new website, http://www.aicausa.org, launched in September. Throughout the planning process we kept two questions in mind, namely, why will people visit our website and what will keep them coming back. This sparked the idea for a new AICA-USA online magazine as a place for original writing by past and present AICA-USA members and affiliates. Our goal was to entice traffic to the site by offering unique, member-driven content that can't be found elsewhere. This has proven an ambitious project, and is still in its initial, experimental stages. Our editor, member Andrea Kirsch, envisions a program that solicits content from various international sections of AICA, to be published in our online magazine on a monthly basis. This will bring international news to our US-based membership and underscore AICA's internationality—an important bonus for prospective members of our section. If your section would like to participate in this initiative, please contact info@aicausa.org.

Our section is in the process of reinvigorating itself and challenging ourselves to better meet the needs of young critics just entering our field. As do our global colleagues, American art writers must function with increasingly precarious working conditions coupled with the burden, in many cases, of substantial student debt. These conditions are symptoms of what's commonly referred to as the "gig economy," a situation where secure full-time employment with benefits is rare, and part-time, freelance, short term contracted work and low-wage internships, the norm. While the advantages of this include flexibility and an invigorating array of different opportunities, in the US, the downside is financial insecurity and lack of benefits like health care.

The growing popularity in the US of writer internships at places that publish art criticism means that art writers—indeed most young writers—often need to work for free or for little pay in order to "break into" our profession. While any writer can start to build an audience autonomously through their online presence, this does not always lead to income or legitimization of their contributions to critical discourse.

In an increasingly virtual world, freelancers may work from home or an isolated environment, with the result that meaningful contacts with other writers are fewer. With our new website and expanded programing in the real world, we aim to assist these emerging writers through professional connections and solidarity. Our new email listserv, via Google, is but one way AICA-USA is building this community through digital platforms. Here members can share ideas, opportunities and critical discourse.

What AICA has to offer its members supersedes global museum access. Now, as when AICA was founded, solidarity though connectedness and community is essential to the field of art criticism. We are actively sharing members' activities and writing on social media and on the website. Through our digital platforms, we get out the word to members about our programming initiatives. We know the value of face-to-face contact with others working in the field, which is an important benefit for AICA members, especially critics new to the field. In Spring 2018, we organized a field trip to Washington, D.C. where our 2017 AICA-USA Distinguished Critic Lecturer Paul Chaat Smith led members through his much-lauded exhibition, *Americans*, at the National Museum of the American Indian; and AICA-USA member John Elderfield led us through the exhibition *Cézanne Portraits*, that he co-curated with Mary Morton at the National Gallery of Art. To cap off this 2-day visit we garnered VIP passes to the National Museum of African American History and Culture. More recently we organized a members-only viewing of Shimon Attie's river installation, *Night Watch*, focusing on New York's refugees and asylum seekers.

The way we represent AICA online reflects how we conceptualize and present the organization to the world, and for this reason, we wanted to share with you our section's experience in bringing new life to our virtual presence and to our actual one.

Hyperallergic: A Model for Art Criticism and Cultural in the Digital Age

Holly Crawford

What, after all, does thumbs up, thumbs down matter when winners are preselected before the critical votes are in? In this economy, it can appear that the critic's job is to broadcast names and contribute to fame.
—Holland Cotter, *New York Times*, 2014.[1]

Hyperallergic is a current day response to art and cultural Cotter's critique about money and the current state of art criticism. It is a Brooklyn-based blogazine that is focuses on art and cultural criticism.[2] Their site states: "Hyperallergic is a forum for playful, serious, and radical perspectives on art and culture in the world today," and *"Sensitive to Art and Its Discontents."*[3] It was founded on the 14th of October 2009 after a year of thinking and planning by Hrag Vartanian and Veken Gueyikian, the partners who created it. They further say on the site that it is a space that will give the art world and surrounding culture a playful, radical and serious look "by focusing on publishing quality and engaging writing and images from informed and provocative perspectives."[4] All this is the mission within a digital daily format. But what do art critics think about it? They pay writers, but less than other publications.

In a survey of 300 critics in 2017, Mary Louise Schumacher in the NeimanReports, wrote that *Hyperallergic* was on the top of their list of highly regarded publications and

---

[1] Holland Cotter, "Lost in the Art-Industrial Complex," https://www.nytimes.com/2014/01/19/arts/design/holland-cotter-looks-at-money-in-art.html

[2] In April I interviewed Harg Varkarian and in August I meet with him twice, once in their office in Brooklyn. Many of the facts in the paper are based on comments from my interview and our preceding conversation. All screen shots are with permission of Hyperallergic, August 2018 for this article.

[3] https://hyperallergic.com/advertise/

[4] https://hyperallergic.com/about/

the only digital one. [5] The top of the list included *The New Yorker*, the *Los Angeles Times*, *Artforum*, *Art in America* and *Hyperallergic*.[6] It has also generated attention from fellow critics in the following ways: In *The New Yorker* by critic Peter Schjeldahl in late 2013 referred to *Hyperallergic* as an "infectiously ill-tempered"[7] blog and in 2014 by Holland Cotter as having revived popular art criticism with a move away from publishing advertising copy or academic jargon filled articles.[8] And about the same time, the AICA-USA gave them an award for being an outstanding publication at their annual meeting. Focus, of this paper, will be on primarily on *Hyperallergic* and how they live up to their mission and these praises. What did they build and who seems to be looking?

Since late 2009, they have grown very quickly by word of mouth. So, how have they structured themselves, and what are they doing to have garnered this attention? *Hyperallergic* is structured as a profit company and not a non-profit. They control the two entities. They did not want to raise money and have a board. They wanted autonomy to decide what advertisers they would take and what they would post. Using today's business jargon, they are creative entrepreneurs. They are solely funded and have not issue of sold stock. And there is a they here: Hrag Vartanian and Veken Gueyukian. So, who are they? What are their backgrounds?

Vartanian is an art historian who liked to blog about art and culture and write reviews for art publications. His day job was doing communications for a New York art gallery, which means posting to the website, social media sending out PR to the press. Gueyikian was in marketing for a pharmaceutical company as a "digital marketing strategist."[9] Vartanian wanted to start an online art publishing business and write books, and he quit his day job. In the 4th year, without advertising, Hyperallegic took off and they both quit their day jobs.

What are they doing with the multiple-voiced blogs, essays, and other many other features? The whole site flows and is continuously updated with new stories. Art and culture flowing past you very quickly. This space is about now. It is not about what was.[10]

[5] Mary Louise Schumacher, "Hyperallergic, at Age 9, Rivals the Arts Journalism of Legacy Media," http://niemanreports.org/articles/hyperallergic/

[6] Mary Louise Schumacher, "Hyperallergic, at Age 9, Rivals the Arts Journalism of Legacy Media," http://niemanreports.org/articles/hyperallergic/

[7] Peter Schjeldahl, "Art in 2013," online https://www.newyorker.com/culture/culture-desk/art-in-2013

[8] Holland Cotter, "Lost in the Art-Industrial Complex," https://www.nytimes.com/2014/01/19/arts/design/holland-cotter-looks-at-money-in-art.html

[9] Conversations with Hrag Vartanian and Mary Louise Schumacher, "Hyperallergic, at Age 9, Rivals the Arts Journalism of Legacy Media," http://niemanreports.org/articles/hyperallergic/

[10] Hrag Vartanian informed me, in a conversation in August 2018, that the Morgan Library in NYC is maintaining a digital archive copy of Hyperallergic.

Early on Cotter said that they "combine criticism, reporting, political activism and gossip on an almost-24-hour news cycle."[11] They are the newspaper model rather than the glossy art magazine. But what about "ill-tempered?" There are many examples.

Here are a few. One of the earliest pages on their website that popped up using their search function was from 2011. It was in the Photo Essay section that is a mix of lots of images and a little text. The first thing you notice is the text is crossed out and a comment added. "~~Glenn Lowry speaking while Mayor Bloomberg looks on. Lowry~~ Some other guy (like we care)..."[12] That addition of "(like we care) is an example of an ill-tempered editorial standard, not just the writer."[13]

Screen shot Hyperallergic 2011.[14]

The article on the Armory was a serious review, but it started in an offbeat way. Another example is the Comic Section. It is drawings and commentary on art and the art world by five contributors. It is not a one frame comment, but multiple frames. Commentary reflects this.

[11] Holland Cotter, "Lost in the Art-Industrial Complex," https://www.nytimes.com/2014/01/19/arts/design/holland-cotter-looks-at-money-in-art.html

[12] https://hyperallergic.com/19718/2011-armory-show/

[13] https://hyperallergic.com/19718/2011-armory-show/

[14] https://hyperallergic.com/19718/2011-armory-show/

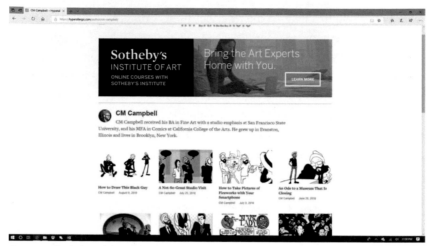

Screen shot Comic pages.[15]

The offbeat, humorous and serious approach are also seen in Vartanian's weekly post called Required Reading. It covers art, culture and politics—things that interest him—with editorial headers like: 'Hmmm," "it's a doozy of white supremacy," and "yes, you read that right…"[16] as editorial introduction to the hyperlinks. This is just another example of his twist on art criticism and political activism.

Screen shot of Required Reading.[17]

---

[15] https://hyperallergic.com/comics/

[16] https://hyperallergic.com/457366/required-reading-387/

[17] https://hyperallergic.com/457366/required-reading-387/

Required Reading (late August 2018). The text here are the editorial comments and part of the hyperlink.

- Democrating portraiture? Hmmm…
- Good luck trying to erase artist Steve Locke, he's not having it, and Adrian Walker of the *Boston Globe* explains why
- Some of the greatest works of Chinese art keep getting brazenly stolen from museums around the world. Is it a conspiracy?
- Writing about Burning Man exhibition in DC, Jillian Steinhauser says in *The New Republic*
- We wrote about the toppling of the infamous "Silent Sam" statue on the campus of the University of North Carolina, but did you know it's history? Writing for *Forbes*, Kristina Killgrove explains
- RELATED: This was the speech read at the inauguration of "Silent Sam," and it's a doozy of white supremacy.
- I love vintage art reviews that get it wrong, like these mixed reviews of Andy Warhol's Campbell's Soup cans
- Priscilla Frank of the Huffington Post took her muppet boyfriend — yes, you read that right — to a new film called *The Happytime Murders*, which is directed and produced by Brian Henson, son of Jim. She writes:
- White Supremacy in heels? Rachel Cargle writes about "tone policing to whitesplaining, the liberal white women's feminism is more toxic than they realize," and continues:
- Taylor Lorenz thinks posting sponsored content on Instagram is a new summer job. She writes:
- There are nuclear weapon nerds? Of course, there are. Paddy Johnson is on it:
- Are Americans becoming hoarders?
- On the 10th anniversary of Georgia's war with Russia, a Georgian condom manufacturer created this special edition:

What else? *Hyperallergic* digitally publishes two editions along with daily or weekly newsletter and posts to FB, Twitter, Instagram and Tumblr. Vartanian is posting. There is a weekday edition and a weekend edition. The weekend edition and its editor and writers are independent of editorial oversight from Vartanian. He does not want complete control with a stamp of his interests and opinions They are free to write and post what interests them without clearing it with Hrag.

The newsletter has 100,000+ subscribers. It is the major vehicle that feeds the traffic to their website, as well as, all the other social media. The newsletter which is free is sent out daily or weekly depending on the subscribers' preferences. The daily and weekly newsletter includes a letter from the editor, Vartanian. The emailed newsletter a recap of the most significant and popular stories of the moment. The website is completely searchable, free and open to all. No password or subscription is necessary to search read the current posts and past posts.

And if you have a desire to buy an art object, *Hyperallergic* has a store. You can purchase postcards with images of the canon or more contemporary objects. It reflects its sense of humor and possible source of revenue, but not the most significant.

Screen shot of the Hyperallergic Store.[18]

Lastly, before returning to the business side of *Hyperallergic*, what is in a name? *Hyperallergic*, what and how would a reader related or think about the name? Have you become allergic to all the hype, money and PR reviews? If you read one more PR review that is solely a description or wade through academic rhetoric you swear will break out in hives? Probably. You were trying to swear off art lately. Probably. Also, Hrag is just that. He is literally hyperallergic to many things from food to the environment. It was a word that he liked and wanted to use.

Here are their current social media stats that allowed them to quit their day jobs.

Hyperallergic Statistics [19]

"In over five years, *Hyperallergic* has attracted over 433,000 Facebook fans, 220,000 Instagram followers, 250,000 Tumblr followers, 135,000 Twitter followers, 1.8

---

[18] https://store.hyperallergic.com/
[19] https://hyperallergic.com/advertise/

million Google+ followers, and nearly 1 million unique visitors per month."[20] These figures are supported by tracking services which added traffic by country.[21] Most of their traffic is in the United States, as you can see, 64.2%. And then: France at 2.9%; Canada at 2.4%; UK at 2.4% and Italy at 2.1%.[22]

Back to business: How do they support this enterprise? Through advertisements that are placed on the site which are seen by about 4 million people. This is Veken Gueyikian's side of the business. In *Hyperallergic*'s second year, Gueyikian formed Nectar (nectarads.com). Nectar currently has nine clients that are internet-based art businesses such as Rhizome that is now part of the New Museum.

A Screen shot of art organization where ads are placed by Nectar:[23]

Screen shot of Spoon & Tamago's website.[24]

[20] https://hyperallergic.com/advertise/

[21] https://www.easycounter.com/report/hyperallergic.com

[22] https://www.easycounter.com/report/hyperallergic.com

[23] https://nectarads.com/publishers/

[24] http://www.spoon-tamago.com/

The same ads flow through all the client's pages which includes *Hyperallergic*.

> The idea was to create beautiful ads that readers would recognize as part of an art-literate community, Gueyikian says, adding that he regards accepting ads for the site as an endorsement of sorts. Many of the arts organizations Gueyikian approached—museums, nonprofits, art schools, art services—had never paid for digital ads before…[25]

Currently, they are predominantly from The Met, advertising a current exhibition and SVA. Nectar posts an extensive and impressive list of sponsors' who have taken out ads over the last 9 years. Here is a partial list from Nectar.

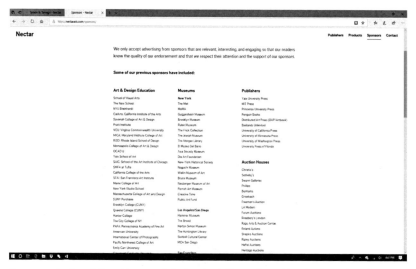

Screen shots of the Hyperallergic and the other Nectar's advertisers or sponsors as they are called on Nectar's site: [26]

These sponsors and clients are the sources of revenue for Nectar and ultimately *Hyperallergic*. It is the revenue that allows then to pay rent, staff, writers and stay in business. Are there other digital models? A different approach is the *ArtsJournal* that started in 1999 by Doug McLennan, who is still the editor.

> The site is a digest of some of the best arts and cultural journalism in the English-speaking world. Each day ArtsJournal features link to

---

[25] Mary Louise Schumacher, "Hyperallergic, at Age 9, Rivals the Arts Journalism of Legacy Media," http://niemanreports.org/articles/hyperallergic/

[26] https://nectarads.com/sponsors/

stories culled from around the internet, including blogs and more than 200 English-language newspapers, magazines and publications featuring writing about arts and culture.[27]

Since 2003, it also has blogs from 60 writers. Most are listed on their site as cultural writers. Some write about visual art too. The two visual writers, John Perreault and Glen Weiss, have not posted since 2015. It has a newsletter, both daily and weekly, and it is free. Their revenue is slightly ad based with subscription element. For $28 a year the newsletter is sent daily or weekly without ads. There are 30,000 subscribers. That is just under $1M a year in revenue from subscribers. ArtsJournal also seems to have significant funding from the Wallace Foundation.

ArtsJournal's traffic is 3.9K daily visitors and 5.48-page views. 77% of their traffic is from the United States, with 3.1% from Denmark and 2.1% from India. Given they are pulling from sources worldwide, one would have expected a larger following from other English-speaking countries.

These are just two of online art blogamazines in the English language with the most traffic. Their ads are different than print art magazine. Art gallery ads are prominently seen in the print magazines, such as *ArtForum* and *Art in America*. Galleries mission is to sell art. They also want reviews to show to buyers. Glossy pages with high end ads from high end products, as seen in *ArtForum*, are important part of the cache of selling art.

They have a presence on FB, Instagram and Twitter, as well as, a website.

ArtForum Statistics:
Traffic by country:

USA	59.3%
UK	4.9%
France	4.7%
Germany	3.9%
Switzerland	2.4%

The most interesting thing about these numbers, and it is true of all these English language magazines, is the geographic concentration of their online following.

As for the print circulation, *ArtForum* and *Art in America*, are not on the list of the top 100 magazines in the United States. Only the *Smithsonian* magazine is ranked in the top 100 and the magazine. The *Smithsonian* magazine has a circulation of 2,054,696. It is ranked 34 right between *Martha Stewart Living* and *Seventeen*. Star magazine is ranked

---

[27] https://www.artsjournal.com/about

at 100. It is a Hollywood tabloid that is owned by the same firm that owns *The National Enquirer*. *The Star* has a circulation in the 900,000.[28]

Art in America started in 1913 and had a circulation 75,000 (in 2008).[29] The model of course if different too. It is a print-based magazine with a subscriptions and advertising in the magazine. *Art in America*'s website traffic is 70.1% US.

Statistics are not a measure of quality. Some will say it is just clicks and traffic. The same can be said for print publication. With print and online publications know one know what is really read. Online you can see the number of pages and what pages are viewed. You can even see the time people sent on the site from couple seconds to hours. But all publications need funding through some source. Most rely on advertising revenue and advertisers what traffic. *Hyperallergic* generates traffic to their site through free newsletter subscribers and from other social media. Without ad revenue, they would be out of business.

Would it be possible to start and online art magazine or blogzine? If you very rich, you might try it, but there are fixed costs. You need to build and maintain a site which is expensive. You will also need an editor, writers and copyeditors. You need one of more persons to layout the article with the images. If you have a comment's section, you need people to read them and delete some of the comments. *Huffington Post* had a staff of a dozen people reading comments, a minimum of a thousand a day, that were posted about various articles. These people worked in two shifts. They tried to have a software program highlight all questionable comments, but as we all know search engines are anything but perfect and hate speech can be very nuanced.[30] How do you get at least a half million followers a month? And that's what you need to attract sponsors who want to place ads unless you are self-funding. There are locations and opportunities. The one that came to mind was *Art.ES* out of Madrid that was published in Spanish and English. Fernando Galan, the founder and editor, had a website that was the archive. The last issue was published early in 2018.

From this research, it seems that it would be possible for a Spanish language magazine go online and stop printing. *Hyperallergic* is one model and one voice, but it is one voice that has a tremendous following. *Art in America* and *Artnews* might move into a stronger online model and, as I have suggested, other publications, particularly art and cultural publication that are not English-centric.

---

[28] http://www.psaresearch.com/images/TOPMAGAZINES.pdf

[29] https://en.wikipedia.org/wiki/Art_in_America

[30] Conversation with Renee Best who was a reader for Huffington for 7 years.
     All screen shots are with permission of Hyperallergic.

An Eco-System of Criticism-Activism to Empower "Overcoming the Past"- Film Discourse and <NN 15> Community Project of Taiwan's White Terror Memory

Yu-Juin Wang

Taiwan's democracy is facing multiple challenges as the debates on how to deal with the dark memory of the 228 massacre and the White Terror gain new momentum after the passing of the new 'transitional justice' law in 2017. Center at the <NN 15> project is an old house in Keelung city where the author's father was arrested as a young college student in 1950 and imprisoned in Green Island until 1960. In short, <NN 15> old house embodies a long-forgotten history which emerges to the public attention via an accidental path. The story of <NN 15 old house> first went public in 2015 via social media and since then has been attracting attention of many citizens who are inspired by the Sun Flower movement in 2014. Among many factors that help to sustain the public interest in <NN 15> is film, especially European films related to "Vergangenheitsbewaeltigung" (overcoming the past). Via discussion and debates on films that were public screened at various film festivals, as well as at the National 228 Memorial Museum, the author observed that that an increasing number of citizens are undergoing their own "overcoming the past" process by addressing the critical question of nationalism, reconciliation and social welfare etc. European feature and documentary films like "Ida" (2012), "Vita Activa: The Spirit of Hannah Arendt" (2015), "Nicky's Family" (2011), "Labyrinth of Lies" (2014) etc. provide an easy access to the complicated history of Europe in the Age of Extreme of the 20th century. Two perspectives of "overcoming the past" that are seldom reflected in the current (official) discussion of "transitional justice", but received good attention via these films are (1) the relation of memory to dementia, and (2) the relation of memory to social innovation for the future generation. As the <NN 15> project develops, with films stimulating critical reflection and inspiring citizen action, a cosmopolitan solidarity is formed to encourage more global-local life story sharing. This paper will conclude with a vision of more innovative co-working of critics and activist, within and beyond national borders.

Xiao Lu's Dialogue

Damian Smith

The photograph captures the moment when Chinese artist Xiao Lu fires a live pistol round in to her sculptural installation work titled *Dialogue*. The year is 1989, and Xiao Lu's life is about to change. What she has done—in the capital of Mainland China, within living memory of the Great Proletarian Cultural Revolution, and at a time when the push for social reforms is gathering apace—is something momentous, entirely radical and deeply individual. And, it is this break with conformity, this sweeping articulation of self, that makes the shooting an entirely dangerous scenario, in fact, far more so than the act of ensuing destruction. This is a work with a history; it is a work with a future, and it is a work with a predictive capacity, in as much as it foreshadows those issues of individual liberty that continue to be fought over in China today.

This year's Congress Theme is 'Art Criticism in the age of Virtuality and Democracy', with the two sub-themes being 'Art criticism in the age of virtuality' and 'Art discourse facing challenged democracy'. Now, as Xiao Lu's shooting intervention took place in a country that is ruled by a one Party, Communist system, one might wonder as to why an analysis of it has been chosen for inclusion. And as the internet only came in to existence in 1989, one might further query this example. On this latter point, the shooting intervention needed no internet to propel it into the virtual realm. The gesture spread across China in the manner of a viral meme. Even if you hadn't seen it, news of this crazy individual unloading a gun in the National Museum was spreading by word of mouth. So, let us not confuse the virtual with the internet, as indeed, humans have been conjuring the virtual long before we had the technology to do it in the contemporary sense. And what of this 'challenged democracy'? From today's perspective, and at the time of its enactment, Xiao Lu's work seems entirely symbolic of the Democracy Movement in China. It was radical. It was transgressive. And it occurred without consideration of the structures that had been mustered in a bid to maintain social order. However, I would not like to fall in to the trap, as others have done, of linking Xiao Lu's work to the Democracy Movement in any explicit way. Indeed, her steadfast pursuit of her 'own thing' makes this work doubly transgressive. It aligns with no one but the artist herself. And let's not kid ourselves. Pulling out a gun in a national museum and firing it, anywhere in the world, is going to get you arrested. But what this statement masks—issues of gender and the situation of women as actors or protagonists in the public domain, and the uncanny reverberations of an artwork that is both specific and hard to pin down—are the themes that I would like to unpack today, and specifically, how they intersect with issues of democracy and virtuality.

The history of Xiao Lu's shooting intervention takes shape in relation to the events surrounding the artist's participation in the ground-breaking exhibition 'China Avant Garde', staged in 1989 at the National Art Museum in Beijing. It was there, in the country's most important art museum, that the subsequent ricocheting effects of Xiao Lu's performance-based intervention, wherein the artist fired a pistol into her installation work, a piece moreover that bore the same *Dialogue* title, which places Xiao Lu at the precise epicentre of momentous and historic events. China's internal and collective plea for an authentic and engaged public discourse, which in 1989 was reaching fever pitch, was somehow embodied in that moment. A lone woman, in the sacrosanct museum, had in a single instance, demolished any polite semblance of debate, be it public, private, political or artistic. After turning herself in, Xiao Lu was arrested, and her infamous pistol shot, just four months before the June 4 uprising, would go down in history as the 'first shots fired in Tiananmen'.

The fact that Xiao Lu's gesture was largely personal in nature did not prevent her shooting intervention from being read, both by the state security apparatus and local art critics, as fundamentally political. For instance, Song Liwei, the editor of the Chinese contemporary art magazine, *Zhongguo Meishu Bao*, wrote in its eleventh issue, in 1989, that "the artistic character of the incident resides in its demonstration of the degree of elasticity of the Chinese legal system" (Merlin & Xiao 2018). And indeed, it was at this point we see the widespread, and entirely inaccurate presentation of the shooting as being the work of Tang Song and Xiao Lu. For an artist whose interests were directed to the challenges and pitfalls of communication, this was a bitter irony.

The misinterpretation would scarcely be challenged until the publication of Xiao Lu's memoir, again titled 'Dialogue', which appeared two decades later in 2009. In the intervening years, Xiao Lu would take refuge in the Australian city of Sydney and her publication would ultimately reveal the challenges within her own life that led up to the fateful shooting intervention.

Xiao Lu's *Dialogue* project is now iconic in the context of Chinese contemporary art. However, I feel compelled to consider it against wider parameters, and especially, in terms of other pivotal works. To say the least, Xiao Lu's *Dialogue* is canonical of this period, and this will help to locate it within today's discussion. Certainly, it is not too great a leap to perceive Xiao Lu's initial 1989 installation, her subsequent shooting intervention, later photographic suite titled *15 shots*, 2003 and published memoir as constituting a singular and highly complex artwork that is stretched out in time. By virtue of this unfolding, the comparison that springs to mind is Marcel Duchamp's portmanteau piece *The Bride Stripped Bare by her Bachelors, Even (Large Glass)*, 1915-1923. Duchamp's work encompasses its initial creation, the subsequent damage that the piece sustained in transit, which the artist perceived as the moment in which the work was 'finally unfinished' and the suite of 94 documents that Duchamp published under the title 'The Green Box', to explain some of his thinking around the creation of *The Bride Stripped Bare*. Similarly, Xiao Lu's project is enacted in stages and is accompanied by a memoir that might also be read as a guide to the *Dialogue* installation, shooting and photographs. It is uncanny also that Duchamp's work was similarly shot by the artist, in his case with the aid of a toy canon, and the work's *prima face* narrative concerns the fraught relations between men and women, as did Xiao Lu's original installation.

Just as Duchamp's work alludes easy categorisation, indeed it seems almost *sui generis*, one finds it difficult to locate Xiao Lu's work within the neat demarcations of contemporary Chinese art. I emphasise too, that this resistance to categorisation underscores the originality of Xiao Lu's practice, its refusal to congeal into something as easy as terms like 'democracy' or 'freedom' might imply. The work embodies a compulsive motivation. Explosive. Unbridled. Stemming in large part from unconscious processes, the artist is attacking her own work, but also, her own self-image, as she fires into a mirror. And that elusive nature is refreshing as it is liberating. According to Xiao Lu, "I did not necessarily intend to do the gun firing the way I did. I really cannot explain clearly why I did it; it is as if the whole thing was predestined."

And if we return to that question of categorisation, we see that while the *Dialogue* installation and shooting took place in 1989, the subsequent photographs and memoir were produced in the ensuing decades, so simply locating it within the context of the 1980s avant-garde is not especially accurate. Indeed, for the critic and curator Li Xianting, Xiao Lu's gunshot signalled the end of the ten-year period of 'New Wave Art'. In the case of this photograph, from 2004, the split composition, positive in one half, negative in the other evokes a myriad of dualities—not least of all self and other, and yin and yang. It announces also the work's particular displacement in time, the moment and temporality continually in juxtaposition and play. Neither has Xiao Lu ever identified with the Cynical Realist or Political Pop art movements of the 1990s. But what is this work if not a cynical and profoundly world-weary response to the experience of existing within a fractured and at times dissembling society?

It is ironic too that the threat to Chinese society—and what is this work if not a threat?—would not come from without, as one might imagine when contemplating those earlier and rather insular images produced during the Cultural Revolution. For instance, Shen Jiawei's *Standing Guard for our Great Motherland,* 1974. Instead, the peril came from within the artistic and cultural heart of the nation's capital.

Further still, what could be more political than this plea from one who had experienced personal betrayal at the hands of those in whom she had hoped to trust? This is made clear in the artist's memoir. Xiao Lu details being seduced by a friend of her parents, to whom she had turned for support as a young and unworldly student. In other contexts, Xiao Lu's performance-based gesture would not be overlooked for its essentially feminist credentials. Not only has this seldom been the case with commentaries on Xiao Lu, but the shooting was initially perceived as a collaborative work that featured her then partner Tang Song. As Xiao Lu later explained, one theory at the time suggested that:

> *Dialogue*, born out of a woman's emotions, is simply worthless. The same work, however, is deemed extremely meaningful and valuable when Tang Song added his political and social interpretation, saying that it tested the flexibility of Chinese law and so on (Merlin & Xiao 2018).

This imposition of an assumed male authority served not only to disempower the artist, but effectively co-opt and silence her position as both an artist and as a woman radically engaged with her own society.

Again, one would hardly think to associate Xiao Lu with 'surrealism' as a descriptive term, as one might when studying the practices of some of her contemporaries, like Guan Wei, Ah Xian or Chen Qingqing. And yet, what could be more disjunctive, more alive with the bizarre interplay of one reality imposing itself on another, than a solitary artist, unloading her pistol into an enigmatically conceived installation in a Chinese art museum in the momentous year 1989? Xiao Lu's surreal moment seems utterly contemporary to us and perhaps in being so, it is easy to forget how such a gesture—this performance of aesthetic terrorism—might echo the destruction of artworks during the Cultural Revolution, the likes of which had threatened even the great institutions including the National Art Museum. Neither was this the first time that iconoclastic tendencies had been unleashed in the Middle Kingdom, where numerous campaigns against Buddhist artworks and imagery can also be identified. Xiao Lu's gesture therefore is not without context in the long sweep of Chinese history. In both literal and figurative terms, her shooting intervention is decidedly iconoclastic.

And what might Xiao Lu's project suggest about the coming Chinese art? As much as her pistol shot so precisely embodied the tensions of 1989, a firing that signalled entirely its own moment in time, Xiao Lu's action was also a high velocity projection into the rapidly approaching future. No subsequent dissenting gesture could escape comparison with it, and indeed many have fallen short of its mark. In comparison, Ai Weiwei's well-known *Dropping a Han Dynasty Urn*, 1995, registers as a staged and rather empty expression of iconoclasm, its shock value quickly subsiding into gesture. Aimed squarely at tomorrow, Xiao Lu's emancipatory action seems to embody what the Cuban novelist Alejo Carpentier (1904 –1980) saw in the bloodstains of upheaval, that "a revolution is not argued about, it's done". But as we now know, the aftermath of 1989 was never going to include an expansion of social freedoms, let alone broader participation in the political process. Rather, as we see in this photograph by the contemporary Beijing photographer Chen Man, participation in Chinese society today is in large part mercantile and consumerist, but not, as Xiao Lu's work might suggest, inclusive of expanded gestures of the self. And that is where her work persists, as a push for personal freedom and as a viral meme that required no internet to propel it.

Arctic Environmental Challenges through Virtuality

Jean Bundy

Virtuality is an art critic's visual/verbal research and communication tool when assessing climate change. The movie *Letters from Juliet* (2010) is Hollywood's version of simulacra. The plot builds around Veronese women called 'Secretaries of Juliet,' who answer love letters left under Juliet's balcony. Juliet, of course, is Shakespeare's fictitious character and, like Elvis, has become real by virtue of cult-popularity and consumer culture expanded by the Internet. After the film has left theaters, it can be downloaded endlessly, making actors virtual deities.

Sociologist Jean Baudrillard (1929-2007) who felt multifaceted simulacra was a 'game with reality' wrote, "the world is literally taken as it is and 'Disneyfied' in other words is virtually sealed (Baudrillard 54)." While Baudrillard's disenchantments with modernity contain truisms, the fact is we are forever stuck in an electronic world and might as well use it advantageously. Still Baudrillard insisted, "Reality absorbed the simulacrum and now adorns itself in all of the rhetoric of simulation. The simulacrum has become reality—a travesty." (Baudrillard 171).

Baudrillard didn't think the painterly Sublime descriptive enough either, yet it explains early distortions of reality before the digital age (Baudrillard 114). Today's virtuality possesses traces of late eighteenth century philosopher Edmund Burke's (1729-1797) defined Sublime. Visually associated with Burke, David Caspar Friedrich's painting *Wanderer above the Sea of Fog* (1818) presented uncontrollable Nature, demonstrating that when standing on the edge of a precipice, environmental forces, interpreted as raging seas, can be safely appreciated. It was Andy Warhol (1928-1987) who at the cusp of the computer age reconfigured the Sublime by enlarging multiple newspaper images, turning shock into virtuality's banal entertainment which Baudrillard feels becomes all too 'hyperreal' and 'destroys the illusion' (Baudrilliard 114). Whereas Friedrich's *Wanderer...* gives spectators pause, the knowledge that his picture is really just make believe, never leaves the viewer's mind, while Warhol provides spectators with purposeful confusion. Baudrillard proposes, "The modern hero is not the hero of the artistic sublime, but rather the hero of the objective irony of the world of commodity, the world that art incarnates in the objective irony of its own disappearance (Baudrillard 103)." Commodity and virtuality have become compatible bedfellows.

Unlike Friedrich's painting which is one contemplative canvas constructed by one guy, the computer is an expansive landscape that has even made Friedrich's painting go viral. Digital picture making brings the Sublime into personal space, as witnessing climate change's horrific hurricanes and fires from a video monitor, is certainly safer.

Well, the bad guys have virtuality in their tool boxes too. Upon taking office, the Trump administration deleted climate change data from their websites, rejecting all scientific opinions on Global Warming. They are now pouncing on the 1973 Endangered Species Act which in my Arctic neighborhood will have overarching consequences. (*NYTimes,* 1/20/17; 7/22/18). But, sometimes knowledge gained from smart devices does contribute to a cleaner environment. Recently, print and electronic media announced *'Strawless in Seattle',* a movement which prohibits restaurants from distributing plastic straws and utensils that contribute to killing marine life (*Seattle Times,* 9/8/17). *'Strawless…'* was picked up by *National Public Radio,* who expanded on how, "the world throws away more than a billion pounds of plastic every day (*NPR,* 6/30/18). NPR's host Scott Simon added that other cities were now contemplating going *'Strawless'.*

Pictures have a profound effect and often are an impetus for change, especially when placed on the Internet. Burke believed the origins of art, along with Sublime and Beauty, were inseparable from Nature (Bromwich 62). According to Burke, "If we can comprehend clearly how things operate upon one of our senses; there can be very little difficulty in conceiving in what manner they affect the rest (Phillips 128)." Images of plastic-strangled wildlife or photographs of disappearing coral from Australia's Great Barrier Reef give web surfers an instant yet lingering mental image. Biologist Edward O. Wilson (b. 1929) argues that human taste and smell are weak senses and therefore people have had to reach out to science, technology and design in order to compensate (Wilson 269-270). Wilson feels, "A quality of great art is its ability to guide attention from one of its parts to another in a manner that pleases, informs, and provokes (Wilson 271)." Wilson associates 'biophilia' with aesthetics because for centuries depictions of the natural world cropped up as repetitive patterns. (Wilson 269-272). However, oversaturation of imagery is a downside of virtuality that can lead to complacency.

Scientists and Artists Address Arctic Global Warming

Virtuality in all its forms cooperates with reality as it helps to alert large numbers to serious issues, even if electronic equipment can't solve every problem. In the Arctic climate change is evident in all waterways, wildlife and vegetation. The Tundra holds frozen water while mountains capture glaciers; thus land and sea are affected by melting, and pH-imbalances. According to science writer Ned Rozell, in 2013 scientists from Dartmouth College, the Universities of Maine and New Hampshire, drilled 600 feet into Alaska's Mt. Hunter. Core samples showed that, "snow at two-plus miles elevation is now melting more than at any time since the 1600s (*ADN*, 05/26/18)." This past summer the Department of Fish and Game curtailed King salmon fishing in South Central Alaska, even at the height of tourist season, after seeing insufficient species return to spawn (*ADN*, 6/21/18; 7/17/18).

Four artists working in the far North and one exhibition draw attention to the climate changing Arctic. An excerpt from their video *Envoy* (2016) by Rap artist Allison Akootchook Warden (Iñupiaq), and Sitka filmmaker Nicholas Galanin (Tlingit/Aleut) show a stressed caged Polar Bear frantically pacing in a not so politically correct zoo. Until recently, zoos kept animals confined as amusing specimens, giving little thought to their welfare. The Polar Bear has become the poster child of Global Warming as Arctic sea ice, the bear's habitat, is melting. Ironically, zoos may be the only places Polar Bears will thrive. In the Galanin/Warden footage the matted bear who resides alone in a concrete jungle represents environmental carelessness at its worst, as well as man's lack of foresight and humanity. Not the cuddly creatures that appear in Disney footage or Coke commercials, Polar Bears deserve our help. Viruality does have its ironies as melting is benefitting Point Hope, Alaska where high speed Internet cables have been embedded into Arctic sea beds, giving the tiny town of 700 access to the world through the passing digital linkage between London and Tokyo (*NYTimes*, 12/2/17)

The photograph, *Subsistence, 2017*, by artist Brian Adams (Iñupiaq), seeks humanity beneath surfaces as Adams explores age-old sustainability, store bought versus harvesting of the wild, while maintaining harmony with the environment. Mary Rexford is pictured outside her Western style Kaktovik home, as opposed to a grass/sod/driftwood dwelling. She appears in Native dress, preparing Thanksgiving dinner by separating/freezing outer layers of Bowhead whale blubber. Peeking through the snow are plastic tubs. In Alaska, it's common to use backyards as storage, harking back to nomadic living when everything gathered was stored nearby, then utilized. Controversy arises about Natives who continue to hunt the Bowhead Whale when they can buy groceries. Today, the indigenous have gasoline engines for hunting/fishing as well as plastics for food storage, products that never saw a true subsistence lifestyle. Rexford stands as a testimonial to women who still turn kill into edible and wearable goods, appropriating all parts, thus respecting the environment and preserving ancestral cultural heritage. Rexford too has adapted to virtuality, note her satellite dish.

University of North Carolina, Charlotte, professor Marek Ranis' transparent digital print, *Faith* (2017), pictures an inverted oil rig superimposed against an Arctic sunrise/sunset that becomes a metaphor for explaining frictions between mineral exploration and Norwegian Sami reindeer herders. Made to resemble stained glass, the photograph conjures sacred spaces. But this upside down rig is awkward looking, making viewers stop and think. Ranis merges metaphors of beauty with destruction, which apply to natural and man-made arenas. Machines that extract needed oil, providing Norway with wealth, are also capable of massive air and water pollution. The gorgeous landscape behind the rig, produced by the sun's energy, can also generate devastating consequences without man's assistance. Harkening back to early twentieth century Heideggerian discussions on the potency of the machine age, then fast forward to the twenty-first century, contemplating whether progress has been made when it comes to utilizing technology (natural and man-made) safely and efficiently, seems appropriate (Heidegger, Technology). The tug between preserving raw beauty and harnessing Nature occurs throughout all Arctic communities. In Norway reindeer grazing pastures are being turned into mineral development patches. In Alaska the debate about whether to allow copper mining in Bristol Bay, home to commercial and recreational salmon fishing, continues with the conundrum that providing jobs to indigenous locals, who can't rely on total subsistence, may pose environmental consequences if a mine were to leach toxins.

UCLA professor/photographer Rebecca Mendez scrutinizes ever changing landscapes: windblown grass lands, crashing water falls, cracking Polar ice, taking the Sublime to new heights by integrating her soul into natural environs. To Mendez, "the journey, in itself, is the medium" (Mendez). She documented migratory patterns of Arctic Terns who travel in a figure-eight pattern 44,300 miles from pole to pole, yearly. Populations have diminished from insufficient catch/eat and oceanic trash strangulations, as warmer, acidic waters have drastically changed habitats. In 2013, Mendez built *CircumSolar Migration 1,* a circular video screen, which she positioned on a Southern California beach. By projecting at night, the rim of the screen vanishes into darkness and thus the location of Arctic Terns in flight becomes immaterial. It is any place they visit, and everyone's problem to fix. She declares, "all living things exist within cyclical, migratory patterns that we should respect rather than ignore" (Mendez).

"Alaska is on the great circle route for shipping between North America and Asia," which means discarded waste accumulates in the Arctic (Plastic 138). Anchorage Museum's show *Gyre: The Plastic Ocean,* 2014, exhibited art from recycled detritus, slow to breakdown in landfills and salt water, as well as photographs of sea birds killed by ingesting plastics or becoming fatally entangled. Nicholas Mallos, director of Trash

Free Seas, presented bottle caps found at Gore Point, Alaska that read: New Zealand, Japan, Taiwan/China etc. Trash does circulate (Plastic 94, 95). Marine cleanup foundations exist but don't begin to make a dent in the mess caused by deliberate, accidental or environmental spillage (Plastic 142). Alaska's, 1989 Exxon Valdez Oil Spill destroyed Arctic aquatic life and increased oceanic pollution. A positive result was the creation of Seward's Alaska Sea Life Center, a tourist destination, education facility and an emergency room for aquatic mammals. Modern fish nets pose health hazards to ocean-going creatures, as webbing is not made of natural fibers and thus doesn't decompose. The mesh can be lost in a storm, or deliberately discarded at sea continuing to entrap sea life. Australian artist Sue Ryan's sculpture *Ghost Dog*, 2012, is made from abandoned fish nets, beach thongs and wire (Plastic 149-159) reconfiguring waste into art as seen in the recent Whitney exhibition, *Between the Waters,* 2018, which can, like the show *Gyre...* be Googled indefinitely after closing.

Virtuality helps artists and critics to be earthly aware and engage in conversations. But in the nineteenth century Arctic scientific-tourist travel, like the famous Harriman Expedition, 1899, produced maps, drawings and diaries, but information gleaned was initially available only to an elite few. Today, University of Colorado's Mark Serreze can share NASA satellite data with Internet audiences. For example, in 2016, St. Patrick Bay ice caps on Canada's Ellesmere Island, "covered only 5% of the areas that they did back in 1959 (Serreze 24)." And Marek Ranis has woven satellite photos into woolen carpets. Viewers can better relate to escalating Arctic/Antarctic melt when shown reality on rugs, common household items.

In 1867, and 1883, Swedish navigator Adolf Erik Nordenskiöld explored Greenland, encountering early Arctic pollution. He was puzzled by black powder floating in water holes situated in the ice, which would later be identified as coal dust, a by-product of the Industrial Revolution. (Hatfield 174-175). Since 1982, satellite visibility has greatly improved and can also record increased vegetation or 'shrubbification,' on the Tundra, another culprit contributing to carbon greenhouse gases as thawing continues (Serreze 56, 57, 218).

Visually explaining changes to the Tundra can be also understood in the recent Anchorage Museum show *Murmur: Arctic Realities,* 2018. Artist John Grade built a faux Pingo (15' x 38' x 42') from recycled yellow cedar. Grade offers visitors the chance to experience a Pingo in situ by providing 'HoloLens' goggles that virtualize sights and sounds of the Noatak National Preserve. A Pingo, Inuit for small hill, is like a 'cyst' upon the Arctic Tundra. They are formed by water thawing/freezing, gradually erupting permafrost about two centimeters yearly, but taking centuries to attain over 200 feet in height and 2,000 feet in diameter. Pingos are increasing, possibly due to gases from underground vegetable decomposition. Grade's Sublime is not somewhere out there while you stand safely on a precipice; it becomes inescapable with its Global Warming messaging.

Virtuality with all the electronic choices is a tool to implement change. It also takes a fearless art community, as art written, imaged, sculpted, or performed is a means to address social and political issues. Hungry museums will accept money from controversial sources. David Koch, a conservative philanthropist, is a Metropolitan Museum trustee who gave $65 million to renovate the Museum's Fifth Ave Plaza (Metropolitan, 9/10/14).   Universities cave to pressure from alumni and boards as seen when Polk State College, Florida rescinded adjunct professor Serhat Tanyolacar's *Death of Innocence,* because it referenced the Trump administration, unfavorably (*CAA,* 3/15/18).

Protesting, once relegated to street demonstrations and placards, explodes because of virtuality. Last summer's soccer match interrupted by Pussy Riot went viral on social media (*NYTimes,* 7/15/18). French philosopher Henri Lefebvre (1901-1991) wrote on art's relationship to social space before electronic simulacra; nonetheless he's still relevant, writing:

> Nothing disappears completely, however; nor can what subsists be defined solely in terms of traces, memories or relics. In space, what came earlier continues to underpin what follows. The preconditions of social space have their own particular way of enduring and remaining actual within that space.... "What is the fantasy of art? To lead out of what is present, out of what is close, out of representations of space, into what is further off, into nature, into symbols, into representational spaces. (Lefebvre 229-232)

Virtuality has expanded the power of art, to heighten social awareness; reality has been demoted, only if allowed.

References

Baudrillard, Jean. The Conspiracy of Art. Semiotext(e). New York,   2005. Print.
Bromwich, David. The Intellectual Life of Edmund Burke, From the Sublime and Beautiful to American Independence. Belknap Press of Harvard University Press, Cambridge, Massachusetts, 2014. Print.
Decker, Julie and Anchorage Museum, Gyre, The Plastic Ocean. Booth-Clibborn Editions, London, 2014. Print.
Hatfield, Philip J. Lines in the Ice, Exploring the Root of the World. McGill-Queen's University Press, Montreal & Kingston, 2016. Print.

Heidegger, Martin, The Question Concerning Technology and other Essays, William Lovitt, trans. Harper Perennial, New York, 1977. Print.

Lefebvre, Henri, The Production of Space. Blackwell Publishing, Malden Mass, 1991. Print.

Phillips, Adam, Ed. Edmund Burke, A Philosophical Enquiry. Oxford University Press, New York 2008. Print.

Serreze, Mark C., Brave New Arctic, The Untold Story of the Melting North. Princeton University Press, Princeton, New Jersey, 2018. Print.

Wilson, Edward O. The Social Conquest of Earth. Liveright Publishing Corporation, New York, 2012. Print.

Articles

CAA News Today, An Interview with Artist Serhat Tanyolacar on Censorship at Polk State College, College Art Association.
http://www.collegeart.org/news/2018/03/15/an-interview-with-artist-serhart-tanyolacar-on-ce. Web. March 15, 2018

Davenport, Carol. With Trump in Charge, Climate Change References Purged from Website. New York Times.
https://www.nytimes.com/2017/01/20/us/politics/trump-white-house-website.html Web. January 20, 2017.

New York Times Editorial Board. Donald Trump Has Endangered Species in His Sights.
https://www.nytimes.com/2018/07/22/opinion/editorials/zinke-interior-endangered-species...Web. July 22, 2018

Hollander, Zaz. From Bad to Worse: State Announces More King Salmon Fishing Shutdowns for Susitna Valley, Anchorage Daily News.
htpps://www.adn.com/outdoors-adventure/fishing/2018/06/21/from-bad-to-worse-state-announces-more-king-fishing-shutdowns-for-susitna-valley/ Web.   June, 21, 2018

Tunseth, Matt. Fish and Game Restricts King Salmon Fishing to Catch-and Release on Kenai, Kasilof Rivers, Anchorage Daily News.
https://www.adn.com/alaska-news/2018/07/16/fish-and-game-restricts-king-fishing-to-catch-and-release-on-kenai-kasilof/. Web. July, 16, 2018

Kang, Cecilia, Melting Arctic Ice Makes High-Speed Internet a Reality in a Remote Town. New York Times.
https://www.nytimes.com/2017/12/02/technology/from-the-arctics-melting-ice-an-unexpected-digital-hub.html.   Web. December 2, 2107

Metropolitan Museum's New David H. Koch Plaza Opens to the Public September 10

Metropilitan Museum. https://www.metropolitanmuseum.org/press/news/2014/plaza-opening. Web. September 10, 2014

Nechepurenko, Ivan and Melissa Gomez. Pussy Riot Members Detained After Running Onto Field at World Cup Final, Police Say, New York Times.
https://www.nytimes.com/2018/07/15/sports/soccer/pussy-riot-world-cup-final.html.   Web.

July 15, 2018.

Rozell, Ned. Snow and Ice Samples from Mount Hunter Show a Record of a Colder Past, Anchorage Daily News,
    htpps://www.adn.com/alaska-news/science/2018/05/26/snow-and-ice-samples-from-mount-hunter-show-a-record-of-a-colder-past. Web. May, 26, 2018

Ryan, John, Seattle Bans Most Plastic Straws in Restaurants. National Public Radio.
    https://www.npr.org/2018/06/30/624911805/seattle-bans-most-plastic-straws-in   restaurants, Web. June 30, 2018.

The Last Straw? Seattle will say goodbye to plastic straws, utensils with upcoming ban. The Seattle Times.
    https://www.seattletimes.com/seattle-news/the-last-straw-seattle-will-say-goodbye-to-plastic-straws-utensils-with-upcoming-ban/ Web. September 8, 2017.

Artists' and Exhibitions Cited

Anchorage Museum. Gyre: The Plastic Ocean, Exhibition
    https://www.anchoragemuseum.org/exhibits/gyre-the-plastic-ocean/

Anchorage Museum. Murmur: Arctic Realities
    http://www.anchoragemuseum.org/exhibits/murmur-artic-realities/

Mendez, Rebeca. (artist). https://www.aiga.org/2017-aiga-medalist-rebeca-mendez
    https://www.anchoragemuseum.org/about-us/museum-journal-archive/rebeca-mendez-explores-landscape-boundaries-and-culture/

Whitney Museum of American Art. Between the Waters
    https://www.Whitney.org/Exhibitions/BetweenTheWaters

Contemporary Art, Democratization and Social Change:
Politics of Art in Postcolonial Buddhist Sri Lanka

Sabine Grosser

Nearly half a century after the ending of colonial rule, during the 90s of the twentieth century, a new art scene and art discourse developed in Sri Lanka influenced by the continuing civil war of this time.

Ten essential aspects will be identified in the form of ten hypotheses that characterize the developments in the Sri Lankan art scene by the turn of the millennium working for a peaceful, democratic society. It will be exemplified how this generation question social structures and power relations and not only contribute to the development of a new art discourse but also to the ongoing democratization process of the society.

My considerations are based on the insights and research that I have been able to do in the country during my five-year stay between 1997 and 2002, and which I am still updating with observations from outside.

A View from the Outside: Some Methodological Remarks

In the last twenty years, I have been observing the development of contemporary art in Sri Lanka. Beginning in 1997 working as a DAAD[1] Senior Lecturer at the University of Kelaniya. During five years—until 2002—I had the chance to become an eye witness of the development of a vibrant art scene in this country—the so-called 90s generation. During this time, I collected material in situ and designed a research concept that involved my experiences. In 2010 my writings were structured in my publication about *Contemporary Art and the Culture of Commemoration in Sri Lanka*, with focus on its developments at the turn of the centuries.[2] My considerations here are based on those

---

[1] DAAD Deutscher Akademischer Austausch Dienst / German Academic Exchange Service.

[2] Grosser, Sabine. Kunst und Erinnerungskultur Sri Lankas im Kontext kultureller Globalisierung – Eine

findings updated by additional material until today.

In my research, I develop a multi-perspective approach to contemporary art in Sri Lanka and especially the art movement at the turn of the centuries. An original methodological approach was developed referring not only to art historical methods but also considering methods of social sciences.[3] To avoid a generalising subsuming and to meet the work of every artist the book does not give a survey or puts a theoretical framing over the considerations but chooses an inductive approach and concentrates on the oeuvres of five artists: two female artists, Anoli Perera and Druvinka Madawela, as well as three male artists, Koralegadara Pushpakumar, Chandraguptha Thenuwara and Jagath Weerashinghe.

The readings and analyses show that those five artists portray a new generation that developed nearly half a century after the colonial regime. The term *'90s trend*, *'90s generation* or *'90s movement* seems beyond dispute and the term is used in the ongoing discussion (compare for example Weerashinge 2012).

In the following, I will use ten hypotheses to characterize how the *'90s generation* strengthens the process of peace and democratization in the country. I'll concentrate on three artists Anoli Perea, Chandragutha Thenuwara and Jagath Weerasingh.

1. Most Artists of this Generation Derive from the New Middle Class.

Especially Anoli Perera[4] describes her artistic work based on her personal life experience as a woman in the socio-cultural context of the newly-established middle class in Sri Lanka.[5] The term stands out because in the Sri Lankan context it is usually used in the sense of a positive self-designation and is not disparagingly connoted as in the German linguistic context. Most artists of the *'90s generation* come from the emerging middle class[6], belong to the same generation, were fortunate enough to study abroad

---

multiperspektivische Betrachtung als Beitrag zum transkulturellen Dialog. Oberhausen: Athena Verlag, 2010. (In the following: Grosser 2010)

[3] Acknowledging that it would be not possible to undergo the outside perspective, this methodological approach was outlined in detail (compare Grosser 2010, 9–96). To briefly mention some of the central methodological considerations: In order to put the outside point of view into perspective artist interviews were included, because the artists are understood as experts in their own lifeworld, who construct their own role models. Those interviews are also quoted in this paper. The complete interviews you may find in this book in English language (Grosser 2010, 477 – 532: http://www.athena-verlag.de/controller.php?cmd= detail&titelnummer=414 (15.11.2017)).

[4] Anoli Perera was born 1962 in Colombo and describes herself as a self-taught artist.

[5] Compare for example the interview with Anoli Perera, printed in: Grosser 2010, 485–492.

[6] Arunatilake, Nisha / Omar, Mufaris: The Sri Lankan global middle class – trends and effects on the economy.

(either in the USA or the former Sovjet Union) —usually with the help of scholarships—and came back to the country around 1990.

In the local Sri Lankan context, the term "middle class"[7] stands for the breaking up of a subtle caste system, which assigns people to solid groups, even though the Sri Lankan constitution states that all men and women are equal. It is a consequence of the postcolonial changes in the society (after the Independence of Ceylon from the British in 1948), combined with major political reforms in the 1970s: The land reforms brought on by the government of Sirimavo Bandaranaike who limited private owner ship of land and the reforms towards a free market by the government of J. R. Jayewardene. The formation of a new "middle class" offers the artists an opportunity to redefine one's own position within a democratic society—and as we can see in the interviews they are very much aware about this development. The artists understand their responsibility towards the society as a mission from their parent's generation. Usually, a different career goal was pursued, such as a doctor or diplomat, and coincidences influenced the development towards the artistic profession.

Excursus: Differences to the '43- Group

In contrast to the '43-Group, an artist group founded immediately after the colonial era. The members of the '43-group came mainly from the upper classes, who usually studied abroad due to the family background, especially France, and who adopted and adapted to the cultural habits of the ruling colonial rulers, such as playing the piano or painting as part of a good education:

> ... the background of the 43 group was mainly influenced by the apparently aspireable middle class culture of the colonial rulers: Up to the 1970s, the official visual art scene belonged largely to the privileged colonialized elite, those with the means to purchase paintings and the leisure to learn to appreciate them. ... But all were educated enough to

---

Back ground paper written for the State of the Economy 2013 of the Institute of Policy Studies of Sri Lanka. Colombo 2013. https://www.researchgate.net/publication/278021521_The_Sri_Lankan_global_middle_class_-_trends_and_effects_on_the_economy [accessed Aug 15 2018].

[7] Upper class made up primary of landowners, the Upper middle class of educated professionals holding traditional jobs such as Lawyers, Doctors, Army officers, Academics, senior Civil Servants and police officers; and merchants. The political leaders of the new Dominion of Ceylon came from these two classes. Lower middle class made up persons who were educated but held less prestigious, but respected jobs such lower level public servants, policemen, and teachers.

support themselves with 'white collar' employment, even to travel abroad. Among the 43 Group, all spoke English well or reasonably well, and all but Manjusiri had Christian, not Buddhist, backgrounds." (Dissanayake 1998, o. S.)

2. Most Members of the So-called 90s Movement are Willing to Take Social and Political Responsibility.

Jagath Weerasinghe[8] and Chandraguptha Thenuwara[9] describe themselves most clearly as political artists. They come back to Sri Lanka in 1992 after studying in the USA and the Sovjet Union willing to change the situation in their country.

With their art they give a public, political statement: For example Chandraguptha Thenuwara with his painting "*Mirror Wall*" (oil on canvas, 159.5 x 140.3 cm, 1992), mediating his reaction to the news of the pogrom against the Tamils. In the interview, he describes the artwork as his statement to the former political situation.

The title Mirror Wall refers to a rock face in Sigiriya, with the same name, on which visitors have left their messages for centuries. He interprets this Graffiti as political statements which have been covered with paint. The emptied bucket in the painting points to this imaginary action. According to the artist, the image of the emptied bucket also generally represents the "absence of something". The carelessly spilled paint could also evoke the association with needlessly spilled blood.

The artists analyse the changing situation, take a new perspective on the political and religious traditions and introduce a new attitude into the art scene: The responsibility of the individual for the ongoing violence in the society, connected with the reflection of their own role as an individual in the society.

3. In a Destabilised Postcolonial Surrounding the Artists Position Themselves in a very Personal Way.

The starting point and motivation for the artists are their personal experiences. Like

---

[8]   Jagath Weerasinghe was born in 1954 in Moratuwa, a small village close to the capital Colombo; educated as an archaeologist at the University of Kelaniya, he later studied fine arts in Washington D.C., USA. Today he works as artist and teaches art and archaeology at the Postgraduate Institute of Archaeology, University of Kelaniya, Sri Lanka.

[9]   Chandraguptha Thenuwara was born in the southern part of Sri Lanka in 1960 and is married to Kumudini Samuel. She is a prominent human rights activist and Tamil. This important conjunction takes a significant influence on his political attitude.

Jagath Weerasinghe explains:

> My topic has always been (pauses) ... it has always been
> myself. ...You can not have a very strong line between private and
> public ... it comes into your private stuff ... But these are the two ways
> that I look at my subject matter ... but my subject matter is always
> myself.[10]

The artist describes his situation as highly influenced by Buddhist traditions and at the same time destabilised by the postcolonial context, as well as the long lasting political violence in Sri Lanka.[11] In his paintings, he combines his examination of the virulent topic of war and violence in his country with his personal positioning as a Buddhist. He addresses this topic for example in the early painting *Broken Stupa* (1992)[12], which shows a scattered stupa standing symbolically as prominent symbol for Buddhist culture in Sri Lanka.

The stupa — originating from India — developed its specific form (in the shape of a bell) in Sri Lanka and is understood as a core part of the local temple architecture. The stupa represents the cosmos and the Nirvana. In Weerasinghe's painting it represents his dilemma as a Buddhist in a country affected by the civil war: The stupa, a core symbol of Buddhism, is present but destroyed.

But this painting can also be read as a rebellion against the western ideals of classical modernism, which the student was taught by his Sri Lankan teachers H.A. Karunaratne and Stanley Abeysinghe. Those modernist postulates include the "perfect composition" or the attempt to "depict any kind of reality". Those formal postulates don't correspond with the artist's experience of a fragile, unclear and fragmented surrounding. In the interview he states, "And why do I think that I can make a perfect painting when everything else in the world is totally screwed up and collapsed ... "[13]

4. New Topics are Introduced by the Artists in the Public Discussion.

Until the end of colonialism, contemporary social and political topics hardly played a major role in the pictures of Sri Lankan art.   During the 1990s the ongoing civil war in

---

[10]   Interview with Jagath Weerasinghe, printed in: Grosser 2010, 264.

[11]   Grosser 2010, 265–267.

[12]   Jagath Weerasinghe 1992. The Broken Stupa, Acrylic on Paper, 54 x 40 cm.

[13]   Interview with Jagath Weerasinghe 2002, printed in: Grosser 2010, 516–532.

Sri Lanka (1983–2009), its impact on the society and the question of the responsibility of an artist, as well the impacts of globalisation, became the dominating topics in the local art scene. For example in Chandraguptha Thenuwara's *Dance of Victory*[14] and two years later Jagath Weerasinghe's *Who are you Soldier?*.[15]

Both artworks use helmets, body parts and crouches as symbols for the operators of war: the soldiers. However, the fighters are not depicted as personified figures, heroes or victors but as victims. The parts of the painting remain fragmented, symbolizing wounded bodies, damaged by war.

Jagath Weerasinghe works with, for him typical during this time, muted and broken colour palettes and a fragmented composition. The helmet, the body parts and the hand raised in premonition, like a warning sign, are clearly recognizable and stand in bright contrast to the diffuse background, almost resembling a warning. The colour palette reminds of bush-fighting and blood. The dark green and red tones increase their effect through an intense complementary contrast. By the question: Who are you Soldier the artist speaks directly to the viewer: Who are you, son, father, husband—whose insignia of a soldier's life is recognizable in the picture? Via the message contained within the artwork, the individual person is addressed, aiming to remind him of his individual societal responsibility.

Two years later Chandraguptha Thenuwara questions the role of the soldier with the title: *Dance of Victory*: What remains after an alleged victory, when the injured winners have staggered away from the battlefield. The figures do not appear as heroes but seem vulnerable and pitiable. For his work the painter uses a very clear, easy to decode visual language, staying loyal to his intensive colour palette of yellow and orange hues.[16]

---

[14]   Acrylic on Canvas, 152,5 x 173,5 cm.

[15]   Oil on canvas, 48 x 60 cm.

[16]   Both artists choose the easel painting as prominent medium of the art scene in Sri Lana during the nineties. In both paintings, the pictorial subject matter is not depicted in a naturalistic sense, but rather realised with a certain degree of abstraction; but still distinctly decodable pictorial symbols can be identified. Despite differing colour-palettes, clear colours and an expressive flow characterise both of the artist's working methods. At the first glance, the paintings might remind a Western observer of classical Modernism, especially Expressionism. When we consider Jagath Weerasinghes remarks about his Sri Lankan teachers mentioned before, it may be noticed that, not only with the theme, but also with the chosen artistic expression, he again places himself against the local reception of the classical modernism of his teacher generation — like described in the last passage, against a clear composition, a clear colour palette and so on.

5. The Artists Increasingly Obtain a Public Role in the Society, Whilst Creating a New Role Model of an Artist.

However, the artists are not only introducing new topics and new artistic techniques into the art scene, furthermore they construct a new role model of an artist in the local context, who tries to take influence on the society and its development in various ways. Again Jagath Weerasinghe describes his role as an artist in the society on multiple levels:

"First as an activist in art and politics, second as a teacher and third as an artist. These roles mix together, boundaries are blurred." (Interview with Jagath Weerasinghe 2002, printed in: Grosser 2010, 516–532)

His colleagues also take on this role: Chandraguptha Thenuware is the founder of the Vibhavi Art Academy in 1996—a non-governmental and non-profit institution, established as an alternative and independent art school, Anoli Perera is one of the founding members of Theertha International Artists Collective, organising a gallery, international exchange including an educational art program for the rural areas.

6. The Ongoing Civil War Takes a Catalytic Effect on the Artist's Efforts and Unifies also Those with Different Opinions.

New art places develop during the 1990—like the Heritage Gallery, a non-profit art space, or the Barefoot Gallery by Dominik and Nazreen Sanzoni. They intensify the public discussion; more and more artists raise their voice, like Kingsley Gunatillake, Tissa de Alwis or Muhanned Cader—to introduce some more names.

Younger artist like for example Pradeep Chandrasiri, born in 1968, enrich the discussion. He himself a victim of a torture camp, connects to the local visual context with his installation *Broken Hands*: He uses the very common clay as material for the hands lying on wooden piles in different heights. In combination with charcoal, oil lamps and beetle leaves he evokes impressions of local everyday culture which is not only limited to temples or museums.[17]

Or Sujith Rathnayake, born 1971 in Ranna. He refers in his artwork to the aesthetics of the local print media of this time, which ruthlessly publishes images of scattered body parts of suicide bombers. The artist uses media prints in his artwork and combines them with his own gestural paintings: With the title *After the Town Hall Bomb* 2000 for instance he relates to an assault on Chandrika Kumaratunga Bandaranaike in in front of the town hall in Sri Lanka's capital Colombo.

---

[17] Pradeep Chandrasiri 1997. Broken Hands, installation with wood, charcoal, oillamps, nails, clay, Bethel leaves.

Tamil artists are not visible in the local art scene in Colombo during the nineties as the country is divided. Only in 2002 the Paradise Road Gallery shows a one-man exhibition of Thamotharampillai Shanaathanan. This prominent artist was born 1980 in Jaffna, studied art in India at the University of Delhi and currently works at the Art Department of Jaffna University. In his art work, he combines Tamil traditions with postmodern thinking. One major topic is the interrelatedness of the individual with its surrounding.

The political discussion and examination of war has a connecting effect on the artists. Despite their different opinions, they unite in order to take a public stand.

7. The Artists Choose Consciously from Various Artistic Styles to Transfer Their Ideas and Experiment with New Art Forms, Like Installations, Performances or Mobile Art Projects to Find the Best Way to Express Their Ideas and to Reach a Bigger Audience.

During the 1990s, the panel painting in oil or acrylic is the predominant medium of the art scene, stylistically influenced by the local debate about modernity, with distinct colours and an expressive painting style with a mostly fragmented composition. The focus is set on the contextual statement and the communicated message of the painting. The strong connection between the political and personal level is a characteristic.

At the turn of the millennium more and more artists discuss the possibilities of art as a political instrument. Increasingly the question, which artistic instruments would accomplish the intended effect on the viewer, comes into focus. The artists more and more reflect on their role in society by discovering various possibilities of art and using cultural events as political forms of action.

They use varying stylistic elements and techniques to create easy to understand, decoded, attractive pictures which leave no doubt regarding their message.

Chandraguptha Thenuwara explains:

> C. T.: ... sometimes I have to do political work and same the human figure.
> S. G.: You divide these two aspects or you bring them also together?
> C. T.: I'm trying now to bring them together. Sometimes you need modern art forms, sometimes you need the orthodox conventional art forms to deliver a message. I'm lucky I can do both. If I need a figurative expression, I can do it. I have the skill and the training, because that I have an advantage doing that kind of thing ...and that's why I might have

to repeat the same thing again and again to simplify the work and do more political exhibitions than exhibitions not only to show *your* capacity as an artist.[18]

The first installations at the Heritage Gallery[19] in Colombo enrich the discussion: Chandraguptha Thenuwara's *Barrelism* and Jagath Weerasinghe's *Yantra Gala and the Round Pilgrimage*[20].

Excursus: Yantra Gala and the Round Pilgrimage

Jagath Weerasinghe refers in his installation to his Buddhist background and combines artistic, political and spiritual aspects. He describes, that the idea for this work *Yantra Gala and the Round Pilgrimage* initially occurred in his mind,

"… organising a ceremony for a group of parents, whose children had disappeared and murdered in 1989-90 at torture camps at Embilipitiya. … most of the mothers came wearing white saris and holding a picture of their lost child. These women reminded me of mothers going to temples with flowers, held in their hands. Their white saris made it so severe a feeling. Instead of flowers, now they are carrying the photograph of a child who is now murdered. The irony in this situation sank deep into my heart. What made them go from place to place in search of their lost children, as if they were doing the annual round pilgrim of sacred places? One of the mothers asked me crying, 'Is nobody concerned with our suffering?' My work began from this question." (Weerasinghe 1999)

The exhibition consists of different components: The Yantra Gala (91.4 x 91.4 x 61 cm), a relief titled Altar Piece (182 x 46 x 12 cm) and eight paintings (each 86.4 x 55.9 cm). The Yantra Gala in the centre of the room is empty, only the mould reminds of its intentional function as base of a Buddha statue. Jagath Weerasinghe understands the inoperable Yantra Gala as a metaphor of the lost Buddhist Dharma and a symbol for a sacred Buddhist place. Around the stone rice is spread on the ground, reminding of everyday scenes of drying rice on the street. In between the crops, small labels with

---

[18] Sabine Grosser (S. G.), interview with Chandraguptha Thenuwara (C. T.) 2.4.2002, printed in Grosser 2010, 503 – 515.

[19] During the nineties, the Heritage Gallery was an exhibition space in the spirit of a non-profit-oriented gallery for experimental art initiated by a local architect and managed by the artist and graphic designer Balbier Bodth.

[20] Jagath Weerasinghe 1999. Yantra Gala and the Round Pilgrimage. Installation in the Heritage Gallery comprising eight oil paintings on canvas with collage, elements of an altar with wood, resin, clay, gold leaf, wheat, earth.

names of torture and detention camps, as well as names of sacred places in Sri Lanka can be detected. Small green birds made from clay are distributed all over the room, like small symbols of hope. On the central wall the Altar Piece—a relief with another small mould of a Buddha statue and scattered clay flowers and lamps framed by two paintings of a Mal Asabaya—evoke impressions of an altar, which has lost its function.

The eight small paintings show a variation of similar scenes in dark colours highlighted with clear yellow colour: Women in Saris, holding a picture in their hands, an empty speech balloon symbolising their unheard voices and maps of Sri Lanka representing the search of the mothers for their lost children. With the combination of the different components the artist sets an analogy between the search of the mothers and the annual round pilgrimage combining twelve sacred places on the island.

In the installation, the artist takes over components of Buddhist, Sinhala visual culture. The symbols like the Sinhala script, or the sacred components such as the Yantra Gala or the flower altar are familiar primarily to the Buddhist Sinhala population. In this way Weerasinghe achieves the intended effect of the works of art and facilitates the discussion of the own history, especially the violence and injustices in society.

In the local discourse Weerasinghe's exhibition *Yantra Gala and the Round Pilgrimage* is considered as the first installation in the country. (Compare Grosser 2010, 286–288)

8. The Artists Understand the Galleries and Public Places as a Space for Freedom of Expression.

Public space and mobile concepts for exhibiting art play an increasingly important role: like for example the concept of a mobile exhibition of flags *Artists Against War: Flag-Project-Workshop* (Noothana Sithuvam Vansaya) designed by a group of Sri Lankan artists and presented at various public places of political interest or Chandraguptha Thenuwara's *Barrelism.*

Excursus: Barrelism

In 1997 the artist launched his ongoing series of camouflage works entitled *Barrelism*. The ending -ism reminds us ironically of various Isms in art history. The first artwork in this series was an oil painting titled *Camouflage* (100 x 149.5 cm). Human figures holding crutches arise like silhouettes in between the camouflage patterns.

The symbol of the Barrel is connected with personal experiences of the artist. As a child living in the eastern province he saw burning barrels alongside the road used by workers building streets. Promising the opportunity to meet friends and relatives more easily and getting connected with the world. During the civil war this positive symbolic meaning changed: In Colombo the barrels painted in camouflage colours and installed as checkpoints became part of the urban landscape, disturbing the accessibility of places, limiting the freedom of movement. In the interview Thenuware describes his association of the barrels with vessels that hold the blood of people.

Gradually the artist became more interested in the barrel as an object, its object hood and locality. He uses the cylindrical container with a height of 35 inches and a diameter of 23 inches in his artwork in a newly defined context:

> In fact, the tar barrel is not an innocent object anymore. It symbolises state power and Sinhala racism. You can see that the yellow colour is widely used for painting of military barrels. Generally, the meaning of camouflaging an object is to avoid drawing special attention to it or to hide it. But the yellow colour draws one's attention quickly. For example, the major colour, which is used to paint road signs and pedestrian crossing lines, is yellow. Then, what is the purpose of yellow coloured military barrels? To show the power. Thanks to the overwhelming presence of barrels, the government maintains its power over the masses. On the other hand, barrels provide security for the centres of power. I have tried to express this reality through the image of barrels.[21]

With the intention to provoke a discussion in the society the public space gains high importance for his art-work. As plans for his first public installation of barrles, the *Monument for the Innocent Victims of War* in front of the Galadari Hotel in Colombo were disturbed due to a bomb blast there—Thenuwara used the open space in front of the Vibhavi Art Academy for the installation instead, opposing the bureaucratic state power.

In order to address as many different people as possible Chandraguptha Thenuwara uses various artistic styles and techniques to transmit his ideas—as already mentioned in the last hypothesis and as it also becomes clear in the *Barrelism* project. Most important for him is the intended political message. Most consequently he uses the barrels which are used by the military for building their checkpoints and disturbing the public life in the capital Colombo and combines them with his paintings, like in the installation *Woman in*

---

[21] Interview with Thenuware, Medis 1999.

Barrelistic Area or refers to them like in the graphic *Barrelism Tourist Map*[22].

Excursus: New Concepts of Commemoration in Public Space

Within this process also new concepts of commemoration in public space are introduced on the island. Already during the ongoing conflict two memorials are inaugurated: *The Shrine of Innocents* (1999) by Jagath Weerasinghe close to the parliament lake and Chandraguptha Thenuwara's *The Monument of the Disappeared* (2000) in Raddulowa. Both memorials have very different concepts and stories. Both are dedicated to all victims of the lasting conflict. But the first is very much involved in local power plays. The latter one is more dedicated to grass root structures in a global context and uses transnational networks. Therefore, the story of those two places shows very clearly the advantages and disadvantages of both systems. In 2015 the *Shrine of Innocents* is abandoned, and *The Monument of the Disappeared* is still involved in regular official commemoration ceremonies.

9. The Artists Cooperate with Other Groups in the Society to Spread Their Ideas.

The artists form coalitions with other groups of society. They reflect on their role in society and use their public role consciously. Increasingly people accept them in this role. The artists turn into the voice of public opinion, which agitates for peace politics over the years.

Cultural events are used effectively as political instrument. For example, when Dr. Neelan Thiruchelvam, a lawyer, politician and human rights activist became a victim of a political assassination in 1999 various groups of the society unified and reacted promptly with the Neelan Thiruchelvam Commemorative Programme—an Art Exhibition for Peace and Reconciliation (2000) and with a street art painting at the place of the assassination. The Vibhavi Academy of Fine Arts (founded by Chandraguptha Thenuwara) organises the exhibition in cooperation with the Centre for Ethnic Studies (ICES) and the Law & Society Trust & Thiruchelvam Association.

---

[22] Chandraguptha Thenuwara 1997. Barrelism Tourist Map, mixed media.

10. The Artists Use Mass Media and Digital Media to Extend Their Influence. Networking—also Beyond National Borders—Becomes an Important Strategy.

In addition to exhibitions, lectures and briefings, means of advertising are increasingly being used: An association of industrialists launched with the slogan *Sri Lanka First* a large-scale print and TV advertising campaign with full-page newspaper advertisements and commercials for peace. An impressive climax of this campaign was a human chain from the airport to the southern tip of the island. Public opinion is clearly addressed against the war during this time. Artists are used in this action as key figures and emerge as central figures in the newspaper pictures.

Public opinion turns in this time clearly against the war. Political change is expected with the election of Ranil Wickramasinghe in December 2001. Already in February 2002 the new prime minister agrees to an official ceasefire. Also after the ceasefire the artists continue their work: In 2002 they run the exhibition ART PEACE at the Lionel Wendt Gallery in Colombo and in 2003 artists from Colombo organise together with colleagues from Jaffna the first exhibition in a city that has been inaccessible for many Sri Lankan for a long time. This positive development is interrupted in 2006 with the re-intensification of the war. Finally, the civil war is ended militarily after 26 years in May 2009. But even now in 2018 many artists of this generation continue their political work and engage not only in dealing with the trauma of war. For example, at the beginning of 2015 artists were campaigning for a political change in the country: as they were disappointed that the political elite did not change its politics fundamentally but old structures continued.

These considerations support the view that democratization is understood today as an active process that is shaped and sustained by many individuals. Artists can influence this process on different levels, as shown by the example of Sri Lanka.

References

AFAD (Asian Federation Against Involuntary Disappearances). 2011, October. *Attempts to Destroy Monument of the Disappeared in Sri Lanka, A Grievous Offense Against Victims and Their Families.* https://afadsecretariat.wordpress.com/tag/monument-for-the-disappeared/ (Last accessed on 1 July 2016).

AFAD (Asian Federation Against Involuntary Disappearances). 2012, October. *The Monument of the Disappeared in Sri Lanka: A Struggle of Memory Against Forgetting.* http://afad-online.org/news/10-statements/59-the-monument-of-the-disappeared-in-sri-lanka-a-struggle-of-memory-against-forgetting (Last accessed on 1 July 2016).

Assmann, A. 1999. *Erinnerungsräume, Formen und Wandlungen des kulturellen Gedächtnisses.* München: C.H. Beck.

Arunatilake, N. / Omar, M.. 2013. The Sri Lankan global middle class – trends and effects on the economy. Back ground paper written for the State of the Economy 2013 of the Institute of Policy Studies of Sri Lanka. Colombo 2013.

Bandaranayake, S. 1986. *The Rock and Wall Paintings of Sri Lanka.* Colombo: Lake House Bookshop.

Belting, H. 1988. `Das Werk im Kontext`, in: Belting, H.; Dilly H. and Kemp W. (eds.,): *Kunstgeschichte. Eine Einführung.* Berlin: Reimer Verlag, 222 ff.

Bhabha, H. K. 1994. *The Location of Culture.* New York: Psychology Press.

Boehm, G. 2004. `Jenseits der Sprache? Anmerkungen zur Logik der Bilder`, in C. Maar and H. Burda (eds.,) *Iconic Turn. Die neue Macht der Bilder.* Köln: Du Mont. 28–43.

Bogner A.; Littig B. and Menz W. 2005. *Das Experteninterview. Theorie, Methode, Anwendung.* (2) Wiesbaden: Springer.

DaCosta Kaufmann, T.; Dossin, C. and Joyeux-Prunel, B. (eds.,) 2015. *Circulations in the Global History of Art. Prunel, Studies in Art Historiography.* London: Routledge.

Dewhirst, P.; Kapur, A. 2015, March. *GENDER JUSTICE: The Disappeared and Invisible. Revealing the Enduring Impact of Enforced Disappearance on Women.* https://www.ictj.org/sites/default/files/ICTJ-Global-Gender-Disappearances-2015.pdf (Last accessed on 1 July 2016)

Dharmasiri, A. 1988. *Modern Art in Sri Lanka: The Anton Wickremasinghe Collection.* Colombo: Associated Newspapers of Ceylon.

Dissanayake, S. B. 1999. `Paintings and Painters of Sri Lanka 1948-1998: Independence's Step Children Looking Beyond Post Modernism`, in The George Keyt Foundation (ed.). *Moods and Modes: Fifty Years of Sri Lankan Painting.* Publication information unavailable.

Gasparini, M. January 2014, updated February 2016. *Interview with Monica Juneja about Global Art History.* http://trafo.hypotheses.org/567 (Last accessed on 21 May 2017)

Geertz, C. 1987. `Dichte Beschreibung. Bemerkungen zu einer deutenden Theorie von Kultur`, in: Geertz C. *Beiträge zum Verstehen kultureller Systeme*, Frankfurt a. M. 1987 (1. 1973), 7 – 43.

Grosser, S. 2004. `Changing Worlds: Music, Women and Fine Arts in Postcolonial Sri Lanka`, in: Baumann M.P. and Claus-Bachmann M. (eds.,). *WOM (The World of Music)* 46 (3) Bamberg: University of Bamberg, 101 - 111.

Grosser, S. 2008. `Contextualising Contemporary Sri Lankan Art / Le Contexte de l'Art Contemporain au Sri Lanka`, in: Mona Bismarck Foundation (ed.). *Expressions d'Indépendance, Exhib. Cat., 4.4. - 12.7. Paris,* 51 - 75.

Grosser, S. 2010. *Kunst und Erinnerungskultur Sri Lankas im Kontext kultureller Globalisierung– Eine multiperspektivische Betrachtung als Beitrag zum transkulturellen Dialog.* Oberhausen: Athena Verlag.

Grosser, S. 2015, October. *Re-considering the Responsibility of an Artist in a Postcolonial, Buddhist Society – looking at Sri Lanka.* http://www.seismopolite.com/re-considering-the-responsibility-of-an-artist-in-a-postcolonial-buddhist-society-looking-at-sri-lanka (Last accessed on 1 July 2016)

Hall, S. 1999: `Kulturelle Identität und Globalisierung`, in Hörning, K. and Winter R. (eds.,).

Widerspenstige Kulturen. Frankfurt a. M.: Suhrkamp, 393 – 441.

Halpé, A. 1977. `The Tortuous Path: Modernity and Alienation in Sri Lankan Art`, in: George Keyt Foundation (ed.). *Felicitation Volume.* Publication information unavailable.

Harrison, G.: Democratization. https://www.britannica.com/topic/democratization (15.8.2018)

Krieger, V. (ed.) 2008. *Kunstgeschichte und Gegenwartskunst. Vom Nutzen und Nachteil der Zeitgenossenschaft.* Köln/Weimar/Wien: Böhlau Verlag.

Martin, J.H. 2005. `Modernität als Hindernis für die gerechte Beurteilung der Kulturen`, in: Heinrich-Böll-Stiftung (ed.) *Reader der internationalen Kulturkonferenz: Idenität versus Globalisierung. Haus der Kulturen der Welt, Berlin 20. – 22. Januar 2005.* Publication information unavailable.

Medis, D. 1999, November. *A conversation with Sri Lankan artist Chandraguptha Thenuwara.* http://www.wsws.org/articles/1999/nov1999/cam-n19.shtml (Last accessed on 16 June 2003).

The George Keyt Foundation (ed.) 1999. *Moods and Modes: Fifty Years of Sri Lankan Painting.* Publication information unavailable.

Oshani, P.A.L. and Wijethissa, K.G.C.P. 2015. *Conceptual Policy Framework for Urban Parks in Sri Lanka with special reference to the Diyatha Uyana Urban Park.* Kelaniya: University of Kelaniya, Sri Lanka.

Perera, A. 2000a. Reclaiming Histories ..., in: Sapumal Foundation, Exhib. Cat. (ed.) *Reclaiming Histories: A Retrospective Exhibition of Women's Art.* Colombo. Publication information unavailable.

Perera, A. (ed.) 2000b: *Artists Against Violence: An Art Exhibition for Peace and Reconciliation, Catalogue of the Neelan Thiruchelvam Commemorative Exhibition, Exhib. Cat.,* Colombo. Publication information unavailable.

Perera, A. 2000b: *A new order: contemporary visual art in Sri Lanka, in: Art Asia Pacific* (26): 72 –77.

Perera, Anoli, State of Sri Lankan Art, Frontline 16, Februar, Chennai, India, 1999, 13 – 26.

Perera, A. 1997. `A Socio Political Reading of Yantra Gala and the Round Pilgrimage, an Exhibition of Paintings and Installations by Jagath Weerasinghe, Heritage Art Gallery, Colombo`, Daily News and Sunday Observer. Publication information unavailable.

Perera, S. 2001. `Public Spaces and Monuments: Politics of Sanctioned and Contested Memory, Paper presented at the conference 'Current Anthropological Research in Sri Lanka``, in: *PRAVADA (Sinhala)*, Vol. 19 – 20. Publication information unavailable.

Sri Lanka Brief 2012, February. *Expression of Protest against the Destruction of the Shrine of Innocents.* http://srilankabrief.org/2012/02/expression-of-protest-against-the-destruction-of-the-shrine-of-innocents/ (Last accessed on 1 July 2016)

Author unavailable 1999. `Embilipitiya agony – parents of missing children still sullen`, in *The Island.* Publication information unavailable.

Thenuwara, C. 2005. *Barrelism: A response to the Militarization of Urban Space.* Unpublished lecture at the workshop `Gendering Urban Space in the Middle East and South Asia`, organised by Institute for Gender and Women Studies American University in Cairo and Shehr Network, February 2005 in Cairo.

Thenuwara C. 2001. `Brilliant Politically Inspired Artist`, in: *The Island*. Publication information unavailable.

Turner, Caroline (ed.) 2005. *Art and Social Change. Contemporary Art in Asia and the Pacific*. Canberra: Pandanus Books.

Turner, Caroline 1998. Asian Modernisms, in: *Art AsiaPacific* Vol. 17: 20-21.

Weerasinghe, J. 2011, November. *Shrine of the Innocents: [DIS\RE] APPEARENCE of a memorial*. https://theerthaartists.wordpress.com/2011/11/12/shrine-of-the-innocents-disre-appearence-of-a-monument/ (Last accessed on 1 July 2016)

Weerasinghe, J. 2002. *Moments of Cultural Impact: a Socio-Political Reading of Contemporary Art Practice in Sri Lanka, Khoj International Artists Workshop*. http://www.khojworkshop.org/sana_m_jagath.htm (Last accessed on 5 December 2002).

Weerasinghe, J. 2012. *What now – after the '90s Trend?*. http://colomboartbiennale.com/2012-2/becoming-speakers-forum/ (Last accessed on 25 May 2017)

Weerasinghe, J. 1999: *"Yantra Gala and the round pilgrimage"*. http://www.visualarts.qld.gov.au/apt3/artists/artist_bios/jagath_weerasinghe_a.htm (Last accessed on 28 May 2017).

Welsch, W. 1995. *Aesthetics Beyond Aesthetics*. http://www2.uni-jena.de/welsch/papers/W_Welsch_Aesthetics_beyond_Aesthetics.html (Last accessed on 30 May 2017)

Welsch, W. 2007: *Transculturality – the Puzzling Form of Cultures Today*. http://www2.uni-jena.de/welsch/papers/W_Wlelsch_Transculturality.html (Last accessed on 30 May 2017)

Williams, J. 1999. `The Construction of Gender in the Paintings and Graffiti of Sigiriya`, in: Dehejia, V. (ed.): Representing the Body. Gender Issues in Indian Art. New Delhi: Kali for Women (Woman Unlimited), 56 - 67.

A Theater - in Absence

Felix Ho Yuen Chan

In September 2017, the Guggenheim Museum in New York announced that it would pull three works involving the use of animals from its much-anticipated survey, *Art and China after 1989: Theater of the World*. Among them, Sun Yuan and Peng Yu's video *Dogs That Cannot Touch Each Other* entered the most heated realm of controversy [figure 1]. Having first been staged as a 5- minute performance in 2003, this work is no stranger to controversy. Sun and Peng had tried to restage the performance in the 2004 Gwangju Biennale, but were only able to exhibit an edited video due to the constraints of resources and the fear of backlash. Nevertheless, American critic Michael Rush instantly slammed the video documentation of the performance as "snuff film." "The video should be removed immediately and confiscated." Rush writes ferociously in his "Report from Gwangju 2004" for *Artnet.com*, "…Someone in China is not paying attention" (artnet.com/Magazine/features/rush/rush10-19-04.asp).

Since then, this piece—this theater—has remained silent for thirteen years while Chinese contemporary art has slowly risen as a global player, until it reappeared in the announced checklist of Guggenheim's ambitious, large scale exhibition. This time, *Dogs That Cannot Touch Each Other* stirred a tsunami of reactions on the international stage. The controversy not only spirals out of the ethical practice surrounding an "artwork", but also extends into the characterization of a nation's modernity. The outraged voices unanimously pointed out the exploitation of animals as a glorified mode of art making, claiming that it should have no place at an exhibition in the United States. *Dogs That Cannot Touch Each Other* incited an immense wave of anger from animal rights organizations and netizens; according to the museum, many threats were even issued against employees of the museum, indicating that harm would visit them if the piece should remain in the exhibition. The museum ultimately decided not to display it, merely signaling its absence by its white-on-black title shot included in the exhibition.

What has been missing in the Guggenheim controversy and its aftermath is a thorough investigation of the origins of *Dogs That Cannot Touch Each Other* and the journey of Sun and Peng, a commentator of a cross-cultural dialogue on globalism who have consistently use socially conscious art forms as activism for the past two decades. Too much specificity need to be worked through in order for us to understand this piece in particular and the crisis it brings to "global art" as a legitimate curatorial premise in the age of globalism.

The Emergence of Sun Yuan and Peng Yu

Since their debut, Sun Yuan and Peng Yu have used deliberately controversial, discomforting materials to call forth an unfiltered analysis of humanity, social realities, and the conditions that we create. In retrospect, their creative progression is not one of increasing indulgence of ethical transgression; rather, the duo have scaled their spectatorship as they expanded their activity on an increasingly globalized platform.

Around 2000, Sun Yuan and Peng Yu emerged with a younger generation of performance artists, following the famed "Beijing East Village," a performance-oriented collective that arose in 1992 and abruptly ended in 1995. Like their predecessors, Sun and Peng engaged with the body, specifically body mutilation and animal carcasses as allegory for hyper-suffering and violence. Upon graduation from the oil painting department of Central Academy of Fine Arts (CAFA) in Beijing, Sun and Peng, like many of their peers, immediately disassociated themselves from traditional academy pedagogy to produce confrontational installations and performances, which at the time were still considered to be inferior art forms among Chinese academies. The duo's first credited collaborative work was *Body Link* [figure 2], presented at a group sculpture exhibition *Indulge in Hurt*, curated by Li Xianting at CAFA in 2000.

To commemorate their recent decision to get married, Sun and Peng sat next to each other and simultaneously transfused 100cc of blood from their own bodies into the corpse of Siamese twin babies that they managed to acquire through connections of a friend at a university hospital as a medical sample. To date, *Body Link* remains the duo's first and last performance for the duo to present themselves as the subjects of the work to date. With such a shocking debut serving as their artistic manifesto, they went on to conduct unfiltered analyses on the brutal truth of the human conditions and relationships. Their conceptual exploration would later expand to encompass a wide range of media. Many of these projects constituted studies of specific materials and exploitations that exhaust or distort their physical properties.

In Sun and Peng's oeuvre, works featuring dogs as analogue to human existence appeared early in their career. The first was created for *Fuck Off*, an exhibition organized by artist Ai Weiwei and critic Feng Boyi at Donglang Gallery in Shanghai in 2000.

Taking advantage of a relatively liberal city, *Fuck Off* marked a collective effort to announce the oppositional and confrontational nature of Chinese avant-garde artists. Many works in *Fuck Off* displayed the grotesque brutalization of bodies in intimate portrayals of torture and violence. Sun and Peng contributed *Soul Killing* [figure 3], a sculpture installation that constituted a physical and spiritual investigation of death. The piece featured a large convex lens, a 500W signal lamp, and a dog that had been bought from a food market and taxidermied. Dramatically lit on top of a white table by an industrial lamp in front of a red curtain, the dog's bruised and bloody but taxidermied body is held by a metal stand. Stuffed in such a way to maintain an aggressive stance, a ferocious canine dynamically lunges with full force at an unknown enemy. The dog's vicious profile is enhanced by the smoke arising from its head, the result of the high voltage lamp placed above it scorching its head through a convex lens. This, according to Sun, is "soul killing": the high-intensity beam of light terminates the soul that escaped from the dog's skull.

In their catalogue statement, the duo declares an ambiguous, koan-like objective, "If the physical body of a dog dies, you must also kill its soul in order to make death permanent."

2003: An Overlooked Ignition Point

The year 2003 marked a conceptual departure for the duo, as they formed the clear focus to spectatorship and began to consider the idea of a theater—an audacious, yet not unprompted move. Notably, the timeline of their creative expansion matches that of the nation and the dystopic energy that the world displayed through many apocalyptic events.

In 2003, Sun and Peng staged two large-scale installations using live animals, exploiting their aggressive nature as a proxy for the theater of human power dynamic under capitalism. One installation was *Paper Tiger*, in which they caged an Asian Tiger at a dangerously close though safe distance from the viewers. The other was *Dogs That Cannot Touch Each Other*, commissioned by Today Art Museum as a performance piece for its exhibition *Secondhand Reality*, curated by veteran curator Gu Zhenqing. Of the same generation as Hou Hanru (one of the three curators of Guggenheim's *Theater of The World*), Gu had successfully organized *Man and Animals*, a series of radical performance art that took place in 2000 throughout public parks in China by using guerilla-tactics. Then, in 2003, he secured a venue at Today Art Museum, a new private museum in Beijing.

By now, it is well known that the so-called "honeymoon" phase between 1979 and 1989 when a reforming China showed much tolerance toward unofficial avant-garde art was ended traumatically by the Tiananmen Square incident of June 4, 1989. However, by 2003, Chinese contemporary art had been legitimized in public spaces thanks to such exhibitions as *Fuck Off* in 2000, along with *Post-Sensibility* curated by Qiu Zhijie and *The First Guangzhou Triennial* curated by Hou Hanru, Hans Ulrich Obrist, and Guo Xiaoyan, both in 2002. Even though the organization of art exhibitions was still heavily controlled by the cultural authorities, Gu intended *Secondhand Reality* to herald an "entrance into people's halls and homes" (*dengtang rushi*, 登堂入室) for contemporary Chinese art. He recalls, in my phone conversation with the curator in February 2018, that with this exhibition he wanted to acknowledge not only contemporary art's entrance into the public consciousness, but also its growingly active engagement with society. That is to say, it was his ambition to assert the efficacy of contemporary art as an uncompromised, investigative tool of social realities.

Notably, in curating *Second Hand Reality*, Gu made commissions central to the exhibition, encouraging the participating artists to conceive site-specific performances and large- scale installations that best addressed contemporary social issues. He worked with the artists to select the best projects from their proposals, while trying to secure sufficient funding for their productions. Through his past collaborations and correspondence with Sun and Peng, Gu had a good understanding of their confrontational and transgressive approach to social topics would fulfill the exhibition's premise.

In Gu's reckoning, several turbulent events informed the exhibition's pressing social agenda. One such domestic event was the SARs virus episode in 2003, when the deadly epidemic broke out around the world, especially in Southeastern Asia. The death toll reached thousands in China and caused a large-scale panic in all major cities. Despite the severity of the epidemic, the Chinese government heavily censored the coverage of the crisis, especially the death, for fear of social unrest. In the same year, on the international front, the U. S. launched its eight-year invasion of Iraq, under a vague pretext of discovering the weapons of mass destruction. The invasion utterly destabilized the Middle East region. The severe lack of transparency in information only amplified the widespread apprehension, felt among Chinese citizens. Although the arrival of the Internet age promised democratic exchange of information and knowledge, the Chinese authorities responded to it by exercising draconian censorship over all media outlets.

However, some positive changes *were* taking place, as China transformed itself from a socialist economy to a major player in global economics and politics in the new millennium. In 2001, China won the bid to host the 2008 Summer Olympics, and joined the World Trade Organization in the following year. These two events signify an unprecedented role of China in the world that would demand responsibilities from the most populous country, which now received global attention and scrutiny. In this context, Gu hoped the radical art forms he intended for *Secondhand Reality* would at once reflect on China's socialist legacy as well as interrogate the impact of globalization on contemporary China.

Dog as Subject

It was in just such a paradoxical and volatile time that Sun and Peng's work began to change.

The duo decided to revisit the subject of dogs, this time to delineate not only the interiority of human existence, but to tackle the façade of a harmonious social order. In planning a project for the exhibition, *Secondhand Reality*, they looked at the taboo tradition of dogfighting. A blood sport banned in England and America, dogfighting was very much alive in China's underground gambling scenes. The violent history of dogfighting had the potential to call forth the truths of uniquely localized situations.

Monica Villavicencio's informative essay, "A History of Dogfighting," for *NPR* (July 19, 2007), explains that, in the West, dogfighting dates back to 12th-century Britain, where dogs were trained for a popular event named "baiting" (npr.org/templates/story/story. php?storyId=12108421) A prototype of dogfighting, baiting was a kind of blood sport where trained dogs went head to head against a chained bear or a bull, to the point where the larger animal either got severely wounded or killed. When baiting was banned by the British parliament in 1835, dogfighting became a legal alternative. Trainers began crossbreeding dogs in order to create "a fast, agile, and vicious animal capable of brawling for hours at a time." Dogfighting quickly spread to the United States shortly before the Civil War. Through crossbreeding of British fight dogs and local species, the American pit bull terriers were created as the ultimate fighting canine. It has since become a popular breed and spread to Latin America, the Middle East, and Eastern Europe.

In China, dogfighting dates back to the Song dynasty. It can still be seen today in some areas. However, since gambling on dogfights is banned and severely punished, this bloody, inhumane tradition has gone underground, spawning a huge and clandestine gambling network that is popular in Beijing suburbs and Guangdong. Among various breeds, American pit bull terriers are imported from overseas to fight against each other, or with other combative species such as the Tibetan Mastiff. To maximize their profit, dog owners often hire trainers, buy treadmills, and even introduce illegal substances to boost the dogs' fighting ability. In preparation for their *Secondhand Reality* project, Sun and Peng made several field visits to the training sites and eventually decided to repurpose the typical treadmill training sequence.

The Chinese title they chose was 犬 勿 近 (*quanwujin*), borrowing from the phrase commonly found in public parks and zoos that warns spectators and visitors to stay away from the animals. Its literal translation is 犬 (dogs) + 勿 (no) + 近 (near), or "Don't come near dogs," wherein "dogs" stand in for various animals in the parks and zoos. Calling their project in English: *Dogs That Cannot Touch Each Other*, the duo appropriated this literal sense and gave an ironic twist to this phrase,

Despite the many challenges associated with producing the performance, including the large physical space the work required, potential legal threats that it might face, and a large production budget, the duo managed to stage three live performances in the museum's recently-restored warehouse site, on the opening day of *Secondhand Reality* on October 8, 2003. After the performance, Sun and Peng kept the performance set up as the relic of the project, along with an edited video they created from the three stagings as part of the work, for the duration of the exhibition.

The edited video begins with a crowd walking into a spacious white hall in anticipation of the performance [figure 4]. Among them were quite a few Western faces, foreign journalists, and renowned scholars and collectors from China and elsewhere. Sun Yuan appears in the beginning, giving instructions to the videographer and taking still photographs himself. Eight bull terriers are on individual treadmills, which had both been borrowed from dog trainers. They are aligned in two rows of four, with the dogs facing one another only a few feet apart but initially separated by opaque screens. Behind each dog is a trainer standing close by. With the ring of a bell, the screens are removed and the dogs are revealed to each other. The canines immediately lunge at their opponents, each running on a treadmill while held in place by a harness and a chain leash.

The remainder of the video cuts between the three performances, with rhythmic switches of camera angles enhancing the intensity with which the dogs furiously and futilely run towards each other. Many shots were low angled, focusing particularly on the rapid rotation of the treadmill wheels and the intense, heavy breathing of the dogs. With the bulldogs' barks filling the white hall, numerous camera flashes come from viewers — many of them showing great excitement for documenting what they see. As each dog continues to frantically sprint toward its opponent, the dog trainers clap and yell, "*Pao, pao!*"—"Run, run!"— to encourage their aggression toward each other. Eventually, Peng Yu rings the bell to signal the end of the 5- minute performance. The screens are placed back between the treadmills and many dogs instantly ceased their running and hostility. After the exhibition, this video has since widely been circulated and become the basis to interpret the performance project.

Nothing short of being exploitative and cruel, the live theater of *Dogs That Cannot Touch Each Other* is easily misconstrued as repulsive by many. Yet, for Sun and Peng, the violence and the human consumption of such brutality precisely mirrored what they perceived as a much crueler world, which constituted the "firsthand" reality. The installation took full advantage of dogs' loyalty to their human masters, and their human-trained aggression toward each other.

Under Sun and Peng's wicked mise en scène, the canines are left with no option but to unleash their aggression and exhaust themselves. Yet, this cruel construction is at best a "secondhand," or derivative, reality. The reality that is truly brutal lies not in the construction of Sun and Peng per se, but in an ominous foreshadow of the actual carnage: once unleashed, the pit bulls will release every ounce of their aggression and do what they are trained and engineered to do—to fight each other till the last of their breaths, for the sake of human entertainment and capitalist desire.

In the video, we can see that the Chinese audience on site shows no visible shock toward the performance, because they were familiar with pit bull terriers and knew that this American species were imported for the purpose of dogfighting. When we understand this, the historical and cultural complexity of the dog breed reveals itself as a critical locus of Sun and Peng's transgressive inquiry on globalism as the new governing order of world politics.

As their largest installation to date, Sun and Peng strategically and self-consciously extended their critique to broader cultural demographics beyond China, demanding us, even in 2003, to read it in multiple ways. The American pit bull terriers used were not only foreign species but also artificial products of a complex breeding that culturally and historically mirrored the inherent aggression of humankind. Ironically, this American dog breed, created to serve in such blood sports as bull baiting and dogfighting, has since been domesticated and beloved by Euro-American households, while its use in dogfighting—and indeed, dogfighting itself—has largely been forgotten in these countries. This alone complicates the reception of the work, especially in American and other Western contexts. Sun and Peng were also aware that indigenous dog breeds still represent a source of meat in many rural areas of China, as in other non-Western rural and impoverished communities. For those people outside the Euro-American context, American pit bull terriers would moreover appear a particularly foreign and vicious animal. Such an immense cultural gap dictates that the reception of the piece will range from anger to amusement to indifference.

In this light, transporting an exercise routine of fight dog training to a fine art museum context becomes an institutional critique of sort. The piece questions whether an art installation is capable of creating unfiltered, raw reality, or merely just producing a perception of it, which is a secondhand version of reality. Ultimately, *Dogs That Cannot Touch Each Other* reveals itself as a theater that portrays the existential crisis of China and its habitants, entering into and wrestling with the complexity of globalization in politics and economics. *Dogs That Cannot Touch Each Other* is a grotesque but faithful allegory of the dystopic force in the world at large. It *is* a theater of the world.

The Guggenheim Backlash

Fast forwarding to 2017, *Dogs That Cannot Touch Each Other* was intended to be part of Guggenheim's landmark survey exhibition *Art and China after 1989: Theater of the World* [figure 5]. The difficulty the work might face had been foreshadowed by Michael Rush's bitter criticism from 2004, touched upon in the beginning of this essay. Indeed, removed from its specific social and artistic context, the work's portrayal of brutality seems inarguably vile to many viewers.

Sun and Peng were among 71 artists and collectives in Guggenheim's exhibition roster.

Positioning its exhibition an up-to-date analysis on Chinese contemporary art, the museum emphasized conceptualism during the span of three decades from 1989 to the present. A project by a major art institution that exerts significant influence, the exhibition was clearly intended to explore ways in which these works could be catapulted into a global audience, as its press release (#1498, dated September 21, 2017) asserted. The question remains: Did the museum succeed in their mission?

Sun and Peng's video *Dogs That Cannot Touch Each Other* was to occupy the final rectangular gallery at the Guggenheim, following the upward spiral of its rotunda. Walking up the streamlined corridor, viewers would have experienced a complex array of multi-media works, which were individually visceral and powerful but, placed next to one another, served rather as caricatures of each turbulent episode of China for the last thirty years. The works were neither arranged in a successive timeline, nor grouped in geographic regions, nor categorized in shared formalist elements. They produced an exciting cacophony, yet failed to coalesce as a story. In the final gallery, where Guggenheim curators often use to create a memorable coda, it felt as though the timeline was inexplicably shuffled again due to the coexistence of Sun and Peng's *Dogs* and Gu Dexin's *2009-05-02*, a 35-panel installation featuring continuous listings of heinous crimes written in the same Communist propaganda font in simplified Chinese, punctuated by the same sentence opener, "we have ..." [figure 6].

At face value, both *Dogs* and *2009-05-02* could coexist as two visceral critiques of "China". In reality, such a pairing compromises the meaning of both pieces due to a fundamental difference of their targeted audiences. *2009-05- 02* is an introspective monologue that solicits curiosity for outsiders, but punches the gut for insiders. For those who do not understand Chinese, the banner merely reads as an "exotic" font that evokes the Mao era and suggests collectivity. For those who are literate in Chinese however, the sentence opener "We have" and the association of ghastly crimes imply the literate viewers' agency in all these actions, thus augmenting possible feelings of the shame and concealment for the Chinese audience who had no choice but to participate in this haunting narrative. This includes the massive death tolls during the ten-year Cultural Revolution from 1966 to 1976, a party led initiative that mobilized the participation of entire society, and the mass dislocation of urban populations during the 2008 Olympics, which many citizens' witnessed on a daily basis and felt mostly powerless to resist against injustice.

Sharing little to no formal or conceptual similarity with *2009-05-02*, the introspective criticism found in *2009-05-02* is exactly what Sun and Peng have sought to deconstruct and animate throughout their entire career. In the decade that followed the creation of *Dogs That Cannot Touch Each Other*, Sun and Peng continued to grapple with the global conflicts and unrests unfolding in the 21st century. As of 2017, the duo had ceased using any animals in their work, the last being the fighting dog performance in 2003. Most notably, Sun and Peng have adopted industrial materials such as barbed wires and cranes as manifestations of manmade aggressions informed by the violent undertone that persists in our day and age. For example, the 2013 performance *Seeing Is Not an Option* featured twelve men, all blindfolded, continuously assembling and dissembling real AK-47's. In the 2008 installation *Freedom* [figure 7], the duo suspended a rubber water hose midair in a steel cage, letting it thrash wildly against the floor and the wall as water burst out of the hose. The piece is widely viewed as an allegory to the Communist regime's political suppression of its citizens. Sun and Peng's goal has always been to create a challenging but unfailingly accessible display of not just a certain cultural audience,but of humanity as a whole. Instead of illustrating Sun and Peng's consistent yet progressive modes of production, or by pairing with two other works that are also critique the age of globalism, it appears that the curatorial team somehow expected two equally controversial yet conceptually opposite works to form a synchronized viewing experience. After the backlash over their piece's ethical violations, and the Guggenheim's subsequent decision to take the work down, the monitor features a black screen, displaying only the title *Dogs That Cannot Touch Each Other* and the date "10, 2003."

In the exhibition, there simply were too few resources provided for viewers to understand Sun Yuan and Peng Yu's evolving identities from an underground avant-garde duo to active figures wrestling in the global art arena. Although *Dogs That Cannot Touch Each Other* was created in 2003 and no longer necessarily reflects the duo's current ethos, it would have supposedly demonstrated the poignant criticism of China's increasing agency in its gradual adoption of the globalized model of cultural and political diplomacy.

Hoping to settle the controversy, the curatorial team issued the following statement (press release #1498, dated September 21, 2017):

> Reflecting the artistic and political context of its time and place, *Dogs That Cannot Touch Each Other* is an intentionally challenging and

provocative artwork that seeks to examine and critique systems of power and control. We recognize that the work may be upsetting. The curators of the exhibition hope that viewers will consider why the artists produced it and what they may be saying about the social conditions of globalization and the complex nature of the world we share.

The Guggenheim's terse defense did very little to appease the public anger and unrest, but instead raises a key question for the institutional parade of globalism, which is now a legitimate curatorial methodology: Do Western geographic surveys of art from non-Western background have the ability to import notions of modernity from the period and locale of "the other"? The critical irony of *Dogs That Cannot Touch Each Other*'s absence from the Guggenheim show lies in that this is the rare work that aims to puncture the optimism of globalism as an equalizer of the oppression and hegemony belonging to the history of imperialism and colonialism. It seeks to question the premature celebration of globalism that consequently motivates institutions to conduct general and regional "artistic" survey exhibitions, intended as value equalizers of all notions of artistic modernity in the "postcolonial" era.

In 2017, however, this critical work from 2003 finds itself in an exhibition that functions more as a clumsy ethnographic, rather than artistic, exploration of Chinese art in the 20th and 21st century. Without rigorously restating the contemporaneous urgency of works such as *Dogs That Cannot Touch Each Other*, the Guggenheim failed to offer crucial contextualization, revealing its self-perception as a Western art venue of intrinsic cultural and political dominance. With its meandering analysis of thirty years of China's artistic history, the museum seems to seek affirmation for their mere ambition to include Chinese contemporary art— through the lens of socially-aware artworks—yet offers hardly enough of a framework for the audience to absorb its nuances. In this light, *Dogs That Cannot Touch Each Other* finds itself entering a wasteland, having to satisfy an abstract desire to establish a certain representation of a region as a cultural remnant, rather than a work with continuous potency and relevance. As avant-garde artists, Sun and Peng had taken the brave initiative to engage with a time and place beyond their own, with or without the aid of a Western institution. However, as a radical conceptualist piece created in China in 2003, its intimate link with a specific complex age of China is lost in translation, in the prosaic prescription, "post-1989." This prescient work will remain as a global theater in absence, until being critically reinserted into a framework that expresses genuine interest in its transgressive display of the avant-garde and its cutting-edge diagnosis of globalism.

Figures

Figure 1. Sun Yuan and Peng Yu, *Dogs That Cannot Touch Each Other*, 2003.
Performance at *Secondhand Reality*, Today Art Museum, Beijing, China, 2003

Figure 2. Sun Yuan and Peng Yu, *Body Link*, 2000.
Performance at *Indulge in Hurt*, Central Academy of Fine Arts, Beijing, China, 2000

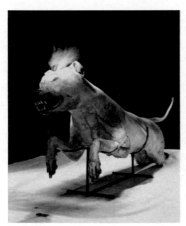

Figure 3. Sun Yuan and Peng Yu, *Soul Killing*, 2000.
Installation view at *Fuck Off*, Donglang Art Gallery, Shanghai, China, 2000

Figure 4. Sun Yuan and Peng Yu, *Dogs That Cannot Touch Each Other*, 2003.
Compilation of video stills

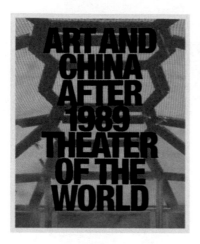

Figure 5. Guggenheim Museum, *Theater of the World*, 2017.
Exhibition poster

Figure 6. Sun Yuan and Peng Yu, *Dogs That Cannot Touch Each Other*, 2003 and Gu Dexin, *2009-05-02*, 2009 (above).
Installation view at *Art and China After 1989 Theater of the World*, Guggenheim Museum, New York, 2017

Figure 7. Sun Yuan and Peng Yu, *Freedom*, 2016.
Installation view at *What about the Art? Contemprary Art from China*, Qatar Museums (QMA), Doha, Qatar 2016

In Search of a Critical Conscience

Ernesto Muñoz

Art defines itself. Art is Art. There are no definitions that match the objectives with which Art is justified, and then any expression far from collective representation, once accepted by society, will become Art.

Watching dance or listening to music or observing a monument does not require a definition to know that Art is being perceived. It is the collective representation par excellence. When the artistic discourse abandons the socially admitted canons, and enters into discussion its validity as such, it will be considered Art, once the society accepts it.

Artistic discourse is not necessarily linked to the political. Each artist as an individual can have a different imaginary of democracy, which may well be even close to the real democracy existing in his country, not necessarily from the base that democracy is a myth. Because in that way art is also a myth and culture will be a myth too.

The artist is essentially a breaker of the reality in which he lives. His way of circumscribing the Art makes him adherent to a cause to which he spontaneously adheres. Hence, artists are commonly referred to as "left". Just wanting to break with the traditional way of making art, leads him along a path, which is often ideologized and transformed into a "dyed artist" politically. But, in any case, it should be considered that the social issue does not necessarily constitute a political position for those who fight for changes that favor the majority of people, such as women's rights or social security. It is not necessarily a "leftist" who ascribes to these struggles, so an artist who communicates in his work a need for changes in questions of social order, is not embarrassing democracy, but is warning him of the need for change.

Then, the artistic discourse will be directed according to collective objectives of people who see in Art, a path of orientation for both the masses and the elite, for changes that must take place in society.

To understand how artistic discourse can influence and constitute a challenge or coustion of the imaginary of democracy, we must analyze the ways in which Art can socially express itself. Thus it is possible to talk about Mass Art, Elitic Art and Political Art.

Mass Art

It is identified as an effort to impose an artistic discourse, a specific group aimed at a particular population, whose goal is to deliver a message, already expected by the people, identified with the welfare economy, which privileges the consumption of goods and services, as a life goal.

The Art of Masses, is incorporated into the collective representation, changing conceptual values such as beauty. Its character of mass acceptance employs pre-established means by society, as necessary for the achievement of states of shared happiness. It is called as a surrogate culture, due to its capacity for replacement, of the original culture proper to a population, brought to the encounter of a momentary satisfaction of their desires for encountering art.

It has achieved a splendor, thanks to the development of communication technologies, which allow it to meet objectives of scope and immediacy in a short time.

Although it is true, it needs technical support and a clear definition of its objectives, leaves aside the individual language of the individual artist and adds efforts, collectivizing the work, so that the expression and the language come to interpret the wishes of the community in pursuit of a prompt response to their entertainment requirements in leisure time.

In the Art of Mass the speech is destined, to maintain positions in the socially accepted, it is possible to mount a show within the framework of "bread and circus", whose purpose is to calm any restlessness of change.

It is said that this Art is concordant with populism, and seeks to have a system of control of the population on a large scale, far from social individualism.

The Art of Masses works under the scheme of an advertising company, where marketing techniques are used, just like the rest of the companies of a neoliberal market system. In this logic, we look for elements of Art that are capable of transmitting messages according to the demand of the public, in terms of entertaining shows. It is consistent with the medium you want to reach.

This type of art, can fairly put in check the imaginary of democracy, when operating in a democratic state, or the dictatorship when operating in a repressive state. Elitic art.

Elitic Art

In Latin American countries they have similarity in their corporate composition since their ascendants were Spanish and Portuguese. They are heirs of the European Culture and maintain their social structures, in spite of the socio-cultural changes that have taken place in each of the Latin American countries. The Creole aristocratic classes, revealed at the time against the kingdoms of Spain and Portugal, achieved along with independence, political power. With this, they maintained their cultural ties with Europe, especially with France. Art born in Latin American countries was elitist, because the Creole aristocracy that ruled accepted it. They could only emerge artists whose work was the pleasure of the aristocracy.

With the passage of time, the Creole aristocracy incorporated the changes of art, which occurred in the rest of the world, with nuances typical of the countries, creating a Latin American Art, which was not very far from European and North American trends, emerged in the twentieth century.

This Art of convenience, or establishment, has a central objective, which is to satisfy the desires of collectors. The work created by conscious artists who create to obtain monetary returns, that is, produce art for a market demand. It is present in Fairs, Halls and Art Galleries. The works of artists cannot be considered as rupturists, but they are avant-garde in the proper sense of the search for beauty, expressed in artistic works.

Undoubtedly, Art for the elites has a discourse in accordance with the imaginary of the prevailing democracy and will not try to use its power in pursuit of radical changes that attempt against the prevailing social structure.

Political Art

Political Art in Latin America has a large number of followers, and is accepted as such in democratic countries, and in this way ideologically engaged artists coexist in both right and left ideas.

Under Sloganes as: "today's society requires ideologies that promote the elimination of inequalities", Art finds followers in artists who work to get the population to become aware and fight for changes destined for purposes such as the one indicated.

There are artists who are members of political parties, for which reason they must discipline themselves to the mandates of the ideology and the leaders. These artists manage to form groups of power within society and their works are considered in many cases in Official Art, which allows them to enter Art for the elites.

When an ideology discovers that through Art, it is possible to get potential followers to join the political party, they look for like-minded artists, to spread their ideas or to give it a character of reliability.

Without a doubt, the discourse of Political Art in some cases may question democracy, given situations such as the discrediting of politics, acts of corruption and the appearance of new actors in politics.

The Art of Latin America and Democracy

In the middle of the twentieth century in Latin America, extreme political changes took place. We heard about both popular governments and dictatorial governments. Some gave way to others. The response of a Marxist-led left government brought with it the onslaught of a dictatorial government. They were difficult years, persecutions, violence, repressions, attacks on human rights, in short, limited experiences, which compromised Art. Later democratic regimes returned to most countries.

The Art of Masses and the Politician in the meantime had a great development. In the governments of the left, artists of similar ideologies were given importance to create a populist art, with the purpose of eradicating the historically prevailing culture. When these governments fell dictatorships made disappear the works of these artists, who were exiled or entered the clandestine art, producing works with rebel content.

The Art and the Use of Communication Technologies.

With the creation of expanded art concepts, artistic criticism has found space in the media, especially in newspaper chains in Argentina, Brazil, Chile, Colombia and Peru.

In this way the critic must obey the dictates of their employers who give importance to Modern Art, facing the Contemporary.

The current criticism made in the Academy, must be nourished obligatorily of the electronic means of communication and in this way, creating blogs manage to set trends.

Much can be speculated on the scope of the media, which is no longer printed and the tendency is to use electronic media. They close newspapers and magazines, because the public prefers reading on the computer or phone. But Art follows the path that the public is willing to use, and it drives it. Networks also have a great interference in art, because it allows artistic discourse to reach the public directly.

But then: what is the role of artistic criticism? . Not always the viewer in its subject matter can capture the Art, and depth of what the artist is trying to make known and the role of the critic is to guide the viewer, in the understanding. Any medium will have an artistic critic considered, in order to generate a communion with its readers, who seek to balance their perceptions with what the artistic discourse delivers.

Trends of Artistic Criticism.

The voices that criticize forget, apparently mockingly, the euphemisms in a time where visuality explodes over the written. There is talk of countries that heal and countries that are cured.

Our knowledge about the artistic discourse in Latin America occurs mainly in the metropolis, being relegated to a second plane, the rest of the cities and localities.

The Universities receive the recognition of the artistic discourse through the criticism of New York, then.

Today in Latin America, the countries have been divided into two blocks, some pursuing Arte Solidario where Political Art is present and others the Elitic Art that pursues collectable works, which inspires merchants to create private Art Galleries, where the artistic discourse is guided, to the pursuit of profit. In this way, the owners of the galleries and media present a form of censorship of artistic discourse, by preventing artistic works that go against collective representation.

On the other hand, the post-truth is present in the political discourse, which is added to the artistic discourse, causing a cognitive dissonance in the collective.

Then the immediate need is to find a conscious critic of the artistic discourse, far from the interferences created by noise of tendencies foreign to the creative task and that overlap in order to obtain undue profits.

美學藝術類

2018 AICA International Congress Taiwan
Art Criticism in the Age of Virtuality and Democracy

主　　編/林志明　教授
校對編審/2018 國際藝評人協會台北世界年會專案工作小組
責任編輯/鄭伊庭
圖文排版/莊皓云
封面設計/楊廣榕

出版策畫/中華民國藝評人協會
發 行 人/宋政坤
法律顧問/毛國樑　律師
出版發行/秀威資訊科技股份有限公司
　　　　　114台北市內湖區瑞光路76巷65號1樓
　　　　　電話：+886-2-2796-3638　傳真：+886-2-2796-1377
　　　　　http://www.showwe.com.tw
劃撥帳號/19563868　戶名：秀威資訊科技股份有限公司
　　　　　讀者服務信箱：service@showwe.com.tw
展售門市/國家書店（松江門市）
　　　　　104台北市中山區松江路209號1樓
　　　　　電話：+886-2-2518-0207　傳真：+886-2-2518-0778
網路訂購/秀威網路書店：https://store.showwe.tw
　　　　　國家網路書店：https://www.govbooks.com.tw

ISBN：978-986-326-632-7
2018年11月　BOD一版
定價：600元
版權所有　翻印必究
本書如有缺頁、破損或裝訂錯誤，請寄回更換

讀者回函卡

感謝您購買本書，為提升服務品質，請填妥以下資料，將讀者回函卡直接寄
回或傳真本公司，收到您的寶貴意見後，我們會收藏記錄及檢討，謝謝！
如您需要了解本公司最新出版書目、購書優惠或企劃活動，歡迎您上網查詢
或下載相關資料：http:// www.showwe.com.tw

您購買的書名：_____

出生日期：_____年_____月_____日

學歷：□高中 (含) 以下　　□大專　　□研究所 (含) 以上

職業：□製造業　□金融業　□資訊業　□軍警　□傳播業　□自由業
　　　□服務業　□公務員　□教職　　□學生　□家管　　□其它_____

購書地點：□網路書店　□實體書店　□書展　□郵購　□贈閱　□其他

您從何得知本書的消息？

　　□網路書店　□實體書店　□網路搜尋　□電子報　□書訊　□雜誌

　　□傳播媒體　□親友推薦　□網站推薦　□部落格　□其他_____

您對本書的評價：(請填代號　1.非常滿意　2.滿意　3.尚可　4.再改進)

　　封面設計____　版面編排____　內容____　文／譯筆____　價格____

讀完書後您覺得：

　　□很有收穫　□有收穫　□收穫不多　□沒收穫

對我們的建議：_____

_____

_____

_____

11466
台北市內湖區瑞光路 76 巷 65 號 1 樓
秀威資訊科技股份有限公司　　　收
BOD 數位出版事業部

⋯⋯⋯⋯⋯⋯⋯⋯⋯⋯⋯⋯⋯⋯⋯⋯⋯⋯⋯⋯⋯⋯⋯⋯⋯⋯⋯⋯⋯⋯

（請沿線對折寄回，謝謝！）

姓　　名：＿＿＿＿＿＿＿＿＿　年齡：＿＿＿＿　性別：□女　□男

郵遞區號：□□□□□

地　　址：＿＿＿＿＿＿＿＿＿＿＿＿＿＿＿＿＿＿＿＿

聯絡電話：(日) ＿＿＿＿＿＿＿＿＿　(夜) ＿＿＿＿＿＿＿＿＿＿

E-mail：＿＿＿＿＿＿＿＿＿＿＿＿＿＿＿＿＿